JOYCE
A GUIDE FOR THE PERPLEXED

The Guides for the Perplexed Series

JOYCE:
A GUIDE FOR THE PERPLEXED

PETER MAHON

continuum

Continuum International Publishing Group
The Tower Building   80 Maiden Lane
11 York Road   Suite 704, New York
London SE1 7NX   NY 10038

www.continuumbooks.com

British Library Cataloguing-in-Publication Data
A catalogue record for this book is available from the British Library.

ISBN: 978-0-8264-8791-9 (hardback)
978-0-8264-8792-6 (paperback)

Library of Congress Cataloging-in-Publication Data
Mahon, Peter, 1971-
Joyce : a guide for the perplexed/Peter Mahon.
p. cm.
Includes index.
ISBN: 978-0-8264-8791-9
ISBN: 978-0-8264-8792-6
1. Joyce, James, 1882-1941–Criticism and interpretation. I. Title.

PR6019.O9Z72538 2009
823'.912–dc22

2009012253

Typeset by Newgen Imaging Systems Pvt Ltd, Chennai, India
Printed and bound in Great Britain by CPI Antony Rowe, Chippenham, Wiltshire

This book is dedicated to my mother,
Joan Mahon

I hope theyre bubbles on it for a wad of money
18.1142–43

CONTENTS

ACKNOWLEDGEMENTS

As ever, thanks to Darcy for putting up with me. I would like to thank Lorraine Weir at the University of British Columbia (UBC) for getting me hooked on Joyce's work in the first place. Thanks as well to Ralph Sarkonak for all his sage advice and support. I would also like to thank my Winter 2008 ENGL 462 Joyce class at UBC for a semester of engagement, imagination and, above all, boundless and infectious enthusiasm: my sincere thanks for making teaching Joyce such an enjoyable experience. Especial thanks must go to Allie, Katie Fitz, Katie C, Jean-Marc, Vish, Kate C, Mike D, Cynthia K, Sara and Allison for their questions, contributions and insights. Oh, and thanks to Rick for being Rick. Finally, a big welcome to my nephew, baby Cormac.

PREFACE

James Joyce's work has, not unjustly, been regarded as some of the most obscure, challenging and difficult writing ever committed to paper; it is also shamelessly funny and endlessly entertaining. This book celebrates the daring, humour and playfulness of Joyce's complex work while engaging with and elucidating some of the most demanding aspects of his writing. It explores the motifs and radical innovations of style that characterize his major works, from his collection of short stories, *Dubliners* (1914), to his famously punny novel, *Finnegans Wake* (1939). By highlighting those aspects of Joyce's texts that engage with issues relating to sexuality, Irish politics, art and the body, it is hoped that *Joyce: A Guide for the Perplexed* offers the new and undergraduate reader of Joyce a Joyce that is contemporary, fresh and relevant.

This book proceeds by examining Joyce's major texts chronologically. Starting with *Dubliners*, moving through *A Portrait of the Artist as a Young Man, Ulysses*, and ending with *Finnegans Wake*, the book introduces its intended reader gradually to the complexity of the Joycean *oeuvre*. Due to issues of space, this book does not explore Joyce's 'lesser' known texts: his 1918 play, *Exiles*, his youthful critical writings or his poetry. Nor does it offer its intended reader a potted synopsis of the author's life and times: that has been done better and in more detail by Richard Ellmann in his monumental *James Joyce* (Oxford: Oxford University Press, 1982) than I could possibly do here and in several lifetimes. Rather, the following chapters are intended to explore, for new readers of Joyce, how Joyce's work moves from an apparently reader-friendly 'realistic' style of writing into a more difficult, reader-taxing style of writing that appears to be anything but 'realistic'. Thus, it is with the new reader in mind that this volume treats some of Joyce's texts in more detail than others: those texts that get the most detailed treatment are the ones that combine likelihood to be read by readers new to Joyce with relative difficulty. As a result, neither the relatively easy-to-read text of *Dubliners*, nor the mind-bogglingly complex text of *Finnegans Wake* – a book that the new reader of Joyce is far less likely to encounter – are treated in exhaustive detail, while texts like *A Portrait of the Artist as a Young Man* and *Ulysses* – the most complex text that a new reader is likely to encounter – are given the bulk of consideration.

This book is thus part *explication du texte*, part appreciation, part theoretical. My theoretical approach to Joyce's texts is informed by certain critical approaches that have grown out of post-structuralist theory. The concluding chapter of this book explores two such theoretical approaches to Joyce's texts that have shaped my reading of his work: queer theory and postcolonial theory. (Other works that have informed my reading of Joyce's texts can be found in the recommended further reading section at the end of the book.) The three above-mentioned 'parts' of the book combine to offer the reader close examinations of key passages from Joyce's major texts that should help to ground and guide him/her. These close examinations are intended to ground and guide the reader – both practically and theoretically – in at least three ways: first, they provide him/her with an opportunity to trace, in the words of the texts themselves, Joyce's complex treatment of the major motifs found throughout his work; second, it is hoped that these close readings will perhaps inspire the reader to dig deeper into Joyce's texts by encouraging him/her to think about how Joyce's stylistic and technical innovations relate to his exploration of his major motifs; third, it is hoped that the readings offered here will help the reader to see that the complexity of Joyce's work is best understood in terms of how its stylistic innovations amount to a profound re-interpretation of how language and literature works. All in all, if this book encourages new readers to read – and perhaps even enjoy – Joyce's work, then it will have done its job.

Finally, a note about the so-called 'Joyce Industry': since Joyce's death, a veritable industry of criticism has grown up around his work. This is something Joyce himself actively encouraged. As Richard Ellmann, the most famous of Joyce's biographers, notes time and again, Joyce was tireless in coming up with schemes and schemas – that invariably relied upon and taxed the friends and family closest to him – for publicizing his work. Even though we are still some several hundred years away from Joyce's joco-serious intention of keeping 'the professors busy for centuries' in order to ensure his immortality (*JJ* 521) – and despite the fact that Joyce's own words regarding that goal have themselves become something of a threadbare cliché – it remains a fact that there is now so much material written on Joyce the man, his life and his work, that it has become impossible for any one person to read, let alone retain, it all. So what is a new reader of Joyce to do? My answer to this question is simply this: a new reader should just begin by reading Joyce's texts. It should go without saying that a book such as the one you are now holding in your hands cannot come close to saying everything that there is to be said about the work of Joyce; the most a book such as this can hope to do is offer the newcomer to Joyce's texts a way into the labyrinth. Above all, have fun; and remember, as *Finnegans Wake* counsels, 'Mind your hats goan in!' (008.09).

CHAPTER ONE

INTRODUCING JOYCE: REALISM AND EPIPHANY IN *DUBLINERS*

Dubliners is Joyce's only collection of short stories; there are 15 stories in all, and critical opinion often notes that they offer the reader – for the most part – a realistic or naturalistic depiction of middle-class existence in Dublin around the turn of the twentieth century. Indeed, the text's depiction of Dublin and its denizens was once considered so 'realistic' that Joyce could not find a Dublin publisher; the text was eventually published in London by Grant Richards in 1914. The stories themselves are criss-crossed by issues that were current in Dublin society at the turn of the century: Irish nationalism, religion, domestic relations, the emergence of an Irish bourgeoisie and art. Several of the characters in *Dubliners* – such as Joe Hynes, Mr Kernan, Bob Doran, Lenehan and Corley – also appear as minor characters in *Ulysses*. Another critical commonplace frequently asserted about *Dubliners* is that each of the stories turns on a moment of an 'epiphany' – the moment when a character comes to a sort of insight. It is also frequently noted that the first three stories in the collection are narrated by children; with the fourth story, 'Eveline', the book switches to a third-person narration, as the protagonist becomes progressively older; and the collection ends with 'The Dead': the overall structure of the book thus moves from childhood to maturity.

In this chapter, I want to reconsider briefly the relationship that the short stories in *Dubliners* have with both 'realism' and 'epiphany'. All references to *Dubliners* (D) in what follows use the pagination of the Penguin Classics edition (2000), with notes and an introduction by Terence Brown.

Simply put, literary realism was a late nineteenth-/early twentieth-century literary technique or style that sought to faithfully represent 'reality' – that is, contemporary middle-class life and society. As a literary style, realism was also a reaction against Romanticism and it favoured the use of scientific and rational methods of observation. Thus, realism as a literary technique was concerned with a particular way of presenting a specific subject matter. Given this definition, it certainly would seem that at first glance *Dubliners* is a classic example of literary realism: the text offers the reader an apparently faithful picture of Dublin and the domestic, social and political ills of its middle class at the turn of the nineteenth and twentieth centuries. At the same time, however, *Dubliners* also seems to challenge the notion of 'realism' right from the opening paragraphs of the first story in the collection, 'The Sisters'. The text's challenge to realism comes through the three words that the young narrator contemplates while he thinks about the impending death of an old priest he had recently grown attached to:

There was no hope for him this time: it was the third stroke. Night after night I had passed the house (it was vacation time) and studied the lighted square of window: and night after night I had found it lighted in the same way, faintly and evenly. If he was dead, I thought, I would see the reflection of candles on the darkened blind for I knew that two candles must be set at the head of a corpse. He had often said to me: *I am not long for this world*, and I had thought his words idle. Now I knew they were true. Every night as I gazed up at the window I said softly to myself the word *paralysis*. It had always sounded strangely in my ears, like the word *gnomon* in the Euclid and the word *simony* in the Catechism. But now it sounded to me like the name of some maleficent and sinful being. It filled me with fear, and yet I longed to be nearer to it and to look upon its deadly work.

Old Cotter was sitting at the fire, smoking, when I came downstairs to supper. While my aunt was ladling out my stirabout he said, as if returning to some former remark of his:

– No, I wouldn't say he was exactly . . . but there was something queer . . . there was something uncanny about him. I'll tell you my opinion. (D 1)

In this complex passage, the young narrator seems fascinated by three words in particular that are typographically singled out in italics: 'paralysis', 'gnomon' and 'simony'. These three words also serve a major structural role in the text: they neatly and quickly introduce the reader to three major themes that run throughout *Dubliners*. As such, these words reveal the lenses through which the 'reality' of Dublin is to be filtered. In other words, the opening paragraphs of *Dubliners* self-consciously reveal the architecture of the book in a way that suggests the 'faithful' depiction of 'reality' is in fact self-consciously artistic. Thus, the paralysis of the priest becomes a metaphor for the many other forms of paralysis – moral, religious, emotional, political and artistic – that afflict almost all of the characters in all of the stories in the collection: the mental paralysis of the young narrator of 'An Encounter' when confronted with a paedophile; the artistic and financial paralysis of Little Chandler, mired in a loveless marriage and a job he hates in 'A Little Cloud'; the emotional and spiritual paralysis of Eveline who is unable to leave her abusive father in 'Eveline'; the financial paralysis of Jimmy who is unable to keep up with the spending of his rich European counterparts in 'After the Race'; the spiritual and alcoholic paralysis that afflicts the Farrington family in 'Counterparts'; the emotional and sexual paralysis that costs Mr Duffy happiness and Mrs Sinico her life in 'A Painful Case'; Irish political paralysis after the political downfall of Charles Stewart Parnell[1] in 'Ivy Day in the Committee Room'. Likewise, the notion of 'simony' – the buying or selling of spiritual offices, pardons or favours – is found throughout the text, although it is perhaps most obvious in the Church's selling of its moral authority to appeal to businessmen in 'Grace'. Simony can also be found in other metaphorical forms throughout the text, where it can refer to the trafficking of other non-religious, but nonetheless spiritual, qualities such as Lenehan's and Corley's self-worth and masculinity in 'Two Gallants', Little Chandler's manhood in 'A Little Cloud', Polly's 'honour' in 'The Boarding House' and Mrs Kearney's daughter's musical talents in 'A Mother'. However, it is the notion of Euclid's 'gnomon' – the geometric figure that remains after a parallelogram has been removed from a similar but larger parallelogram with which it shares a corner – that I want to concentrate on here because it offers not only a way of clarifying and underlining the text's challenge to the conventions of literary realism but also a way reconfiguring the concept of epiphany and how epiphany has traditionally been seen to function in *Dubliners*.

As I mentioned above, the short stories in *Dubliners* are often said to illustrate Joyce's notion of 'epiphany', the definition of which can be found in *Stephen Hero*,[2] his abandoned draft for *A Portrait of the*

Artist as a Young Man. For Stephen Dedalus, the young artist-protagonist of *Stephen Hero*, epiphany is a key component of his 'esthetic theory': 'By an epiphany he meant a sudden spiritual manifestation, whether in the vulgarity of speech or of gesture or in a memorable phase of the mind itself' (SH 216). The epiphany of an object or situation, occurs, according to Stephen, when 'all at once I see it and I know at once what it is: epiphany' (SH 216). 'Epiphany', at least as far as the text of *Stephen Hero* is concerned, suggests the recognition or manifestation of something as complete, whole and unambiguous: that is to say, when something is 'epiphanized', it is recognized for exactly what it is. This definition of epiphany, however, does not seem to mesh very well with the 'epiphanies' that occur in the stories of *Dubliners*, which, more often than not, resist any such clear recognition and provoke a whole host of questions on the part of the reader: what, exactly, does the broken chalice in 'The Sisters' signify? What exactly does the young narrator come to recognize in his feelings for Mahony at the end of 'An Encounter'? Whose vanity drives and derides the young narrator of 'Araby'? What does the Hungarian's announcement of daybreak mean in 'After the Race'? What does the gold coin in Corley's hand at the end of 'Two Gallants' signify? What exactly brings tears of remorse to Little Chandler's eyes at the end of 'A Little Cloud'? And what, exactly, does Gabriel seem to realize at the end of 'The Dead'? There are no simple or straightforward answers to these questions: it thus seems that the 'epiphany' as it is found in *Dubliners* is something fragmentary and incomplete. Read thus, 'epiphany' in *Dubliners* appears to share more with the gnomon that the young narrator of 'The Sisters' mentions in the first paragraph of the book.

Because the geometrical figure of the gnomon can only be constructed by removing a piece from a parallelogram, it can be understood as having a piece perpetually missing from it, allowing it to function 'in' the text as a metaphor for incompleteness or lack. This further suggests that epiphany in *Dubliners* is structured somewhat like a gnomon. The first, and most obvious, of these metaphorical gnomons is announced in the text by the parts of the adult conversation that the young narrator of 'The Sisters' cannot follow, which are marked explicitly by the series of ellipses that repeatedly punctuate the text. Since Old Cotter's elliptical speech in 'The Sisters' (cited above) is offered to the reader as the first example of a metaphorical gnomon in the entire text of *Dubliners*, I want to dwell on it in order to see if it offers up any more clues as to the other important features of the metaphorical gnomon in *Dubliners*.

As Old Cotter's elliptical speech shows, the gnomon is associated with what cannot be safely, easily or completely uttered in words: the frequent ellipses in the text force the reader to confront the metaphorical gnomon as spacing, gaps and silences. Further, Old Cotter's elliptical speech also illustrates that the metaphorical gnomon is a place that is doubly permeated by desire: not only does the young narrator desire to know exactly what Cotter is saying – or rather, not saying – about Fr Flynn's relationship with him, but that which Old Cotter 'speaks' of is itself a place of dangerous or taboo desire that is threatening to the one who desires. The uncomfortable and threatening contours of desire are glimpsed in 'The Sisters' in the disconcerting imagery of the young narrator's dream about Fr Flynn:

> But the grey face still followed me. It murmured, and I understood that it desired to confess something. I felt my soul receding into some pleasant and vicious region; and there again I found it waiting for me. It began to confess to me in a murmuring voice and I wondered why it smiled continually and why the lips were so moist with spittle. (D 3)

The same sort of dangerous – 'pleasant and vicious' – desire is encountered by the young narrator of 'An Encounter', who displays some very odd behaviour in the presence of the 'queer old josser' (D 18) he meets in a field while playing truant from school. And although the ending of 'The Sisters' remains ambiguous and reveals very little – 'It was that chalice he broke . . . That was the beginning of it. Of course, they say it was all right, that it contained nothing, I mean. But still . . . They say it was the boy's fault. But poor James was so nervous, God be merciful to him!' (D 9–10) – it nevertheless leaves open the possibility of the circulation of inappropriate, but nonetheless reciprocated, sexual desires between a young boy and Fr Flynn.

It is possible to see many different variants of these metaphorical gnomons throughout the text of *Dubliners*: one can be seen in the strange 'confused notion' (D 15) that drives the young narrator of 'An Encounter' to search the docks for a sailor with green eyes, only to later find them in the face of a paedophile. The gnomon can also been seen in the examples of 'broken' masculinity that recur in other stories: the remains of Mr Kiernan the tea-taster's tongue after he bites a chunk off it in a drunken fall down the stairs of a pub in 'Grace', the artistically and emotionally castrated figure of Little Chandler in 'A Little Cloud' and Mr Holohan's bad leg in 'A Mother'. Feminine versions of the gnomon can be seen in Eveline's terrified breakdown which leaves her clinging to the railings at the ferry, Polly's loss of her 'honour' in 'The Boarding House', the death of Mrs Sinico in 'A Painful Case', Maria's lack of a husband in 'Clay' and in perhaps the most potent gnomon in the entire text – Gretta's desire for the ghost of Michael Furey in 'The Dead'. All of the metaphorical gnomons in the text can thus be read as sites of failure, regret, decline, loss, repression and sadness; as such, these gnomons – by virtue of their incompleteness – are sites of desire, sites of yearning, and they take on their powerful significance due to their very incompleteness.

This is not to suggest, however, that the stories in *Dubliners* configure desire in terms of a simple absence or loss. On the contrary, desire constantly conjures the ghost of that which is apparently missing, which, of course, makes what is 'absent' strangely 'present' without it ever being simply present or absent: in other words, desire in *Dubliners* is caught in the space *between* presence and absence. And it is this strange confluence of desire and absence/presence that Gabriel grapples with in the final paragraphs of the last story in the collection – 'The Dead'. After Gabriel and his wife Gretta leave the Christmas party at his Aunts' house and return to their hotel, Gabriel's desire for sexual gratification – which has been building all evening – is thwarted by his wife's distracted state. When he pries into her thoughts, he learns to his horror that not only has Gretta been thinking of Michael Furey – a young man who died out of love for her years before Gabriel had even met her – but also that she has never really stopped loving him. Gretta's invocation of Michael Furey threatens Gabriel, powerfully illustrating the menacing 'presence' that something 'absent' can have: 'A vague terror seized Gabriel at this answer, as if, at that hour when he had hoped to triumph, some impalpable and vindictive being was coming against him, gathering forces against him in its vague world' (D 221–2). Gabriel's confrontation with Michael Furey's ghost – that is, with his wife's desire – creates a rupture in Gabriel's world through which other ghosts arrive; and as they enter it, they dissolve that world:

> Generous tears filled Gabriel's eyes. He had never felt like that himself towards any woman, but he knew that such a feeling must be love. The tears gathered more thickly in his eyes and in the partial darkness he imagined he saw the form of a young man standing under a dripping tree. Other forms were near. His soul had approached that region where dwell the vast hosts of the dead. He was conscious of, but could not apprehend, their wayward and flickering existence. His own identity was fading out into a grey impalpable world: the solid world itself, which these dead had one time reared and lived in, was dissolving and dwindling.
>
> A few light taps upon the pane made him turn to the window. It had begun to snow again. He watched sleepily the flakes, silver and dark, falling obliquely against the lamplight. The time had come for him to set out on his journey westward. Yes, the newspapers were right: snow was general all over Ireland. It was falling on every part of the dark central plain, on the treeless hills, falling softly upon the Bog of Allen and, farther westward, softly falling into the dark mutinous Shannon waves. It was falling, too, upon every part of the lonely churchyard on the hill where Michael Furey lay buried. It lay thickly drifted on the crooked crosses and headstones, on the spears of the little gate, on the barren thorns. His soul swooned slowly as he heard the snow falling faintly through the universe and faintly falling, like the descent of their last end, upon all the living and the dead. (D 224–5)

Gabriel's epiphany, not surprisingly, remains incomplete, gnomon-like: he is unable to apprehend the 'wayward and flickering existence' of the absence/presence of the ghosts that Gretta's desire allows into the 'real' world of the text. Gretta's desire thus becomes a force that dissolves both the main character of the story and the reality of the world he inhabits: the dissolution of Gabriel and his world is thus also the 'death' of 'realism' and the revelation of its limitations in grappling with desire. In other words, 'The Dead' ends by suggesting that desire cannot be accommodated by the technique and style of 'realism' since it dissolves both the 'real world' and the 'concrete individual'.

That desire is not something that can be accommodated in realism once again serves to illustrate desire's relation to the gnomon: like desire, the incompleteness of the gnomon cannot be captured in terms of something – an object or a moment – 'in' the realism of the text. As Old Cotter's elliptical speech at the beginning makes clear, the gnomon points forever 'beyond' the text – 'outside' the text – to something not said. This 'pointing beyond the text' can also be read as a 'self-reflexive' movement in *Dubliners* – that is, a movement whereby the text refers or calls the reader's attention to itself as a text that is being read. Read thus, the gnomon makes it possible to read Old Cotter's elliptical speech in the 'The Sisters' as an allegory for how the text of *Dubliners* reveals the limitations of the technique or style of 'realism', and to read the young narrator's frustrated desire to know more as an allegory for the reader's position with respect to that technique or style. In other words, the gnomon's self-reflexive movement once more reveals the limitations of realism, which, as a style, is forced to leave the sort of desire that the gnomon represents as simply unspoken – a 'blank': and, as the ending of 'The Dead' illustrates, because desire dissolves realism, it requires a new style in which realism is supplemented by a certain self-reflexivity. This self-reflexivity nudges *Dubliners* in the direction of the playfully self-reflexive structures of *Ulysses* and *Finnegans Wake* that I discuss in the following chapters.[3]

CHAPTER TWO

A PORTRAIT OF THE ARTIST AS A YOUNG MAN: THE SEXUAL POLITICS OF ART

This chapter examines Joyce's first novel, *A Portrait of the Artist as a Young Man*. *Portrait*, which grew out of an earlier version of the story called *Stephen Hero* that Joyce abandoned in 1905, was first published in serial form in *The Egoist*, a journal founded by Harriet Shaw Weaver and Dora Marsden, from 1914 to 1915, and appeared in book form in 1916. The novel, set in and around the city of Dublin in the last years of the nineteenth century, is a semi-autobiographical *bildungsroman* that traces the intellectual, religious, sexual and artistic development of Stephen Dedalus from a very young boy in chapter I to his graduation from university in chapter V. What follows here explores Stephen's evolution as an artist by picking up and following the thread of his complex engagement with language. In particular, I will concentrate on how Stephen's relationship with language mediates and informs his struggles with the forces of Irishness, sexuality, religion, politics and aesthetics. Throughout this chapter, I have relied on Seamus Deane's excellent annotated edition of *Portrait*, published in 2000 by Penguin Classics. All page references to the text (P) in this chapter follow this edition.

CHAPTER I: LANGUAGE, THE BODY AND POLITICS

Portrait famously begins with a kinetic series of citations and repetitions that serve to underscore the fact that the individual – here, a very young Stephen – is, almost from birth, caught up in a doubled and complex entanglement with language: the language that describes and defines him/her and the language that s/he uses:

> Once upon a time and a very good time it was there was a moocow coming down along the road and this moocow that was coming down along the road met a nicens little boy named baby tuckoo . . .
> His father told him that story: his father looked at him through a glass: he had a hairy face.
> He was baby tuckoo. The moocow came down the road where Betty Byrne lived: she sold lemon platt.
>
> *O, the wild rose blossoms*
> *On the little green place.*
>
> He sang that song. That was his song.
>
> *O, the green wothe botheth.* (P 3)

In addition, these citations – of the formula that traditionally begins a fairytale, of Stephen's father's story, of a song Stephen sings – serve to underscore the fact that the language which describes and defines the individual – by literally turning him/her into a 'character' – also pre-exists him/her. This is not to say, however, that the individual is simply at the mercy of language: even at this very young age, Stephen has already learned to assert his individuality through citation. By repeating the words of others, Stephen changes them, and thereby manages to assume some individuality through those words. Language, then, is doubled: it is at once an impersonal force and the force that creates the individual. By the time Stephen is old enough to go to Clongowes – a boarding school run by the Jesuit religious order in County Kildare – he begins to notice that language's doubleness can also make it a treacherous, and potentially violent, force: Stephen, starting to feel the chill on the playing pitch, puts his cold hands in his pockets, and, as he does so, he becomes aware of how the word 'belt' can mean two very different things: 'That was a belt around his pocket. And a belt was also to give a fellow a belt' (P 5).

The next step in Stephen's relationship to language is illustrated by his contemplation of a 'queer word' – 'suck' – which is also another word that is fraught with double meaning insofar as it can also mean a 'teacher's pet' (P 7). 'Suck' also brings with it an expanded awareness of language: words are no longer simply sounds that are uttered by humans; they are also spoken by other things. When Stephen recalls his father pulling the plug out of a sink full of water, he hears again the sound that the dirty water had made as it passed through 'the hole of the basin': 'suck only louder' (P 8). As he thinks about the word 'suck' and the sink, Stephen finds himself starting to feel cold and then hot, which reminds him of the 'two cocks that you turned and water came out' and the 'names' printed on them – 'cold and hot' (P 8). In other words, as Stephen thinks about the *names* 'cold' and 'hot,' he starts to *feel* cold and then hot: although the narrative does not reveal it for several pages, Stephen is here experiencing the first symptoms of a fever that he has contracted as a result of being knocked into the 'square ditch' (P 7) – the cess pool into which the school's dormitory toilets emptied – by a fellow student named Wells some days earlier. It would seem, then, that for Stephen, language is composed of names that have a peculiarly intimate relationship with the body: the 'names' 'hot' and 'cold' are called forth by Stephen's feverish symptoms and also serve to give those symptoms an identifiable shape.

It is Stephen's fascination with names – specifically, two interlinked names, 'God' and 'politics' – that also makes it possible to see how his first awareness of the realms of religion and politics is inextricable from language. After he finds himself perplexed by his inability to think of what lies beyond the universe, he arrives at God's name: 'still God remained always the same God and God's real name was God' (P 13). Stephen registers a similar frustration when it comes to trying to understand the political controversy that has begun to swirl about the figure of Charles Stewart Parnell (1846–1891). Parnell was the head of the Irish Parliamentary Party and lobbied for Irish Home Rule, the establishment of an Irish legislative body with responsibility for domestic affairs. Parnell's downfall began in 1889 when it became known that he had been having an affair with Katherine O'Shea, the wife of his parliamentary colleague Captain William O'Shea, after O'Shea filed for divorce and cited him as a co-respondent. Once news of the divorce scandal – as it came to be known – began to travel, Parnell lost the support of the then English Prime Minister, William Gladstone, the Catholic Church in Ireland and, eventually, his own party. Although he does not yet understand the details of Parnell's divorce scandal, Stephen nevertheless grasps that the controversy has 'two sides' and that it has a particular name: it 'was

called politics' (P 13). Stephen thus finds himself subject to two enig-
matic names that lie beyond his powers of thought and are a source
of pain: 'it pained him that he did not know well what politics meant
and that he did not know where the universe ended' (P 14). Stephen's
religious and political pain thus anticipates the religious and political
fallout of the Parnell divorce scandal, which will tear his own com-
fortable domestic sphere to pieces: while home for Christmas holi-
days, Stephen acts as terrified witness to the savage religious and
political row that erupts between Mr Casey, a friend of Stephen's
father, and 'Dante' Riordan, a woman who stays with the Dedalus
family, over Christmas dinner. The divorce scandal had the effect
of fusing Irishness with a narrow Catholic conception of morality,
something Dante makes very clear when she rounds on Parnell:
'A traitor, an adulterer! The priests were right to abandon him. The
priests were always the true friends of Ireland' (P 38). Mr Casey, who
has been arguing for the separation of state from Church morality,
responds, 'We have had too much God in Ireland. Away with God!'
(P 39), causing Dante to storm out of the room. Stephen looks to
his father, Simon, only to see him weeping pitifully for Parnell.
Language, in the form of the names of 'God' and 'politics' is thus
experienced by Stephen as a site of painful and frightening religious
and political division.

Even though language causes frustration, pain and division, the
text nevertheless makes it clear that Stephen also experiences language as a force that can reach beyond the limitations of his thoughts
by breaking open new possibilities and paths for thinking, feeling
and acting. After his traumatic brush with Parnell's transgressive
desire and sexuality over Christmas dinner, Stephen returns to
Clongowes for the new term, only to have another encounter with
transgressive desire and sexuality. The students are full of talk about
the fate of five students who tried to run away from school, but were
later caught; they speculate on the reasons for their running away –
stealing money, drinking altar wine and so on – until one student,
Athy, tells the group why they had run away in one word: 'Smugging'
(P 42), a slang term for amorous homosexual behaviour. Although
Stephen does not at first seem to understand what the older students
mean by 'smugging', he nevertheless skirts around its meaning by
repeatedly using other words that suggest illicit sexual behaviour. This
happens as follows: first, Stephen recalls that one of the boys who
ran away, Simon Moonan (whose name suggests 'mooning'), had

one night shown him a red and green apple-shaped ball which was filled with 'creamy sweets' (P 42): the apple-shaped packaging suggests the apple in the Garden of Eden, and thus the loss of sexual innocence. Next, Stephen considers the nickname of another of the boys who ran away: 'Lady' Boyle, so-named because 'he was always at his nails paring them' (P 43). Stephen then goes on to wonder about the place where the 'smugging' supposedly took place: the square, or open toilets behind the dormitory, which empty into the ditch into which Wells pushed him. The square, with its graffiti covered walls, is, Stephen thinks repeatedly, a 'queer' place (P 43). Finally, when Stephen thinks about the boys' punishment – caning – he is very anxious about having to bend over and take his trousers down: 'you always felt like a shiver when you let down your trousers. It was the same in the bath when you undressed yourself. He wondered who had to let them down, the master or the boy himself' (P 45). When taken together, Stephen's thoughts seem to suggest that he has an intuitive grasp of what is involved in 'smugging'. Thus, between the Parnell divorce scandal and the Clongowes 'smugging' episode, language in chapter I acts as a double-edged force that creates and threatens the individual and the family, opening them up to politics, sexuality and desire. And it is with the intertwined forces of language, sexuality, desire and politics that Stephen will struggle for the rest of *Portrait*.

CHAPTER II: THE EXCITATIONS OF WORDS

As Simon Dedalus's financial situation grows ever more precarious due to his drinking, Stephen is forced to leave Clongowes; he thus has a lot of free time at the beginning of chapter II. Chapter II begins by underscoring once more Stephen's relationship to words and narrative. Because he is now older, Stephen is no longer trying to find himself in fairytales; instead, he tries to inscribe himself in longer more complex narratives, such as *The Count of Monte Cristo* (1844) by Alexandre Dumas père (1802–70) (P 64–5). Stephen's imaginative engagement with the text of *The Count of Monte Cristo* has at least four stages: he first responds to the text by making a picture out of coloured paper of the cave in which Edmund Dantes finds his treasure and converts into a hideout; next, after wearying of the picture he has made, he destroys it; the destruction of the picture then allows another 'bright picture' of Marseilles and Mercedes to 'come to his mind' (P 65); the imaginative picture of Marseilles that Stephen creates is then 'refound' or 'cited' in the 'real world'. These four stages thus allow Stephen to recreate his environment as an imaginative citation of Dumas's text: thus, the 'small whitewashed house' (P 65) near his home in Blackrock – a small well-to-do town in south County Dublin – becomes the abode of another Mercedes. But this imaginative recreation of his environment is not passive since he does not simply relive the adventures in the book: 'in his imagination he lived through a long train of adventures, marvellous as those in the book itself, towards the close of which there appeared an image of himself, grown older and sadder' (P 65). In this complex citational interplay, text, imagination and reality become wrapped around each other, and separating reality from fiction becomes very difficult.

The financial woes of the Dedalus family eventually force them to move from Blackrock to the northside of Dublin city, where Stephen begins attending Belvedere College, a secondary school also run by the Jesuit religious order. For Stephen, 'Dublin was a new and complex sensation' (P 69). Stephen connects the new and complex sensation evoked by the city as he wanders along the quays and docks to the 'restless, foolish impulses' (P 69) that continually drive him in search for Mercedes. When he finds a replacement Mercedes in the mysterious figure of 'E—— C——' (who remains unidentified until chapter III, where she is identified as 'Emma' [P 124]), whose glances agitate Stephen's blood and excite his heart, it becomes clear that the new and complex sensation of Dublin is bound up with Stephen's awakening sexuality. Stephen's first attempt to write a poem for Emma fails (P 73–4), and, as chapter II progresses, he becomes more and more subject to 'the stream of moody emotions' that being around Emma conjures in him and which are made all the worse because they 'had not yet found an outlet in verse' (P 81). Poetry – if only he could write it – would seem to function for Stephen in much the same way as masturbation insofar as turning his desire for Emma into words would offer him some sexual release. And, when Emma fails to wait for him after he has performed in a school play, the sexually frustrated poet falls back on a religious gesture: he seeks to mortify his senses with the stink of 'horse piss and rotted straw' in an effort to calm himself (P 91).

The other scene in chapter II that powerfully illustrates Stephen's complex psycho-sexual relation to words is his encounter with the word *Fœtus* while on a trip to Cork with his father, who has gone there to sell off his remaining assets. Simon, who is intent on reliving past glories, brings Stephen to his old university in an effort to find his name carved into one of the desks in the anatomy theatre. However, instead of finding the name of his father, Stephen finds the word *Fœtus* carved into the woodwork, where it produces a strong effect on him: 'On the desk before him he read the word *Fœtus* cut several times in the dark stained wood. The sudden legend startled his blood: he seemed to feel the absent students of the college about him and to shrink from their company. A vision of their life, which his father's words had been powerless to evoke, sprang up before him out of the word cut in the desk' (P 95). It is interesting that the words of paternal authority – Stephen's father – are powerless compared to the word *Fœtus*, a word that is so powerful it produces an imaginative scene that Stephen has serious difficulty in controlling. And it is the lack of control that he has here in the face of an indelible imaginative vision that prompts him to connect the scene in the anatomy theatre to those other moments when his 'monstrous' desires take control of him:

> But the word and the vision capered before his eyes as he walked back across the quadrangle and towards the college gate. It shocked him to find in the outer world a trace of what he had deemed till then a brutish and individual malady of his own mind. His monstrous reveries came thronging into his memory. They too had sprung up before him, suddenly and furiously, out of mere words. (P 95)

Stephen, in an effort to cope with the power of words to shock, disturb, incite and conjure monstrous desires, attempts to ground himself by trying to restore some semblance of paternal authority through invoking his earlier conception of words as names:

> I am Stephen Dedalus. I am walking beside my father whose name is Simon Dedalus. We are in Cork, in Ireland. Cork is a city. Our room is in the Victoria Hotel. Victoria and Stephen and Simon. Simon and Stephen and Victoria. Names. (P 98)

Stephen's attempts to ward off the power of words and their intimate connection to monstrous sexual desires with paternal authority ultimately fail: towards the end of chapter II, Stephen is once again gripped by monstrous desires which take the form of yet more words: 'the inarticulate cries and the unspoken brutal words rushed forth from his brain to force a passage. His blood was in revolt' (P 106). The manner in which Stephen is subject to these desires is worth noting because they recall not only the filthy water of the square ditch at Clongowes, but also his dim grasp of the 'queer' story of 'smugging' in the square at Clongowes: his sexual desire splits off from him to become a 'dark presence moving upon him in the darkness, a presence subtle and murmurous as a flood filling him wholly with itself. Its murmur besieged his ears like the murmur of some multitude in sleep; its subtle streams penetrated his being. His hands clenched convulsively and his teeth set together as he suffered the agony of its penetration' (P 106). In a complex image that echoes the transgressive nature of desire and smugging, Stephen is penetrated – essentially raped – by his desires, by their dark flow of murmurous language. Thus, Stephen's desires do not seem to be easily reducible to a moment of purely heterosexual desire. Stephen's response to this dark language is an orgasm of sexual frustration in which still more words burst out of him:

> [A cry] broke from him like a wail of despair from a hell of sufferers and died in a wail of furious entreaty, a cry for an iniquitous abandonment, a cry which was but the echo of an obscene scrawl which he had read on the oozing wall of a urinal. (P 106)

The word having burst from him he finds himself admitted to another world – the 'quarter of the jews' (P 107) – where prostitutes ply their trade (P 107). The prostitute that Stephen meets takes the lead in their encounter: she kisses him and Stephen succumbs to 'the dark pressure of her softly parting lips' (P 108). Through the prostitute's dark lips, 'the vehicle of a vague speech', comes a dark language of 'timid pressure, darker than the swoon of sin, softer than sound or odour' (P 108). Language is thus indissociable from sex: the dark language of sex that comes through the parted lips of a prostitute is the answer to his filthy verbal ejaculation.

CHAPTER III: FILTHY LANGUAGE

Language and 'the new and complex sensation' of a Dublin in which Stephen can now readily find sex come together in a striking image in chapter III: 'The letters of the name of Dublin lay heavily upon his mind, pushing one another surlily hither and thither with slow boorish insistence' (P 119).[1] This image neatly yokes together Stephen's complex intertwining of sex, language and the imaginative recreation of the environment. His frequent visits to prostitutes establish a 'dark peace' between body and soul (P 110); at the same time, Stephen is acutely conscious of – no doubt informed in some part by his remembrance of the political and religious war that erupted around Parnell's sexual conduct – the conflict between his sexual desires and his Catholic faith: 'he had sinned mortally not once but many times and he knew that, while he stood in danger of eternal damnation for the first sin alone, by every succeeding sin he multiplied his guilt and his punishment' (P 110). And it is his pride – the Satanic sin – in his sins that prevents him from praying to God (P 110).

Stephen's acute awareness of the religious implications of his actions undoubtedly makes him susceptible to the preacher's terrifying fire and brimstone sermons on hell that take place during a religious retreat at Belvedere (P 125–34; 137–46). But it is seeing Father Arnall, one of his former teachers at Clongowes, at the retreat that paves the way for the profound impact of those sermons on Stephen: the sight of Father Arnall prompts in Stephen a stream of visions of his time at Clongowes, and his soul becomes 'again a child's soul' (P 116). Transformed by memory into a helpless child again, Stephen is now especially vulnerable the powerful rhetorical method of the sermon: the composition of place. Composition of place was devised by Saint Ignatius of Loyola (1491–1556) and set down in *The Spiritual Exercises* (1522–1524): the person performing the spiritual exercises endeavours 'to imagine with the senses of the mind, in our imagination' (P 137) a place or object associated with their faith. Using this method, the first sermon catalogues, in terrifyingly cruel and graphic detail, the sight, sound, feel, smell and taste of hell, showing how each sense is assailed by its own particular torment:

[T]he eyes with impenetrable utter darkness, the nose with noisome odours, the ears with yells and howls and execrations, the taste with foul matter, leprous corruption, nameless suffocating filth, the touch with redhot goads and spikes, with cruel tongues of flame. (P 131)

But it is the stench of Hell that explicitly echoes the childhood scene of Stephen's traumatic fall into the square ditch – the open sewer into which runs the outflow from the toilets at Clongowes – in chapter I: 'All the filth of the world, all the offal and scum of the world, we are told, shall run there as to a vast reeking sewer when the terrible con- flagration of the last day has purged the world' (P 129). It would seem, then, that Stephen has already fallen into 'hell' and emerged from its pissy, shitty, stinking waters with a burning fever; and it would also seem that Stephen's traumatic fall into the square ditch/ hell, which is also close to the site where the smugging incident took place, has been informing all of the images of fallenness, filthiness and water that he repeatedly uses to describes sex and desire. Given all this, it is not surprising that Stephen, who spends so much time imaginatively recreating the world around him, is particularly sus- ceptible to the composition of place.

Words and language are very much at the centre of Stephen's terri- fied response to the first sermon:

> He could not grip the floor with his feet and sat heavily at his desk, opening one of his books at random and poring over it. Every word for him! It was true. God was almighty. God could call him now, call him as he sat at his desk, before he had time to be conscious of the summons. God had called him. Yes? What? Yes? (P 134)

Stephen has been so addled by the sermon that he believes he can hear God call him, but does not know what he is saying. Language and words are also at the heart of Stephen's even more terrified response to the second sermon. When he returns home, Stephen goes upstairs 'to be alone with his soul' (P 146); before entering the 'dark cave' of his bedroom – itself a sexual image – he imagines he hears voices: 'He told himself calmly that those words had absolutely no sense which had seemed to rise murmurously from the dark (P 147). He enters his bedroom, and the vision he sees is one in which small, lecherous, goat-like beasts – his sins – move restlessly through a field of weeds and shit (P 148). The beasts move in the same pattern as did the letters of 'Dublin' – 'hither and thither' (P 148; 149) – with 'soft language issuing from their lips' (P 149). The vision is too much for Stephen and he vomits profusely in fear and agony. The invasion of Stephen's body by the words of the sermon thus echoes his rape at the hands of the dark, queer murmurous language that penetrated him so forcefully in chapter II.

The language of the sermons does not merely penetrate Stephen's body – it also splits him in two: the body, according to Stephen, sins unconsciously at first; he then associates the body's subtlety in sinning with the subtlety of the 'serpent' (P 151), which then leads him to imagine 'a torpid snaky life feeding itself out of the tender marrow of his life and fattening upon the slime of lust' (P 151). The thought of being thus split then prompts Stephen to confess his sins, which become words that resemble both ejaculation and shit, transforming the dark box of the confessional into an outhouse: 'His sins trickled from his lips, one by one, trickled in shameful drops from his soul, festering and oozing like a sore, a squalid stream of vice. The last sins oozed forth, sluggish, filthy. There was no more to tell. He bowed his head, overcome' (P 156). Thus spent, Stephen is now free to take communion, and have 'God enter his purified body' (P 158).

CHAPTER IV: THE RETURN OF THE FLESH

Chapter IV deals with Stephen's daily devotions and ritual mortifications of his senses. However, it is possible to foresee the short-lived nature of these devotions given their reliance on sexualized language: after God has 'entered' him (P 158), Stephen's 'ejaculations' of filthy words and semen give way to another sort of 'ejaculations' (P 159) – short exclamatory prayers. At the same time, Stephen's soul is spoken of as female, and when he reads the devotional literature of Saint Alphonsus Liguori (1696–1787) and the Canticle of Canticles, an

> inaudible voice seemed to caress the soul, telling her names and glories, bidding her arise as for espousal and come away, bidding her look forth, a spouse [. . .]; and the soul seemed to answer with the same inaudible voice, surrendering herself: *Inter ubera mea commorabitur* [He shall lie between my breasts]. (P 164)

Given that the devotional literature caresses his soul's breasts – that is, encodes sexual language in its religious language – it is perhaps not surprising that Stephen soon finds himself entertaining yet another 'surrender' of his own (P 165), seeing it in terms of a battle with an incoming tide, awaiting 'the first timid noiseless wavelet to touch his fevered skin' (P 165), only to be saved by 'a sudden ejaculation', which is followed once more by the slow implacable advance of the tide (P 165).

The overlap of sex and religious rhetoric recurs when Stephen later meets with the spiritual director of his school in order to discuss whether or not he has a vocation as a Jesuit priest. The director comments on the dress of other religious orders, using the French for skirts, '*les jupes*', to refer to them, a word-choice that sets off a chain of sexual association in Stephen's mind:

> The names of articles of dress worn by women or of certain soft and delicate stuffs used in their making brought always to his mind a delicate and sinful perfume. [. . .] it was only amid softworded phrases or within rosesoft stuffs that he dared to conceive of the soul or body of a woman moving with tender life. (P 168)

And when the meeting with the director reawakens the smells of Clongowes and the dirty brown water of the baths, Stephen seems to relive once more the fever he contracted after being knocked into the square ditch (P 174). This series of images then resolves into the name he would bear as a Jesuit priest: 'The Reverend Stephen Dedalus, S.J.' (P 174). The name conjures up images of other priests he has known 'shot with pink tinges of suffocated anger' (P 175). It is then that Stephen realizes that he 'would fall. He had not yet fallen but he would fall silently, in an instant. Not to fall was too hard, too hard' (P 175). Thus, even as he rejects religion, the text makes it clear that Stephen cannot help but see his situation in terms of religion: he will fall, like Satan or Adam, into the sin of the world.

Stephen's realization that he will fall comes in conjunction with the possibility of going to University College Dublin. Too excited and impatient to wait for his father to return from the pub with admittance information, Stephen takes off for a walk to Dollymount Strand in north Dublin. As he passes a group of priests on their way back from a swim on the beach, Stephen feels somewhat threatened and resorts to a (slightly misquoted[2]) line of *The Testimony of the Rocks* (1857) by the Scottish geologist and Christian Hugh Miller (1802–1856) to help him pass: 'A day of dappled seaborne clouds' (P 180). This then prompts him to consider language once more:

> Words. Was it their colours? He allowed them to glow and fade, hue after hue: sunrise gold, the russet and green of apple orchards, azure of waves, the greyfringed fleece of clouds. No, it was not their colours: it was the poise and balance of the period itself.

Did he then love the rhythmic rise and fall of words better than their associations of legend and colour? Or was it that, being as weak of sight as he was shy of mind, he drew less pleasure from the reflection of the glowing sensible world through the prism of a language manycoloured and richly storied than from the contemplation of an inner world of individual emotions mirrored perfectly in a lucid supple periodic prose? (P 180)

The questions Stephen poses himself here as he crosses the rickety bridge regarding the importance of the word are intriguing. Significantly, Stephen seems to favour the 'poise', the 'balance' and the 'rhythm' of words above their ability to 'reflect' or 'mirror' either inner or outer worlds: there is thus always more than one world for Stephen. And, when it comes to the ability of words to reflect or mirror inner or outer worlds, Stephen favours their ability to reflect the inner emotional world of the individual, wondering if his choice is not informed by his poor eyesight and timidity.

Once across the bridge, Stephen continues on his way to the seashore, and the text notes his fear of the sea and its tide (P 181). Given his association earlier in the chapter of the creeping tide with the temptation of sexual sin, it is entirely possible that these fears are still the residues of the terror he experienced in chapter III as a result of the sermons. As he nears the beach, he hears 'a voice from beyond the world calling' (P 182). The voice, however, is not God's; it is the combination of shouts from a group of his school-boy acquaintances bathing in the sea, calling his name: 'Come along, Dedalus! *Bous Stephanoumenos! Bous Stephaneforos!*' (P 182). The name the boys choose for Stephen is an interesting reworking of his name in Greek: '*Bous*' is Greek for 'ox', and '*Bous Stephanoumenos!*' means, roughly, 'ox-soul of Stephen', while '*Bous Stephaneforos!*' means, also roughly, 'ox as garland-bearer for sacrifice'. At first, Stephen is repelled by the boys' wet nakedness because it reminds him of the 'dread' he feels in the face of 'the mystery of his own body' (P 182). On hearing their second round of calls, he hears in his name a new association, one that begins to take him beyond his biological father insofar as it awakens the kinship his name has with Daedalus, the artist, inventor and artificer of ancient Greek myth:

Now, as never before, his strange name seemed to him a prophecy. [. . .] Now, at the name of the fabulous artificer, he seemed to hear the noise of dim waves and to see a winged form flying above the waves and slowly climbing the air. What did it mean? Was it a quaint device opening a page of some medieval book of prophecies and symbols, a hawklike man flying sunward above the sea, a prophecy of the end he had been born to serve and had been following through the mists of childhood and boyhood, a symbol of the artist forging anew in his workshop out of the sluggish matter of the earth a new soaring impalpable imperishable being? (P 183)

The new living thing he is to create, it would seem, is in some ways Stephen himself: after all, his new Greek lineage suggests that he no longer really needs his biological parents.

The third call Stephen hears resurrects his soul from the grave of boyhood, thereby making it possible for him to 'create proudly out of the freedom and power of his soul, as the great artificer whose name he bore, a living thing, new and soaring and beautiful, impalpable, imperishable' (P 184). It is in this frenzied spirit that he encounters a girl wading on the beach:

A girl stood before him in midstream, alone and still, gazing out to sea. She seemed like one whom magic had changed into the likeness of a strange and beautiful seabird. Her long slender bare legs were delicate as a crane's and pure save where an emerald trail of seaweed had fashioned itself as a sign upon the flesh. Her thighs, fuller and softhued as ivory, were bared almost to the hips, where the white fringes of her drawers were like feathering of soft white down. Her slateblue skirts were kilted boldly about her waist and dovetailed behind her. Her bosom was as a bird's, soft and slight, slight and soft as the breast of some darkplumaged dove. But her long fair hair was girlish: and girlish, and touched with the wonder of mortal beauty, her face. (P 185–6)

The bird-girl Stephen meets is interesting for a number of reasons; she may or may not be 'real': she can be read as Stephen's first Daedalian creation, a vision of his female soul or a mixture of both. Insofar as she is associated with flight, it is possible to see the bird-girl as a projection of Stephen's new relationship with his name, while the sexualized nature of her appearance reflects Stephen's realization that he must fall into the sin of the world: she bares her legs 'almost to the hips,' exposing her underwear. The sexual aspect of the bird-girl's appearance allows her to merge with the tidal rhythms of Dublin, desire and sin: she gently stirs the incoming tidal flow 'with her foot hither and thither. The first faint noise of gently moving water broke the silence, low and faint and whispering, faint as the bells of sleep; hither and thither, hither and thither' (P 186). The text underlines the bird-girl's association with the rhythms of desire by describing her in language that also moves hither and thither like the tide: her bosom is 'soft and slight, slight and soft'. Stephen's reaction to the bird-girl is also interesting: his trembling eyelids suggest orgasm; his soul swoons in ecstasy amid 'Glimmering and trembling, trembling and unfolding, a breaking light, an opening flower' (P 187). It is also worth noting that Stephen's desire for the bird-girl is, in some ways, lesbian and auto-erotic: his female soul looks with desire on a female form that is perhaps also itself. The appearance of the bird-girl thus complicates even further Stephen's desire, making it very difficult to pin down: it contains elements of heterosexual and male/female homosexual desire that are directed inward and outward; nevertheless, for all its complexity, Stephen's desire is always bound up with language and words.

CHAPTER V: LANGUAGES, POLITICS, AESTHETICS, EXILE

(a) Languages

Given the poetic ecstasy of Stephen's encounter with the bird-girl at the end of the previous chapter, chapter V's opening scene, which centres on a very earthbound image of the artist, sitting in the kitchen, late for his morning lecture, draining 'his third cup of watery tea to the dregs' and surrounded by the debris of a family breakfast that signals ever-growing poverty (P 188), seems almost brutally ironic. Stephen it seems, has not even managed to fly past Clongowes: the hole that has been made in the beef dripping in order to fry bread for breakfast brings 'back to his memory the dark turfcoloured water of the bath at Clongowes' (P 188). This is also the second time that the older Stephen has recalled the aftermath of the traumatic scene of his fall into the shitty, pissy water of the square ditch/hell. The brutality of the text's ironic picture of Stephen in chapter V is amplified when the artist, closing in on age 20 and who on Dollymount strand no longer seemed to need his biological parents because he was forging himself anew in the name of his mythic artificer-father, submits himself to being washed – washed! – by his mother (P 189). Stephen's biological father, in a cutting reference to his son – but one that underscores the fluidity of Stephen's desire – angrily asks one of his daughters from upstairs if 'your lazy bitch of a brother gone out yet', just as Stephen leaves the kitchen (P 189).

Stephen's walk to university, which echoes his youthful translations of Blackrock village and Dublin into the text of *The Count of Monte Cristo*, once again underscores the importance of language: each section of the walk is accompanied by the prose of the German author Gerhart Hauptmann (1862–1946), the prose of John Henry Cardinal Newman (1801–1890), the poetry of the Italian Guido Cavalcanti (1259–1300) and the works of the English poet Ben Jonson (1572–1637) (P 190). Also accompanying him on his walks are the 'spectral words of Aristotle and Aquinas' in which he searches for 'the essence of beauty' (P 190). The text also points out that Stephen's readings of both Saint Thomas Aquinas (1225–1274), a Catholic philosopher who attempted to reconcile Catholic doctrine with the works of Aristotle, and Aristotle himself, are not only slim but also that they have 'rapt him from the companionships of youth' (P 191). One of the few remaining companions that Stephen has is Cranly, and as Stephen continues his journey, he has a vision of Cranly – or, at least half of him: 'Why was it that when he thought of Cranly he could never raise before his mind the entire image of his body but only the image of the head and face?' (P 192). The image of Cranly is also a 'severed head', a 'deathmask', and 'priestlike' because Stephen has repeatedly confessed his 'tumults and unrest and longings' to it (P 192). It would seem, then, at least on some level, Stephen wishes Cranly dead; the vision of Cranly that Stephen has is further complicated by Stephen's careful cataloguing of his friend's face, which lingers on the shape of his nose, the shape and colour of his lips, the shading along his jaws, and his 'dark womanish eyes' (P 192–3). It is as if Stephen's relationship with his friend is worked over by complex attractions that cause him to resent his friend enough to prefer to see him as bodiless and dead. Cranly thus serves to underscore the multivalent forms of Stephen's desire.

Cranly's womanish eyes then open up yet another feminine image to Stephen:

> Through this image he had a glimpse of a strange dark cavern of speculation but at once turned away from it, feeling that it was not

yet the hour to enter it. But the nightshade of his friend's listless-
ness seemed to be diffusing in the air around him a tenuous and
deadly exhalation and he found himself glancing from one casual
word to another on his right or left in stolid wonder that they had
been so silently emptied of instantaneous sense until every mean
shop legend bound his mind like the words of a spell and his soul
shrivelled up sighing with age as he walked on in a lane among
heaps of dead language. His own consciousness of language was
ebbing from his brain and trickling into the very words themselves
which set to band and disband themselves in wayward rhythms[.]
(P 193)

This is a complex moment in the text: Cranly's femininity calls forth
another feminine image: 'a strange dark cavern'. At the same time,
Cranly's image also acts as a poison – 'nightshade' – on Stephen, one
that also robs the words on the shopfronts he passes of their 'sense'
or meaning. These words, drained of their sense by Cranly's poison,
then act as a 'spell' on Stephen, transforming the whole city about him
into 'heaps of dead language', robbing him of his own consciousness
of language, which now begins to flow into 'the words themselves'.
These words rhythmically break apart and reform, dragging from
Stephen one of his poems about ivy (P 193). Although Stephen dismisses his poem as 'drivel', it nevertheless seems that Stephen's complex and ambivalent relationship to Cranly's feminized image and its
poison are a necessary stage in Stephen's poetic method: once the
word 'ivy' is drained of its meaning, rhythmically breaks apart and
reforms, Stephen can then connect it to the word 'ivory' with which
it has no logical or meaningful relationship – just a relationship of
similar sounds and letters. This then allows 'ivory' – not the meaning
of the word nor the thing-in-itself, but the *word itself* – to shine 'in his
brain, clearer and brighter than any ivory sawn from the mottled
tusks of elephants', a shining that then sounds across many languages: '*Ivory, ivoire, avorio, ebur*' (P 193).

(b) Politics

Stephen's morning of thinking about the mysteries of language continues when he finally gets to university and meets the dean of studies
who is in the middle of trying to light a fire (P 200). Stephen, in his
first foray into 'esthetic discussion' in the novel, tries to explain the

need for linguistic clarity by contrasting the use of words in the 'literary tradition' with their use in the 'language of the marketplace'. His efforts run into some unexpected comic and geo-political difficulties:

> – One difficulty, said Stephen, in esthetic discussion is to know whether words are being used according to the literary tradition or according to the tradition of the marketplace. I remember a sentence of Newman's in which he says of the Blessed Virgin that she was detained in the full company of the saints. The use of the word in the marketplace is quite different. I hope I am not detaining you.
> – Not in the least, said the dean politely.
> – No, no, said Stephen, smiling, I mean . . .
> – Yes, yes; I see, said the dean quickly, I quite catch the point: *detain.*
> He thrust forward his under jaw and uttered a dry short cough.
> – To return to the lamp, he said, the feeding of it is also a nice problem. You must choose the pure oil and you must be careful when you pour it in not to overflow it, not to pour in more than the funnel can hold.
> – What funnel? asked Stephen.
> – The funnel through which you pour the oil into your lamp.
> – That? said Stephen. Is that called a funnel? Is it not a tundish?
> – What is a tundish?
> – That. The . . . the funnel.
> – Is that called a tundish in Ireland? asked the dean. I never heard the word in my life. (P 203–4)

Stephen's attempt at 'esthetic discussion' with the dean is hampered by the comical and political treachery of language; in trying to explain the need for a strict definition of terms in aesthetic discussion, Stephen is repeatedly caught out by the doubleness and mobility of language: the same words mean different things in different contexts, the same objects go by different names. He thus comes to see that although both he and the dean speak English, it is not a universal language: it is split with cultural, political and social differences. This prompts Stephen to ponder his Irishness:

How different are the words *home, Christ, ale, master*, on his lips and on mine! I cannot speak or write these words without unrest of spirit. His language, so familiar and so foreign, will always be for me an acquired speech. I have not made or accepted its words. (P 205)

After he leaves the dean, Stephen encounters the political in two forms; the first is when he is pressed by his friend MacCann to sign a petition in support of 'universal brotherhood' (P 212–13): Stephen asks if he will be paid to sign it, which insults MacCann's idealist sensibilities. An argument ensues, and MacCann ends by declaring to Stephen, 'I believe you're a good fellow but you have yet to learn the dignity of altruism and the responsibility of the human individual' (P 215). Stephen's and MacCann's exchange is capped by another student's voice decreeing that 'Intellectual crankery is better out of this movement than in it' (P 215). Stephen's argument with MacCann thus ironically exposes the intolerant practices of those who would preach the notion of 'universal brotherhood'.

Stephen's second encounter with politics brings to a head his longstanding issues with Irish nationalism post-Parnell. Stephen ironically asks Davin, who owns a handbook of fenian – or Irish rebel – military exercises, if he has signed the petition in support of universal peace and brotherhood. Davin makes it clear that he does not see any irony, declaring that he is 'an Irish nationalist first and foremost' (P 218). Puzzled by what he sees as Stephen's inconsistent stance on Irish–English relations, Davin asks Stephen why he is not a nationalist and why he stopped attending Irish classes (P 219). Davin's questions – and the ensuing conversation – are important insofar as they serve to expose the complex intertwining of Stephen's jealous desires with his rejection of the nationalist movement: he left the Irish classes because he saw Emma 'talking and laughing' with the teacher, a priest named Father Moran (P 219). And, once the issue of Stephen's sexual desires is broached, it becomes clear that they have always been too much for Davin to handle: 'When you told me that night in Harcourt Street those things about your private life, honest to God, Stevie, I was not able to eat my dinner' (P 219), to which Stephen replies, 'You mean I am a monster' (P 219). Stephen's choice of the word 'monster' is crucial here: it explicitly recalls the word Stephen twice uses in chapter II to describe his 'filthy orgies' of desire (P 97) – 'monstrous' (P 96 and 98). In other words, the text makes it clear that there is no room for the sort of sexual desires that Stephen expresses and acts upon in the form of Irish nationalism Davin represents: an Irish nationalism that has become morally and sexually stunted due to the Parnell divorce scandal and the Church's response to it. Thus, it is difficult to extract Irish nationalism from the complex entanglements of jealousy, desire and sexuality in the text, and this complexity should be borne in mind when reading Stephen's oft-quoted rejection of nationalism: 'You talk to me of nationality, language, religion. I shall try to fly by those nets' (P 220). Stephen cannot be said to be rejecting Irish nationalism per se; rather, he appears to be rejecting a strain of Irish nationalism that is too narrow and too timid in its conception of desire and sexuality.

(c) Aesthetics

Stephen leaves the realm of politics with Lynch, a fellow student, and, in the peripatetic dialogue that ensues, outlines his aesthetic theory to him (P 221). In many ways, it is possible to see Stephen's theory as his attempt to set up a bulwark against both the disconcerting desires that he continues to find himself subject to and the psychological traumas of the sermons of chapter III. Read thus, Stephen's aesthetic theory is both a form of self-therapy and an attempt to forge a quasi-religion of aestheticism using fragments of the works of Aristotle, Aquinas and, to a lesser extent, Plato and the German dramatist, Gotthold Lessing (1729–1781).

Stephen begins his discussion of aesthetics by trying to define pity and terror:

> Pity is the feeling which arrests the mind in the presence of whatsoever is grave and constant in human sufferings and unites it with the human sufferer. Terror is the feeling which arrests the mind in the presence of whatsoever is grave and constant in human sufferings and unites it with the secret cause. (P 221)

The key word here for Stephen is 'arrest' because 'the tragic emotion is static' (P 222):

> The feelings excited by improper art are kinetic, desire or loathing. Desire urges us to possess, to go to something; loathing urges us to

abandon, to go from something. These are kinetic emotions. The arts which excite them, pornographical or didactic, are therefore improper arts. The esthetic emotion (I use the general term) is therefore static. The mind is arrested and raised above desire and loathing. (P 222)

In other words, anything that does not arrest the mind of the viewer, anything that excites desire or loathing, is not proper art: such things incite to viewer to either move towards it or away from it. One can thus hear in Stephen's thoughts on 'arrest' and 'stasis' an echo of the 'paralysis' explored in *Dubliners* on the aesthetic plane; it is also interesting to note here how often the metaphorics of being outside the law – that is, the metaphorics of arrest and apprehension – pepper Stephen's aesthetic theory. When Lynch says that he once wrote his name across the bum of a statue of Venus in a Dublin museum, Stephen dismisses him as abnormal for having eaten pieces of cow dung at school (P 222). Lynch's 'bum-centric' worldview is what for Stephen marks him as perverse (it is worth noting here that in many ways Lynch is here an echo of Mr Bloom in *Ulysses*): but Stephen should be no stranger to having had shit in his mouth at school given his fall into the square ditch. Stephen, it seems, is thus keen to erase representations of the female bum and shit from his theory because it is doubly kinetic: it is a place of both desire and loathing, a site of sexuality and shit, not thus unlike the square ditch/hell.

That Stephen wants to remove the actions and reactions of the body from his theory becomes clear a page later: 'But we are just now in a mental world' (P 223), and in this mental world, anything that is emotionally kinetic – that excites desire or loathing – is not aesthetic because it produces reactions that are not more than physical (P 223). In other words, desire or loathing are simply reflex actions of the body (P 223) and are thus 'improper' in the realm of aesthetics: that is why, according to Stephen, Lynch's writing on Venus's bum is purely kinetic, reflexive and physical.

One might wonder if the 'verses and cadences' that Stephen recites for Davin and which act as the 'veils of his own longing and dejection' (P 195) can be squared with his aesthetic theory: were they not poetry? One might also wonder how Stephen's theory would deal with the bird-girl both he and the reader encounter at the end of chapter IV; it would seem that insofar as it is suffused with desire, the encounter with the bird-girl cannot constitute a 'true' aesthetic experience according to Stephen's philosophy. This then introduces a difficult problem for the reader of *Portrait*: it begins to suggest that Stephen's aesthetic theory may not be able to fully account for the text of which it is a part. If that is the case, then it would seem that the text is ironically distancing Stephen through his aesthetic theory and not just its presentation of him. It would seem that *Portrait* has begun to anticipate the question of the relation of part to whole on behalf of the reader, a situation that becomes clear when Stephen starts to explain how the 'stasis' of an 'ideal pity' or 'ideal terror' is 'called forth, prolonged and at last dissolved by what I call the rhythm of beauty' (P 223). Rhythm is, according to Stephen, the 'relation of part to part in any aesthetic whole or of an aesthetic whole to its part or parts or of any part to the esthetic whole of which it is a part' (P 223). In other words, the reader's asking him/herself about the relation of Stephen's aesthetic theory to the book in which it is a part is already called for by the text's presentation of that theory. All at once *Portrait* is not only writing about itself, but criticizing itself. With this in mind, the reader might now start to wonder if the rhythmic relations between parts and of part to whole in Stephen's theory are not in themselves kinetic insofar as the viewer has to move 'inside' the object being contemplated from part to part and 'towards' and 'away' from the object when considering the rhythmic relations of part to whole. In other words, it does not seem to be possible for Stephen to remove the kinetic from this theory. And, when the reader considers Stephen's theory in relation to *Portrait*'s many recurrent images of the body, of sexuality, of filth, of desire, of disgust and of terror, it would seem that, short of excising the pages on which these appear, it is impossible to remove the body and its desires from that theory: Stephen's theory necessarily must enter into relationships with the textual imagery of the body and desire that surrounds it. This is not to say that Stephen's aesthetic theory is simply useless; but it stands in ironic contrast to the 'kinetic' text that surrounds it, which serves to underline its status as the aesthetic theory of a young man.

Stephen goes on to define art as 'the human disposition of sensible or intelligible matter for an esthetic end' (P 224), and – following Aquinas – the beautiful as that which pleases the apprehension (P 225), again insisting this apprehension is static. Beauty is 'beheld by the imagination' (P 225) and, since the 'first step in the direction of beauty is to understand the frame and scope of the imagination,

to comprehend the act itself of esthetic apprehension' (P 225), experiencing or apprehending something beautiful is self-reflexive:

> [A]ll people who admire a beautiful object find in it certain rela-
> tions which satisfy and coincide with the stages themselves of all
> aesthetic apprehension. These relations of the sensible, visible to
> you through one form and to me through another, must be there-
> fore the necessary qualities of beauty. (P 227)

Stephen then outlines this process, once again following, for the
most part, Aquinas (*Summa Theologica* I.39.9): '*ad pulcritudinem tria
requiruntur, integritas, consonantia, claritas.* I translate it so: *Three
things are needed for beauty, wholeness, harmony and radiance*' (P 229).
He then sets about explaining this using of the example of the basket
a passing butcher boy wears on his head like a helmet: the first
phase of aesthetic apprehension isolates the basket by drawing a line
around it, separating it from the rest of the world ('not basket'):
'You apprehended it as *one* thing. You see it as one whole. You apprehend its wholeness. That is *integritas*' (P 230); the second phase
involves passing from point to point in the basket, following its formal lines:

> [Y]ou apprehend it as balanced part against part within its limits;
> you feel the rhythm of its structure. In other words the synthesis
> of immediate perception is followed by the analysis of apprehen-
> sion. Having first felt that it is *one* thing you feel now that it is a
> *thing.* You apprehend it as complex, multiple, divisible, separable,
> made up of its parts, the result of its parts and their sum, harmo-
> nious. That is *consonantia.* (P 230)

The third phase is a little more complex; unable to satisfactorily
explain what Aquinas means by '*claritas*', Stephen silently invokes
the Scholastic philosopher Duns Scotus (1270–1308) and his notion
of *quidditas* to explain the basket: 'You see that it is that thing which
it is and no other thing. The radiance of which he speaks in the scholastic *quidditas,* the *whatness* of a thing' (P 231). Stephen's attempts at
defining *claritas* and *quidditas* are related to the notion of 'epiphany'
as it is found in *Stephen Hero.* Before moving on to the final section
of Stephen's aesthetic theory, this is perhaps the place to note the
irony of Stephen's choice of an upturned basket carried by a butcher

boy on his head as an aesthetic example: the basket is misused, the basket is empty, and the basket is full of holes.

The final section of Stephen's peripatetic discussion of aesthetics involves his conception of beauty 'in the marketplace', where the artist must put his work outside himself and before the eyes of others (P 231). There are three forms of art in this context, which, according to Stephen, constitute a sort of progression of artistic form:

> These forms are: the lyrical form, the form wherein the artist presents his image in immediate relation to himself; the epical form, the form wherein he presents his image in mediate relation to himself and to others; the dramatic form, the form wherein he presents his image in immediate relation to others. (P 232)

After Lynch praises Stephen's questions on what can be said to be art for their 'true Scholastic stink' (P 232), Stephen then seems to contradict himself by suggesting that there is not really any such progress of forms at all, least of all in Lessing's discussion of statues in his *Laocoon* (1766): 'The art, being inferior, does not present the forms I spoke of distinguished clearly one from another. Even in literature, the highest and most spiritual art, the forms are often confused' (P 232). This suggests, somewhat ironically, that the neat categories of Stephen's aesthetic theory cannot account for the confusions and complexities of the arts he invokes.

Stephen then goes on to suggest that the first form of art is lyrical, and it echoes the 'rhythmical cry such as ages ago cheered on the man who pulled at the oar' (P 232); in the next form, the epic, 'narrative is no longer purely personal. The personality of the artist passes into the narration itself, flowing round and round the persons and the action like a vital sea' (P 233); the third form is the dramatic, and it

> is reached when the vitality which has flowed and eddied round each person fills every person with such vital force that he or she assumes a proper and intangible aesthetic life. The personality of the artist, at first a cry or a cadence or a mood and then a fluid and lambent narrative, finally refines itself out of existence, impersonalises itself, so to speak. (P 233)

It is perhaps ironic that Stephen should use the sea here as the governing metaphor for how the artist relates to each of these forms because the sea allows the body to flood back into his aesthetic theory; it is clear from chapter IV that Stephen's 'flesh dreaded the cold infrahuman odour of the sea' (P 181), and that that fear has to do with the nakedness of swimmers which reminds him of his dread 'of the mystery of his own body' (P 182). A similar irony attends Stephen's final description of the dramatic form as 'life purified in and reprojected from the human imagination', in relation to which the artist, 'like the God of the creation, remains within or behind or beyond or above his handiwork, invisible, refined out of existence, indifferent, paring his fingernails' (P 233). Not only does the artist become God – yet another reminder to the reader that Stephen's mind is so supersaturated with religion that he is unable to conceive of artistry outside of the confines of religion – he becomes not unlike Lady Boyle – one of the boys involved in chapter I's smugging scandal – so called because 'he was always at his nails, paring them' (P 43). It would seem then, that for all his efforts, Stephen is simply not able to remove kinetic emotions, desires or the body from art: they keep returning, as it were, by the back door.

In many ways, the battle between Stephen's quasi-religious artistic theory and his desire rages around two particular figures for the remainder of *Portrait*: Emma and Cranly. After their walk, Stephen and Lynch return to the steps of the National Library, where there are groups of boys and girls dotted about. The narrative only identifies one figure – Cranly – before Lynch whispers 'Your beloved is here' (P 234) to Stephen. Although Stephen's eyes wander towards an unnamed female figure – undoubtedly Emma – who is standing among a group of girls also gathered at the library door, Lynch's remark seems deliberately ambiguous: there is a split second where it seems that the word 'beloved' indicates Cranly. Stephen's feelings toward Emma are decidedly kinetic: they veer from his feelings of jealousy at having seen her talk to the priest whose Irish classes he stopped attending to feeling as if he judged her 'simple and strange' 'bird's life' and her 'simple and strange' 'bird's heart' too harshly (P 235). Emma is also in Stephen's thoughts when he awakes the next morning ready to write, the words having come to him in the night: 'O! In the virgin womb of the imagination the word was made flesh. Gabriel the seraph had come to the virgin's chamber' (P 236). It is interesting to note how the body – a woman's body – and religion – the Annunciation of the Angel Gabriel to the Virgin Mary that she was pregnant with Christ – combine to furnish the metaphors for

Stephen's imaginative process of artistic creation. The gendering of artistic creation also becomes volatile in this metaphor to the extent that it recalls the Catholic tradition which holds that because she was impregnated by the word of the Angel through her ear, Mary remained a virgin: Stephen thus becomes the 'virgin' visited, penetrated and impregnated by the male semen-word. It is also possible that Stephen's conception of the artistic process as a virgin birth acts, in some ways, as a sort of compensation for his growing alienation from his mother over her increasing devotion to religion. If, for Stephen, the artist is always on some level a maternal and religious figure, then he has found a way to keep both the mother and religion close.

The poem Stephen writes bears further analysis (P 236, 240 and 242–3): it is a villanelle, a 19-line poem of fixed form that consists of five tercets (*aba*) and a final quatrain (*abaa*). The first line is repeated as lines 6, 12 and 18; the third line is repeated as lines 9, 15 and 19, and the first and third lines are joined to form the final couplet of the quatrain. The poem thus has a highly kinetic 'hither and thither' structure; as such, it recalls the movement of the letters of the name Dublin, the movement of the sins in the field of shit, and the movement of the bird-girl's toe as she stirs the tidal waters on the beach. After composing the first three stanzas, Stephen leans back and relives a dance with Emma; this image gives way to his recollection of having run out of the Irish class after he saw her talking to the priest. Stephen's jealousy surges again and breaks 'up violently her fair image', flinging 'the fragments on all sides' (P 239), dispersing Emma into the other images of women who simultaneously attracted and rejected him (P 239). His anger towards Emma becomes a rivalry of priests: the Irish teacher, 'one who was but schooled in the discharging of a formal rite' and him, 'a priest of the eternal imagination, transmuting the daily bread of experience into the radiant body of everliving life' (P 240). The image of the Eucharist draws two more stanzas from him. And as he wonders if Emma has been conscious of his worship of her, Stephen's poetry becomes decidedly kinetic:

A glow of desire kindled again his soul and fired and fulfilled all his body. Conscious of his desire she was waking from odorous sleep, the temptress of his villanelle. Her eyes, dark and with a look of languor, were opening to his eyes. Her nakedness yielded to him, radiant, warm, odorous and lavishlimbed, enfolded him like a shining cloud, enfolded him like water with a liquid life: and like a cloud of vapour or like waters circumfluent in space the liquid letters of speech, symbols of the element of mystery, flowed forth over his brain. (P 242)

Thus enflamed, he completes the final quatrain (P 243). The irony here is palpable: it would seem that Stephen is unable to write his poem in a way that could fit with his aesthetic theory; thus, the text once again exposes the limitations of that theory – namely its proscription of the body and desire.

(d) Exile

Throughout chapter V, language remains for Stephen a source of bliss; later in the text, as he watches birds fly about on Molesworth Street, Stephen begins to ponder the art of augury – the Roman art of divination by watching the flight patterns of birds – and begins to feel vaguely afraid of the future: both in terms of what the birds might portend and the meaning of the portent of his name, the name of the 'hawklike man', Daedalus (P 244). While watching the birds, a snippet of the farewell speech from the play *The Countess Cathleen* (1892) by W B Yeats (1865–1939) comes to him. Stephen's reaction to the words of the speech is a familiarly liquid one of blissful joy:

A soft liquid joy flowed through the words where the soft long vowels hurtled noiselessly and fell away, lapping and flowing back and ever shaking the white bells of their waves in mute chime and mute peal and soft low swooning cry; and he felt that the augury he had sought in the wheeling darting birds and in the pale space of sky above him had come forth from his heart like a bird from a turret, quietly and swiftly. (P 245)

Yeats's words have acted for Stephen as the sign he sought in the sky: all that remains is the interpretation of the sign: 'Symbol of departure or of loneliness' (P 245)?

It is while standing on the library steps as dusk settles that Stephen sees Emma again; when she bows to Cranly as she passes, Stephen begins to suspect that the pair are taking an interest in each other (P 252). As Emma continues on her way through the falling darkness, Stephen recalls – incorrectly – to himself some lines from 'A Litany in Time of Plague' by the English author Thomas Nashe (1567–1601): '*darkness falls from the air*' (P 253). Immediately he feels the stirring of joy: 'A trembling joy, lambent as a faint light, played like a fairy host around him. But why? Her passage through the darkening air or the verse with its black vowels and its opening sound, rich and lute-like?' (P 253). Stephen then begins to recall images of sex and disease from Elizabethan songwriters – apparently without pleasure:

> They were secret and enflaming but her image was not entangled by them. That was not the way to think of her. It was not even the way in which he thought of her. Could his mind then not trust itself? Old phrases, sweet only with a disinterred sweetness like the figseeds Cranly rooted out of his gleaming teeth. (P 253)

Emma's image is thus free from the images that enflame Stephen: it would seem that only now she is 'art' in the sense of Stephen's aesthetic theory. The part that does enflame Stephen – the faded 'sweetness' of these images of sex and disease – remind him instead of the figseeds that Cranly picks from his gleaming teeth. Just as Stephen finishes contemplating Cranly's mouth, he catches Emma's scent on the air and the image of her body becomes entwined in his desire and his 'music' (P 254): she is thus no longer proper art. As his desirous music flows across the image of Emma's body, it is interrupted by a louse biting his neck:

> But the tickling of the skin of his neck made his mind raw and red. The life of his body, illclad, illfed, louseeaten, made him close his eyelids in a sudden spasm of despair: and in the darkness he saw the brittle bright bodies of lice falling from the air and turning often as they fell. Yes; and it was not darkness that fell from the air. It was brightness.
>
> *Brightness falls from the air.*
>
> He had not even remembered rightly Nash's line. All the images it had awakened were false. His mind bred vermin. His thoughts were lice born of the sweat of sloth.
> He came back quickly along the colonnade towards the group of students. Well then, let her go and be damned to her. She could

love some clean athlete who washed himself every morning to the waist and had black hair on his chest. Let her. (P 254)

Stephen squashes the louse – ironically one of those things, along with excrement, that he had considered as a possible work of art (P 232) – and lets it fall. As it falls, he has a mesmerising vision of lice falling from the air and becomes painfully aware of his body, the awareness of which transforms his desire into an uneasy kinetic admixture of jealousy and loathing.

It is while waiting for Cranly to join him for a walk that Stephen seems to first register an awareness of the necessity of engaging kinetic emotions in his art: as he stares 'angrily' at the 'patricians of Ireland' (P 258) through the drawing room window of Maple's Hotel, he wonders how he might

> cast his shadow over the imaginations of their daughters, before their squires begat upon them, that they might breed a race less ignoble than their own? And under the deepened dusk he felt the thoughts and desires of the race to which he belonged flitting like bats across the dark country lanes, under trees by the edges of streams and near the poolmottled bogs. (P 259)

In other words, Stephen wonders how he would engage the desires of those patricians' daughters so as to rework them: the key to this evolving conception of his art is thus the active engagement of female desires.

Stephen finds himself shaken from these thoughts by Cranly's 'strong grip' (P 259), and they begin their walk, during which Stephen's loss of faith and his mother's anxiety over that loss become the topic of conversation. When asked by Cranly if he will receive communion at Easter as per his mother's wishes, Stephen once more asserts his Satanic pride saying, 'I will not serve' (P 260). After Stephen effortlessly rattles off the four transcendent qualities that will distinguish the bodies of saints – 'bright, agile, impassible and, above all, subtle' (P 261) – his friend makes an observation: 'It is a curious thing, do you know, Cranly said dispassionately, how your mind is supersaturated with the religion in which you say you disbelieve. Did you believe in it when you were at school? I bet you did' (P 261). Cranly is certainly partially correct here: Stephen is utterly supersaturated by religion, utterly in its thrall, a circumstance that is underlined by his response to Cranly's question, 'Do you love your mother?' (P 261) – itself an echo of the riddle that so perplexed him in chapter I (P 11): 'I don't know what your words mean' (P 261). In fact, the only thing that Stephen admits to having tried – and failed – to love is God (P 261). However, it later becomes very clear that Stephen is not a non-believer in any simple sense:

> – And is that why you will not communicate, Cranly asked, because you are not sure of that too, because you feel that the host, too, may be the body and blood of the son of God and not a wafer of bread? And because you fear that it may be?
> – Yes, Stephen said quietly, I feel that and I also fear it. (P 264)

Stephen fears that there may be a reality to religion; at the same time, he also feels that he cannot, for the sake of his soul, pay 'false homage to a symbol behind which are massed twenty centuries of authority and veneration' (P 265). Stephen is thus very much in the grip of religion, and he remains caught there by a double-bind of fear and doubt.

The last couple of pages of Cranly's and Stephen's walk are somewhat odd; as they walk, the two of them hear a young servant girl singing the popular music hall song, 'Rosie O'Grady', while she sharpens knives. The servant's song conjures a very peculiar figure out of thin air, which both young men appear to see: 'The figure of woman as she appears in the liturgy of the church passed silently through the darkness' (P 265–6); she is 'slender as a boy' and her voice is as 'frail and as high as a boy's' (P 266). After this mysterious figure of indeterminate sex passes, Cranly takes up the servant girl's song:

> They went on together, Cranly repeating in strongly stressed rhythm the end of the refrain:
>
> *And when we are married,*
> *O, how happy we'll be*
> *For I love sweet Rosie O'Grady*
> *And Rosie O'Grady loves me.*
>
> – There's real poetry for you, he said. There's real love.
> He glanced sideways at Stephen with a strange smile and said:

– Do you consider that poetry? Or do you know what the words mean?
– I want to see Rosie first, said Stephen.
– She's easy to find, Cranly said. (P 266)

Cranly's behaviour here is intriguing: he stresses the 'loves me', calling it 'real love', and gives Stephen a 'strange smile'. What is Cranly trying to say? When Stephen says he 'wants to see Rosie first', Cranly cryptically replies that 'she's easy to find', almost as if to say that 'Rosie' might already be under Stephen's nose. Given that this exchange follows the appearance of a strange singing woman-boy in the text, it is entirely possible that Cranly is the 'Rosie O'Grady' in question. Stephen then turns to look at him, and has the following thoughts:

[I]n the shadow of the trees Stephen saw his pale face, framed by the dark, and his large dark eyes. Yes. His face was handsome: and his body was strong and hard. He had spoken of a mother's love. He felt then the sufferings of women, the weaknesses of their bodies and souls: and would shield them with a strong and reso- lute arm and bow his mind to them.
    Away then: it is time to go. (P 266)

It seems very odd that Stephen sees Cranly's large dark eyes, his handsome face, his strong hard body and his sympathy for women as the very things that will finally impel him to leave Ireland with the famous declaration:

I will not serve that in which I no longer believe, whether it call itself my home, my fatherland, or my church: and I will try to express myself in some mode of life or art as freely as I can and as wholly as I can, using for my defence the only arms I allow myself to use – silence, exile and cunning. (P 268–9)

This declaration prompts Cranly to seize Stephen's arm once more, and Stephen, 'thrilled by his touch', tells him that he has always had the ability to make him confess (P 269). When these incidents are taken together, they strongly suggest that there is an unspoken undercurrent of desire running back and forth between Stephen and Cranly. This undercurrent of unspoken desire – which explains in part Stephen's strange vision of Cranly just before he sees the word 'ivory' as a poetic word (P 192–3) and which Lynch's comment on page 234 has also hinted at – comes closest to being uttered when, after they apparently share the vision of the woman-boy, Cranly stresses the 'loves me' at the end of 'Rosie O'Grady'. When Stephen says that he is not afraid to be alone or leave another, even if that means making a mistake, Cranly asks if that also means 'not to have any one person [. . .] who would be more than a friend, more even than the noblest and truest friend a man ever had' (P 269). When Stephen asks him if the 'more than friend' he speaks of is himself, Cranly's response goes unspoken: 'Cranly did not answer' (P 269).[3]

The style of the narrative changes immediately after Cranly's silence: the third-person narrator disappears and Stephen begins to speak in his own voice as a first-person narrator. Stephen's narration consists of an irregular series of fragmented diary entries that begin on 20 March and end on 27 April, the day Stephen leaves Ireland. That Stephen gets to speak in his own voice for the final pages of the text suggests that the young artist is on the cusp of beginning to find his own voice and freedom. But the text's ironic portrayal of Stephen overtakes him one last time. The irony here is not cruel, but rather affectionate; it serves to remind the reader that even though the 20-year-old artist-god is about to take flight in the company of his mythical father, he still needs his earth-bound mother to pack his case:

26 April: Mother is putting my new secondhand clothes in order. She prays now, she says, that I may learn in my own life and away from home and friends what the heart is and what it feels. Amen. So be it. Welcome, O life, I go to encounter for the millionth time the reality of experience and to forge in the smithy of my soul the uncreated conscience of my race.

27 April: Old father, old artificer, stand me now and ever in good stead. (P 275–6)

CHAPTER THREE

READING *ULYSSES* I: FROM 'TELEMACHUS' TO 'THE WANDERING ROCKS'

Ulysses, first published in February 1922 to coincide with Joyce's 40th birthday, is often cited as the quintessential text of literary modernism. Modernism is an umbrella term that is used to refer to the period of artistic experimentation and innovation that flourished, mainly in North America and Europe, from approximately 1890 to 1930. Modernism was also a particularly widespread phenomenon, affecting practically every form of art – literature, architecture, theatre, sculpture, film, painting, music and so on. *Ulysses* is a poster child for modernism: it continually challenges the preconceptions and conventions of nineteenth century literary realism through its playful experiments with plot, character and style, and it is these experiments that have given *Ulysses* its reputation as for being a book that is hard to start and even harder to finish. The book's somewhat (in)famous reputation is not entirely unwarranted; even for a reader familiar with Joyce's *Dubliners* or *A Portrait of the Artist as a Young Man*, *Ulysses* can seem to mark a radical departure from his previous work.

So what makes *Ulysses* so hard to read? The following two chapters will concentrate on specific passages from the text and offer close readings of what makes them difficult – their stylistic experiments and innovations. It should be borne in mind, however, that the text's 'difficulty' is, to a certain extent at least, part of the point: no amount of explication will make *Ulysses* completely and easily understood; a certain amount of resistance to sense and meaning will always remain. The reader of *Ulysses* will thus have to learn to live with (and, ideally, will learn to love) a certain amount of incertitude.

Throughout this and the following chapter, I will reproduce parts of what is known as 'the Gilbert schema' to introduce each episode of *Ulysses* as it comes up for discussion. The Gilbert schema is named after Stuart Gilbert, the author of *James Joyce's* Ulysses (New York: Knopf, 1930; revised edition, New York: Vintage, 1952) – the first landmark study of *Ulysses* – where it first officially appeared. Gilbert's schema – which never appeared attached to any edition of *Ulysses* published during Joyce's lifetime – revealed how the chapters or episodes of *Ulysses* had secret names that corresponded to episodes found in Homer's *Odyssey*: episode 1 was called 'Telemachus', episode 2, 'Nestor', episode 3 'Proteus', etc. The schema also gave the location of each episode, the approximate time at which each episode begins, the style or technique each was written in, the bodily organ it featured and so on. But Gilbert's schema was neither the first nor only version of such a schema, however. For instance, Sylvia Beach, the publisher of *Ulysses*, had been somewhat secretly circulating a version of the schema to readers of Joyce's text for a number of years. Joyce himself reluctantly loaned versions of the schema to trusted associates who were giving talks or lectures on the book.[1] These once quasi-secret correspondences have now become such commonplaces in Joycean criticism that it is difficult to believe that Joyce was ever completely sincere in his hesitation to make them public.

The existence of the Gilbert schema, however, is important because it tells the reader something interesting about the text s/he is about two read: first, it suggests that *Ulysses* is not, despite numerous references to its being 'encyclopaedic', a completely self-contained text. There has always been quasi-secret extra- or intertextual material that exists beyond the covers of the book that can aid a reader in making his or her way through the text. Second, the story of the schema's circulation suggests that Joyce wanted (a) his readers to be aware that such extra-textual material existed and (b) to guide them in their uncovering of such material. Thus, Joyce was, from the very beginning, more than ready to play extra- and intertextual games with his critics, commentators and readers. Uncovering this wealth of quasi-secret material has driven the Joyce industry for the last eighty-odd years. Many Joyceans have spent their lives identifying, chasing down and cataloguing this extra-textual material, which includes the historical, ceremonial, meteorological and everyday events that took place in Dublin, in Ireland and around the world on 16 June 1904 (the day on which *Ulysses* takes place), a vast array of

musical, popular culture, theological, philosophical and literary allusions and references, an extensive use of foreign languages, an exhaustive exploitation of Dublin's urban and human geography, and so on.
In fact, there is now so much extra-textual material that it would
simply be both unfeasible and impossible to reproduce it here. Fortu-
nately, much of this material has conveniently been collated and catalogued in one place – Don Gifford's *Ulysses Annotated* (Stanford:
University of California Press, 1989). I strongly recommend that any
serious twenty-first century reader of *Ulysses* get his/her hands on a
copy of Gifford and read it alongside Joyce's text: it will be of invalu-
able help with those things that a reader who is *not* Joyce himself
cannot but help find alienating. For this reason alone, Gifford is
worth the investment. For reasons of space in much of what follows,
I will assume that the reader at least has access to a copy of Gifford
simply because if I were to try and point out every single allusion in
the passages being discussed, there would be little room for analysis
of what the text is actually *doing*. With Gifford's help, however, the
reader will be freed from worrying about not catching or understanding a particular allusion; s/he will then be in a good position to begin
encountering the radical games Joyce plays with not only the boundaries of the book, but with the reader and even language itself.

All references to *Ulysses* follow the Gabler Edition (Vintage, 1986)
and are given parenthetically in the text according to episode number
and line number (e.g., 11.120–50). One final note: due to copyright
restrictions on Joyce's work, I am unable to reproduce in full the passages of *Ulysses* that are discussed in the following two chapters.
Those passages of *Ulysses* that are particularly complex or resistant
to paraphrase and which therefore should be read in full alongside
the discussion are highlighted by the following icon: ☙.

Episode 1: Telemachus
Scene: A Martello Tower in Sandycove, County Dublin
Time: 8 a.m.
Organ: None
Technique/Style: Narrative (young)

For a book of its size, the reader might be surprised to learn that
Ulysses takes place in quite a confined space and time: it charts, with
an astonishing degree of naturalistic detail, the actions of two characters – one already familiar to readers of Joyce – Stephen Dedalus,
the protagonist of *Portrait* – and a completely new one – Leopold

Bloom, an advertising salesman – as they go about their business in and around Dublin, between the hours of 8 a.m., 16 June 1904 and approximately 2 a.m., 17 June 1904. The book itself is divided into eighteen chapters or episodes which are grouped into three parts: part I comprises episodes 1–3, which revolve around Stephen, part II is made up of episodes 4–15, which essentially revolve around Mr Bloom and part III consists of episodes 16–18; 16 and 17 deal with the meeting of Stephen and Mr Bloom, while episode 18 is devoted to Mrs Bloom's – Molly's – monologue.

According to the Gilbert schema, the first episode of *Ulysses* is named 'Telemachus', after the son of Odysseus (whose name later becomes Ulysses in Roman myth), the warrior-king hero of Homer's epic ancient Greek poem, the *Odyssey*. The *Odyssey*, which was probably written towards the end of the eighth century BC, charts the trials and tribulations of Odysseus, who, after the fall of Troy, has spent nearly ten years trying to get back home to his wife and son. Believing Odysseus to be dead, an aggressive group of men moves into his palace in an effort to court his wife, Penelope, who, believing her husband to be still alive and on his way home, does her best to resist them. As the *Odyssey* begins, Telemachus, with his life under threat from Penelope's suitors, copes with his feelings of vulnerability, unhappiness and displacement by dreaming of his father's return.

The Stephen the reader meets in the first episode of *Ulysses* is in a somewhat similar situation to Telemachus: he grapples with overwhelming feelings of alienation – political, personal, artistic, historical – from the world around him. The Stephen of *Ulysses* is thus quite different from the Stephen who writes the diary entries that make up the last pages of *Portrait*. For the Stephen at the end of *Portrait*, the world seems to hold out the promise of artistic fulfilment: he had taken his first steps towards becoming an artist by composing a complete poem; his mother had packed his suitcase and he was poised to go and encounter 'for the millionth time the reality of experience' and 'forge in the smithy of [his] soul the uncreated conscience of [his] race' (P 275–6). So, it is something of a shock to meet him once again in Dublin, on the rooftop of a Martello tower – a short, thick-walled defensive fort built on coasts throughout the British Empire in the nineteenth century – the abode of his friend, Malachi 'Buck' Mulligan, a medical student.

Mulligan begins his morning with a shave and the celebration of a mock-mass, intoning '*Introibo ad altare Dei*' – 'I will go up to the altar of God' (1.5) – the phrase that a Catholic priest (prior to Vatican II) would have used to open the mass. Stephen, clearly an unhappy young man, appears on the roof in answer to the nickname given him by Mulligan – 'Kinch'. Mulligan, who is stark naked under his floating dressinggown, irreverently plays the part of the celebrant of the mass, while a shaving bowl plays the part of the chalice, and a razor crossed with a mirror plays the part of a crucifix (1.1–29). If 'Father' Mulligan is the celebrant, then Stephen appears as his mass server, an altar-boy/servant, which mocks Stephen's defiant declaration to Cranly in *Portrait*, 'I will not serve' (P 260). Further, Stephen's condition of servitude under Mulligan the false 'Father', means that he did not succeed in his attempt at the end of *Portrait* to fashion a spiritual – an artistic – father for himself by invoking the Greek god Daedalus – 'Old father, old artificer' (P 276). Stephen's reintroduction here in the context of the mass is thus savagely ironic; the irony of Stephen's position as server becomes even more caustic when it is recalled that the Stephen of *Portrait* conceived of himself – in contrast to an imagined rival for E— C—'s affection whom he viewed as 'a priested peasant' – as a true 'priest of eternal imagination, transmuting the daily bread of experience into the radiant body of everliving life' (P 240). Stephen, unable to conceive of being an artist outside the bounds of being a priest and artistic production outside of the transubstantiation of bread and wine into Christ's body and blood, loses out once again to a priest – 'Father' Mulligan. Thus, this latest version of a (false) priestly rival is also yet another false 'Father'. If, however, the reader is *not* familiar with *Portrait*, then much of this biting irony is lost; this situation suggests that, unlike the relationship between *Dubliners* and *Portrait*, the relationship between *Portrait* and *Ulysses* introduces something 'new' into the experience of reading Joyce: a sort of continuity *between* texts, which only serves to underline the point made above about how *Ulysses* should not be read as a 'self-contained' text. To read *Ulysses* is to (re)read several texts at once.

As the mock mass continues atop the Martello tower, the savagely ironic treatment of Stephen is tempered somewhat by the text's suggestion that Mulligan is unfit to play the role of artist-priest: Mulligan, realizing that he has forgotten to add water to his chalice-bowl – an oversight that then causes him problems with effectively transubstantiating the shaving soap into the body of Christ – whistles down to an as-yet-unseen third party – Haines, an Englishman and student at Oxford – in order to get him to turn on the tap: 'He peered sideways up and gave a long slow whistle of call, then paused awhile in rapt attention, his even white teeth glistening here and there with gold points. Chrysostomos. Two strong shrill whistles answered through the calm' (1.24–7). Here, in the middle of Mulligan's ineffective attempts to perform transubstantiation, an unusual word – Chrysostomos – intrudes into the text in a manner that seems calculated to trip up the reader. The word appears without quotation marks and it does not seem to be a word spoken by the third-person narrator who carries on as if the unusual word has not been said. All of a sudden, on the very first page of *Ulysses*, what had seemed to be a simple enough scene in which two young men mock the rituals of the Catholic Church now demands the reader's closer attention.[2]

If one looks more closely at 'Chrysostomos', it does not seem to be a random intrusion; first of all, it seems related to the context of the mock mass insofar as it is a partial echo of the word Mulligan uses to describe what he is trying to make appear – 'Christine', a sort of feminized Christ. If the reader turns to Gifford, s/he will find that the word 'Chrysostomos' is a Greek epithet meaning 'goldenmouthed'. It would seem, then, that a momentary glimpse of Mulligan's gold fillings has prompted an associative narrative link with 'Chrysostomos' which, as Gifford also notes, has associations with rhetorical prowess (Dion Chrysostomos, c.50–c.117, a Greek rhetorician) and Church history (St John Chrysostomos, 345–407, an early church father). But this information does not yet tell the reader where this oddly intrusive Greek word might have come from. Given that the word can be connected to both Church history and the history of rhetoric, it could easily be associated with Stephen Dedalus. Since the word does not seem to be spoken out loud – Mulligan does not respond to it – it can be read as one of Stephen's thoughts. Read in this way, 'Chrysostomos' would be the first moment in the novel where the reader is dropped into the 'interior monologue' – the apparently unmediated stream of a character's perceptions, words and thought processes.

Even though Joyce always insisted that he was not the inventor of the interior monologue – claiming instead that he first came across it in *Les Lauriers sont coupés*, a book written by the French author Édouard Dujardin[3] – it is easy to imagine how the unannounced intrusion of a character's thoughts into the narrative would have been experienced by one of his early readers as something of a jolt, especially when compared to how characters' thoughts were conventionally presented in novels: instead of simply giving the una-dorned word 'Chrysostomos,' a more conventional narrator might say something like, '"Chrysostomos," Stephen thought to himself as he caught a glimpse of Buck Mulligan's gold fillings'. *Ulysses*, which has used more conventional narrative technique up to this point in the text (and will do so for the rest of its duration), also disturbs those conventions, by offering what appears to be the unmediated thought of its main character; it is thus a text that employs and disrupts literary conventions at once. However, that is not all; the word 'Chrysostomos' is not unambiguously the first example of interior monologue in the text: because the narration surrounding 'Chrysostomos' does not seem to be connected with it, there is room to suggest that the word is neither clearly nor completely Stephen's. It is possible – even if it might seem a little far-fetched at first – that the word 'Chrysostomos' also marks the first stirrings of a different, much more disruptive force in the text, a force that is reducible nei-ther to the text's narrator(s) nor any of its characters. What I suggest here, in other words, is that when re-read in the light of the textual disruptions that force themselves on the reader from episode 7 ('Aeolus') onwards, 'Chrysostomos' can be read as the *first* of those disruptions. Read in this way, right from its first page, *Ulysses* wants to play disruptive games with its reader.

After the disruption of 'Chrysostomos', the text of *Ulysses* settles down and behaves itself for the next couple of pages. The narrative progresses in a rather conventional fashion, dutifully reporting who says or thinks what and providing the reader with the reason for Stephen's return to Dublin after his artistic flight to Paris: his moth-er's painful and protracted death from liver cancer (⧖ 1.77–122). This passage also makes clear the differences between Mulligan's and Stephen's financial and emotional conditions. Mulligan's 'wellfed' frame – and its brightly coloured clothing – stands in stark contrast to Stephen's threadbare black jacket and black secondhand trousers; he is clearly still in mourning for his dead mother.[4] Mulligan is clearly aware of this – he sings 'Who Goes with Fergus?', the same song that Stephen sang for his mother in lieu of a prayer at 1.239–41[5] – which suggests that his repeated invocations of the great sea-mother seem designed to hurt Stephen. They cause Stephen, who cannot look at Dublin Bay without seeing it as the china bowl that held his mother's death vomit, to once again relive both the guilty nightmare in which his decomposing mother comes back to chide him for not kneeling to pray for her and the brutal horror of her last weeks of suffering. Stephen will wrestle with the grief and guilt he feels over his mother's death for the remainder of the book.

After provoking his feelings of guilt and horror, Mulligan reveals that he and a drinking companion spent the previous evening in a pub jokingly suggesting that Stephen's state of mind is the result of syphilis of the central nervous system (g.p.i, or general paresis of the insane) (1.125–37). Mulligan then shows Stephen his reflection in the mirror: 'Stephen bent forward and peered at the mirror held out to him, cleft by a crooked crack. Hair on end. As he and others see me. Who chose this face for me? This dogsbody to rid of vermin. It asks me too' (1.135–7). Here, in the middle of Mulligan's mock-medical diagnosis of Stephen – some fifty-odd lines after the word 'Chrysos-tomos' has intruded into the text – there is another disruption. Once again, the disruptive lines here are not simply the 'voice' of the third-person narrator; this time, however, they are easily attributable to Stephen, who looks at himself in Mulligan's cracked mirror, sees his bed-head ('Hair on end'), and begins pondering his uneasy relation-ships with his lineage, his unclean body and his subservient position with respect to Mulligan ('dogsbody'). Unlike the situation with the word 'Chrysostomos', this is the first unambiguous moment of Stephen's interior monologue: the reader is dropped into the stream of Stephen's perceptions, words and thought processes.

Threaded through this first unambiguous use of the interior monologue is the cracked mirror Mulligan has stolen from his ser-vant's room (1.148). This mirror, well known and much discussed by Joyceans, quickly becomes a complex image of the relative inferiority of 'Irish art' when compared to that of Ireland's then[6] colonial master, England (❦ 1.138–59). The exchange that takes place here between the two young men warrants careful unpacking since it carries a lot of philosophical and socio-political baggage. Ever since the ancient Greeks, Western art has been criticized or praised as mimesis – the reflection or imitation of 'reality', whether that reality is understood as the outward appearance of an actual object, its hid-den spiritual truth/significance, or both. Given this long debate about art-as-reflection-or-imitation, Mulligan's mirror can thus be read as a symbol of artistic production in general. What makes the mirror of artistic imitation peculiarly Irish, however, as Stephen's bitter quip makes clear, is the fact that it is the 'cracked lookingglass of a servant' (1.146). But what is the reader to make of Stephen's diagnosis of the state of Irish art? In order to come to grips with Stephen's bitter analysis of the fractured inferiority of Irish art it is worth considering what prompts it: Mulligan's allusion to the rage of Caliban, which draws on Oscar Wilde's Preface to his *The Picture of Dorian Gray* (1890).[7] In the Preface, Wilde (1854–1900), who enjoyed a career as a brilliantly entertaining Irishman in London up until he was jailed for sodomy in 1895, pointedly mocks English philistinism in matters of art. The reference to Wilde thus mixes art with the historical, economic and colonial tensions between Ireland and England. Read in this way, what takes place on top of the Martello tower becomes an allegorical parallel of Wilde the Irishman's downfall at the hands of the English philistinism he had once mocked: Mulligan, delighted by Stephen's quip, tells him to repeat it to the 'oxy [or Oxford] chap downstairs' – Haines, the Englishman – and then ask him for a guinea. In other words, Mulligan wants Stephen to perform the witty Irishman – Wilde – for the Englishman in return for cash. This cash, the text makes clear, retains the whiff of colonial exploitation: Haines (whose name recalls the French for 'hate', *la haine*) is 'stinking with money' only because of his father, a capitalist of the Empire who, according to Mulligan's quasi-comic caricature of him, made his money ('tin') in a 'swindle', selling jalap, a Mexican drug that accelerates defecation, to Zulus (1.156–7).

One might also wonder if what Mulligan desires is not Stephen's humiliation since he certainly does not seem to be short of cash: there are numerous references to how well-fed Mulligan is, how overabundantly well dressed he is, his gold fillings, his servants, etc. Given Mulligan's financial security, it is perhaps not surprising that Stephen sees in his urging sufficient reason for making a break from his friend, a thought that prompts Stephen's recollection of Cranly from *Portrait* (1.159). And it is his willingness to pimp Stephen for money that ironically makes Mulligan the servant – a fact underscored later in the episode when he cooks and serves Haines's breakfast – to a certain Englishness, even as he plays the master with respect to Stephen. Further, Mulligan's willingness to use Stephen to entertain his English guest can also be read as reinforcing his status as false artist: since the mirror he wields is one that he has stolen from his servant's room, any artistic ability Mulligan may display is already symbolically stolen from his servant, who would thus be another, albeit feminized, image of Stephen. In other words, because Mulligan – the servile false artist – wields with abandon a stolen cracked mirror, the art he makes will never be a 'perfect', 'complete' or 'true' artistic image when compared to that of the English master.[8] Read in this way, Mulligan's grand project to liberate Ireland by 'Hellenising' it (1.158) – making it more 'Greek' – would appear to be just another way of enslaving and thus betraying it all over again.[9]

As if to underline the problems inherent in the process of Hellenization, another narrative 'crack' appears in the text immediately after Stephen's and Mulligan's exchange about the mirrors and art (❧ 1.160–80). This narrative crack, which begins with 'Young shouts' and ends with the invocation of a 'new paganism' that would seek a return through the *omphalos* (1.176) – the Greek word for 'navel' – is worth careful consideration. *Omphalos*, the name Mulligan has given the Martello tower (1.544), is inextricable from the wisdom and culture of ancient Greece: among other things, the word *omphalos* is used in the *Odyssey* to refer to Calypso's island, while the same word referred to the seat of the oracle at Delphi. The positioning of this narrative crack is also important: it appears just after Mulligan mentions to Stephen the 'hazing' of the hapless Clive Kempthorpe at the hands of his fellow students at Oxford ('Magdalen' is one of Oxford University's constituent colleges). The crack's position thus clearly mocks the notion of a Greek neo-paganism by revealing its Englishness and privilege; at the same time, the crack also mocks as hopelessly out-of-touch the criticism of Matthew Arnold (1822–1888). Arnold, who was famous for his emphasis on taste and restraint, is oblivious to the energetic excesses of moneyed young students: while Kempthorpe is being 'debagged' – having his trousers cut off in a sort of mock castration – Arnoldian criticism is happy to stare contentedly at floating particles of newly mown grass. This textual crack could, at first glance, be read as Stephen's re-imagining of Kempthorpe's ordeal, perhaps after hearing a version of it from Mulligan; however, there is nothing in this shard of text that makes it absolutely certain that these are Stephen's thoughts. In fact, it is possible that this crack in the text already announces – in the same manner as the word 'Chrysostomos' – the larger, more disorienting cracks that interrupt the reflective surface of the text with increasing frequency after 'Hades', the sixth episode. That is, since neither Stephen nor Mulligan appear to be 'aware' of what is going on in the crack – both continue their conversation around it as if it had not occurred – its interruption of the narrative seems to be aimed at the reader insofar as it draws attention to the act of reading.

What this narrative crack reveals then is that despite his desire to Hellenize Ireland, Mulligan still remains the Irish servant of the colonial master, Haines. And, insofar as he remains a servant to Mulligan, the servile false artist, Stephen, the 'true priest of the imagination', remains an Irish artist. Thus, there is something of a 'sameness' that binds Mulligan and Stephen together as Irish servants. In fact, this 'sameness' seems underlined by the balanced way in which they use their 'art' to protect themselves: 'Parried again. He fears the lancet of my art as I fear that of his. The cold steel pen' (1.152–3). And yet, there are significant differences between these two Irish servitudes: Stephen is acutely aware that his servitude is inextricable from the colonial politics of Britain and Ireland – he knows that he is the 'servant of a servant' (1.312);[10] Mulligan, however, does not appear to be at all aware of his own servitude. Mulligan's role as the 'gay betrayer' of Ireland who is in league with 'her conqueror', Haines (1.405), becomes clear when he mocks the old milk woman, whom Stephen describes using the traditional allegorical and poetic names for Ireland – 'Silk of the kine and poor old woman, names given her in old time' (1.403–4).[11] Stephen's servitude also differs from the unwitting servitude of the servile and treacherous false artist in that he does not seem to be particularly keen to entertain Haines for money even though actually he needs it. In fact, Stephen's artistry can be read as something of a necessary protection – an apotrope – that he wields against Mulligan's odd combination of mastery and servility. 'Art' is thus no longer something that happens in a realm that would be divorced from 'the real world': for Stephen, art is a strategic means of survival, but not just for any price.

Mulligan's inability to see his own servitude and betrayal is perhaps the main reason why he, the false artist-priest, does not fully grasp the power of the cracked stolen mirror he carries so lightly. Instead of passively and transparently reflecting the world – the conventional understanding of the task of art – the cracked surface of the mirror disrupts reflection by drawing attention to that which is doing the reflecting – the mirror itself. In other words, it is the cracks in the mirror that are important, the 'Irish cracks' that Mulligan, in his desire to please and be like his English master, cannot see – indeed, it was Stephen who had to point them out to him. Stephen, on the other hand, grasps his Irishness through his keen awareness of his servitude, the awareness of the cracks in his art. These cracks, however, can be understood to hold out the possibility of an Irish art that would no longer be either unproblematically reflective or uncon-sciously servile. To the extent that they would disrupt the simple reflection of reality, the 'cracks of Irish art' would appear in the text as what fractures the reader's experience of the book's perfect (and thus transparent) reflection of 'reality'; thus, these cracks – which do not really 'reflect' anything – would draw the reader's attention to the blemishes in the book's reflective surface, disrupting the reader's passive consumption of a 'true' transparent reflection of the real world. In this way, *Ulysses* calls itself to the reader's attention as a piece of non-servile Irish art, making the reader aware of the actual book that s/he has in front of him/her. This is not to say, however, that the Irish art of *Ulysses* is something that would desire to be 'purely', 'quaintly' or 'timelessly' Irish. Quite the contrary. If one turns again to the two major 'artistic cracks' that have already inter-rupted the text – the mysterious *Greek* word, 'Chrysostomos' and interior monologue that Joyce regarded as a *French* innovation – it becomes clear that 'Irish art' needs a combination of ancient, modern and foreign words and literary innovation in order to emerge. Yet this 'foreignness' does not erase the Irish component of this art – it would be absurd to say so given the prominence of Ireland and Dublin in particular to Joyce's works. Instead, it would be more accurate to suggest that by using, say, the 'Frenchness' of the interior monologue, the text of *Ulysses* begins to construct a 'modernist' 'Irish' art that can no longer be simply reduced to Ireland's past colonial relation-ship with England. In this way, the book seems to offer itself – that is, the style in which it was written – as the solution to the predica-ment of Irish art that it (through Stephen) diagnoses. This way of offering a solution to the problem of Irish art should also serve to remind the reader that the *form* of *Ulysses* – the style or manner in which it is written – is inextricable from colonial politics; it should also remind the reader that *how Ulysses* is written is every bit as important for reading the text as the narrative *content* is. The text of *Ulysses* thus rejects the typical opposition of form and content.

Because this form of Irish art can no longer be grasped purely in terms of Ireland's colonial relationship with England or the colonial master's form of reflection, Stephen, just before he leaves Haines (the colonial master of Ireland) and Mulligan (Ireland's gay betrayer and the false artist who has usurped his place) at the bathing area, effec-tively becomes Telemachus when he realizes that he no longer has a place in the *omphalos* (1.733–44). It is also worth noting that the verse Stephen says to himself as he leaves Mulligan and Haines – '*Liliata rutilantium./Turma circumdet./Iubilantium te Virginum.*' – is part of the Latin Prayers for the Dying and marks the second time he has prayed for his mother during the first hour of the day (see 1.276–7).[12] It would seem that Stephen is, on some level, trying to please his dead mother by praying for her in death, something he had refused to do for her in life.

Episode 2: Nestor
Scene: The School, Dalkey
Hour: 10 a.m.
Organ: None
Art: History
Technique/Style: Catechism

The second episode of *Ulysses*, 'Nestor', is named after the master charioteer that Telemachus seeks advice from in Book II of the *Odyssey*. However, the Nestor figure that Stephen encounters in *Ulysses* – Mr Deasy, the headmaster of the private boys' school where Stephen works – is an anti-Semite and considerably less helpful than the Nestor Telemachus meets. In the following discussion of 'Nestor', I will focus on what can be considered as the next series of cracks in the reflective surface of the text that a reader might find most difficult to negotiate: the usurped Irish artist's interior monologue on the complex relationship between being, memory, history and literature. In tracing Stephen's thoughts on these things, it becomes possible to flesh out what is at stake in the non-servile form of 'Irish art' that began to take shape in the previous episode.

We meet Stephen as he comes to the end of his lesson, a mixture of history and literature. The first lines of episode 2 take the form of a catechetical classroom exchange of questions and answers between Stephen and one of his pupils, Cochrane, on the fate of Pyrrhus. Pyrrhus (318–272 BC), a Greek general, was asked by the city of Tarentum, a Greek colony in southern Italy, to lead their struggle against the Romans (⏃ 2.1–17). Pyrrhus' battle against the Romans at Asculum (279 BC) was successful but it effectively broke his army, giving rise to the cliché, 'to win a Pyrrhic victory'. Using the lesson about Pyrrhus as a starting point, Stephen embarks on an interior monologue on the difference between an event that takes place in history and what happens to it when it is remembered in the form of words: 'Fabled by the daughters of memory. And yet it was in some way if not as memory fabled it. A phrase, then, of impatience, thud of Blake's wings of excess. I hear the ruin of all space, shattered glass and toppling masonry, and time one livid final flame. What's left us then?' (2.7–10). The difficult relationship between the event of history and the phrase (2.15) or words used to remember it, is already announced in the text by a pun: the corpse-strewn plain (2.16) of memory is found in a gore-scarred book (2.12: 'gore' in its obsolete sense can also mean 'dirt' or 'filth'). Stephen immediately conceives of the destruction of the historical event by language in terms of two texts by the poet, artist and mystic, William Blake (1757–1827): *The Marriage of Heaven and Hell* (c.1790) and *A Vision of the Last Judgment* (1810). In *The Marriage of Heaven and Hell*, Blake prophesied that the world would end consumed by fire – recalled by Stephen in his image of destroyed buildings and flames. Stephen thus seems to worry that the excess of the artist's words are a form of 'impatience' that would come to destroy the event, leading him to wonder, 'what's left us then?' Stephen's thoughts about how the art of the phrase comes to destroy the 'event' of history neatly link up with his conception of himself as the artist-priest of the imagination who 'transmut[es] the daily bread of experience into the radiant body of everliving life' (P 240). In other words, Stephen now seems to worry that the artist's transmutation of experience may be responsible for producing a certain 'dull ease of the mind'. In an effort to counter this formation of habit, Stephen posits that the historical event of Pyrrhus' victory 'was in some way if not as memory fabled it'. Stephen thus confronts the artistic and historical problem of language: events are changed by the very act of remembering them in the words of history or art; language is at once a creative and destructive force. It is also worth noting that Stephen's description of the corpse-strewn plain is his application of the Ignatian technique of composition of place (as was discussed in the last chapter): Stephen thus once again makes art even as he worries about what it does.

After another student, Armstrong, has tried to answer Stephen's question about 'the end of Pyrrhus' (2.18) by connecting the sound of Pyrrhus' name with the sound of the word 'pier' – 'a kind of bridge sir' (2.33), Stephen makes a joke about a pier being 'a disappointed bridge' that his class fails to understand. This short exchange foregrounds issues of puns and riddles. Stephen resumes his complex musing on the notion of history by considering the possibilities – the 'what ifs' of what has not taken place: what if Caesar had not been stabbed? What if Pyrrhus had not been knocked off his horse in Argos by a tile thrown by a woman? – that the event that did take place has ousted (☙ 2.48–53). Here Stephen confronts the strange notion of the 'infinite possibilities' that never managed to become particular moments in history; such possibilities are not historical precisely because they have been 'ousted' by history.

Stephen's thoughts are here interrupted by the pleas of his students for a story or a 'ghoststory' (2.54–5). Stephen's refusal to tell one is interesting here insofar as it can be read as an echo of the position of the reader with respect to the text of *Ulysses*: like Stephen's students, readers of *Ulysses* may also be expecting a 'story' in which there would be a clear narrative progression from event to event; instead, readers are presented with a narrative that keeps on getting inter- rupted by chunks of history or poetry and opaque snippets of a phil- osophically complex interior monologue on the difficult relationship between history and language. These interruptions – insofar as they fracture the narrative surface of the text – recall the non-reflective cracks in the mirror discussed above; that is, they serve to draw the reader's attention to the actual, physical text of *Ulysses* in front of him/her by interrupting the story. And, through a strange process of self-reflection, the readers of *Ulysses* become students of its cracked Irish mirror, which, just like Stephen, refuses to unfold a story with- out interruption or fragmentation.

Once the class returns to reciting lines from 'Lycidas' (1638) by John Milton (1608–1674), Stephen returns to his thoughts on history and the problem of whether or not the 'infinite possibilities' that have been 'ousted' by the event of history can even be said to possible 'seeing that they never were' (☙ 2.67–76). A solution to this difficult problem is suggested to him by a 'phrase' of Aristotle: 'It must be a movement then, an actuality of the possible as possible' (2.67). Stephen here draws on Aristotle's definition of motion in 3.1 of the *Physics*: 'The fulfilment of what exists potentially, in so far as it exists potentially, is motion – namely of what is alterable *qua* alterable.' Aristotle's definition of motion – itself a famously difficult problem for interpreters of his work – suggests that motion is any kind of change or alteration; thus, motion is 'actualized' by being in motion: once there is no more change, there is no more motion. Stephen adapts this definition of motion to the non-historical 'infinite possibilities': in short, he suggests that these possibilities remain 'actual' only insofar as they remain non-historical possibilities. These possibilities cannot 'be' in the 'past': if they were, they would no longer be possibilities, they would be historical events. Stephen's thoughts on history thus seem to open a link between language and history as destructive forces. In other words, the event of history is perhaps not completely unlike language since it too 'ousts' the infinite possibilities of what did not come to pass. Stephen does not say that these infinite possibilities are destroyed: they thus seem to exist as ahistorical possibilities. It is thus possible to hear in Stephen's thoughts the echo of something that is perhaps no longer simply a part of the 'nightmare' of 'history' (2.377). Stephen, however, does not develop his thoughts on history any further here; instead, his thoughts turn to the time he spent in Paris at the library of Saint Genevieve reading two specific works of Aristotle: *On the Soul*, which describes the soul or mind, by analogy with the hand ('the tool of tools'), as the 'form of forms' (2.75–6); and the *Metaphysics*, which describes the 'prime mover' as thought thinking of thought (2.75). Stephen's use of Aristotle's definition of the soul as the form of forms is of particular interest here: it suggests to him that the 'soul is in a manner all that is' (2.75); in other words, the soul is – in a way that is he does not define here – 'everything'. Stephen's conclusion seems to extrapolate from Aristotle's definition the following proposition: if the soul is the form of forms, then everything that has a form also has a 'soul' in some way. Further, if the soul is 'in' everything, then everything is the soul: this suggests that the soul is not unique; nor is it isolated.

If, as I suggested above, Stephen's refusal to tell his students a story echoes the reader's relationship with the text of *Ulysses*, then the sheer impossibility of solving Stephen's riddle about the fox burying his grandmother (≥ 2.103–15) without knowing the answer to it perhaps serves to make clear that the reader-student will need extra guidance from the teacher-text. Interestingly, and uncannily, *Ulysses* already seems to have prepared for such a student-reader, laying out a place for him/her in the text: the place of Cyril Sargent, the pupil who stays behind and comes to Stephen needing help with his '*Sums*' (2.128). Like Sargent, the reader-student must follow Stephen's lead, (re)tracing his solutions to the 'algebra' problems that he works out for Sargent's benefit (2.139–67). With Sargent at his side, Stephen works out an algebraic problem that recalls Mulligan's exasperated description of his attempt to tease out the relationship between the artist – Shakespeare – and his art – the character of Hamlet – as 'algebra' in episode 1 (1.555–7):

Across the page the symbols moved in grave morrice, in the mummery of their letters, wearing quaint caps of squares and cubes. Give hands, traverse, bow to partner: so: imps of fancy of the Moors. Gone too from the world, Averroes and Moses Maimonides, dark men in mien and movement, flashing in their mocking mirrors the obscure soul of the world, a darkness shining in brightness which brightness could not comprehend. (2.155–60)

There are a number of things to notice here in Stephen's lesson for Sargent. The lesson forges a link between Stephen's theory of art and the figures of algebra, which the Moors – a somewhat dated term used to refer to the Muslims of the Islamic Iberian Peninsula and North Africa who were of Arab and Berber descent – were thought to have introduced algebra into Europe during the Renaissance. Stephen then imagines that the figures of algebra come alive as 'imps' as they cross the page in a Moorish dance ('morrice') wearing 'quaint caps of cubes and squares'. Since these algebraic figures appear to have an occult ability to come to life, Stephen associates them with the 'mocking mirrors' – shiny reflective surfaces such as a crystal ball or water, that produce distorted reflections from which the future could be divined – used by two non-Christian thinkers, the Spanish-Arabian philosopher Averroes (1126–1198), who strove to reconcile Aristotle with Muslim orthodoxy, and the Jewish philosopher Moses Maimonides (1135–1204), whose famous *Guide for the Perplexed* tried to reconcile Aristotle and orthodox Judaism.[13] These occult mirrors not only once again recall the cracked mirror of Irish art, but also make it possible to see Sargent's lesson at Stephen's side as a *mise-en-abyme* for *Ulysses* in at least two ways. First, the characters of Stephen and Mr Bloom, insofar as they are composed of printed marks on pages – the pages of *Ulysses* – mysteriously come to life just like the imps of algebra do as the reader reads the text; second, the 'quaint caps' of the dancing imps allow them to be read as miniature Stephens and Mr Blooms, whose hats are frequently mentioned throughout the text. Thus, the student of the new Irish art of *Ulysses* must also learn to play with algebra and the occult mirrors of non-Christian philosophies if s/he is to 'faithfully move the unsteady symbols' on its pages.

Given his references to Sargent's ugliness and weakness (which only *amor matris* – the love of the mother for the child and the child for its mother – could appreciate (2.163–7)), it might seem, at first glance anyway, that Stephen, a figure for the teacher-text, does not like his students very much. These thoughts, however, should not be taken as an implication that the teacher-text thinks itself superior to its reader-students. On the contrary, the text makes drawing such a conclusion particularly difficult: not only does it go out of its way to heap irony on Stephen's artistic ambitions in the first episode, it also makes it very apparent that Stephen sees himself reflected in the mirror of the small student sitting at his side (⧂ 2.168–77). However, just because Stephen sees his childhood stooping beside him does not mean that he and Sargent are at one or exactly the same: as the text also makes clear, despite what they may have in common or may now share, they remain different people, separated by the unbridgeable gulfs of time and secrecy – different lived experiences. At the same time, this implies that the teacher cannot ever become superior to the student, since s/he is always potentially a student, and must remain open to another teacher who may also happen to be a student.

That the teacher remains a student to a teacher who may also be a student is underscored by Stephen who, after Sargent has left for the hockey field – no doubt in for a bit of a bruising – goes to Mr Deasy to receive his wages. While in the headmaster's office, Stephen endures Deasy's anti-Semitic remarks on how the Jews are 'killing' England and his racist belief that the Jews have dark complexions as proof of their 'sinning against the light' of Christianity (⧂ 2.373–86). Deasy's anti-Semitism is also bound up with the view of the German philosopher George Wilhelm Friedrich Hegel (1770–1831) which held that all history is progress towards the manifestation of the light of the (Christian) God. In this totalizing reading of history, all that remains non-Christian is caught up in a suspicious 'darkness'. Stephen, who, intuitively connects his artistic practice with the 'dark practices' of Averroes and Moses Maimonides, counters Mr Deasy's Christian understanding of the world and history in at least three ways: first, he turns Deasy's own racist criteria on him to suggest that since everyone could be said to have sinned against the light, everyone is, to some extent, 'Jewish' (2.373); second, Stephen's assertion that history is 'a nightmare' from which he is trying to awake effectively challenges Deasy's belief that all history is progress towards the eventual 'great goal' of the manifestation of God (2.377; indeed, Stephen's conversation with Deasy reveals that his conception of history is not even desirable insofar as it is rooted in anti-semitism, racism and sexism); third, by suggesting that 'God' is nothing other than the shouts of the students on the hockey pitch, Stephen practically destroys Deasy's teleological understanding of history as progress (3.382–6): if God is nothing other than the cheers of students scoring hockey goals, then 'he' is no longer 'God'; nor can 'he' be the 'great goal' of history because 'he' is, as it were, already here as 'not-God'. Not surprisingly, Stephen's lack of faith in history as moral progress leads Deasy to question his fitness for the teaching profession (2.401–7). Stephen, in response, explicitly places himself in the role of a learner who has nothing to learn from a teacher like Mr Deasy, who can offer only clichés, racism and sexism when confronted by complex questions and deep-seated doubts. Stephen leaves Mr Deasy's school with his wages and Deasy's missive to the editor of the *Evening Telegraph* on foot and mouth disease, intending not to return.

Episode 3: Proteus
Scene: Sandymount Strand, Dublin
Hour: 11 a.m.
Organ: None
Art: Philology
Technique/Style: Monologue (male)

The third episode of *Ulysses*, 'Proteus,' takes its name from Book IV of the *Odyssey*, which finds Telemachus at the court of King Menelaus, who tells him the tale of how he got back from Troy. Menelaus, who had washed ashore on the island of Pharos unsure of which god he had offended, found help in the form of the daughter of its ruler, Proteus, who told him that her father had the gift of prophecy. To make Proteus speak, Menelaus had to try to grab hold of him as he took different shapes – animals, fire, water and so on. Using this method, Menelaus eventually learned from Proteus how to find his way back home.

In episode 3, the reader accompanies Stephen to Sandymount Strand on the southern edge of Dublin Bay. Once alone on Sandymount Strand, Stephen, yearning for physical connection, contemplates how the apparently simple act of perceiving the world is actually a philosophically complex and inherently creative process. Stephen's desires and thoughts are themselves obsessively kinetic or 'protean' throughout this episode: they shift and move associatively – a word is often enough to cause him to change tracks; they are fascinated by other modes of protean shape-shifting such as the mysteries of transubstantiation – the conversion of bread and wine into the body and blood of Christ in the Eucharist; and they view the world as a shifting text to be read through the lenses of philosophy, history and literature. Stephen's thoughts as he walks along are thus super-saturated with dense and frequently elliptical allusions to the works of philosophers, writers, Church Fathers and heretics: I once again refer the reader to Gifford for the fullest catalogue of Stephen's many allusions in this episode, the sheer amount of which make this by far the most difficult for the reader to manage. The density of Stephen's web of allusion is neatly illustrated by the first two paragraphs of the episode discussed below. This density is also important: it serves to reinforce the sense of Stephen's isolation and alienation from the world around him, something he also notes to himself in this episode. The density of allusion also effectively multiplies the cracks and splits in the reflective surface of *Ulysses*, amplifying the text's disruption of a colonial form of art and endlessly deferring meaning outside of the book the reader has in front of him/her. In other words, these cracks can be read as the further elaboration of the non-reflective Irish art that has been taking shape over the past two episodes. My discussion of this episode will concentrate on how this episode elaborates this art by fragmenting the artist 'himself'.

Stephen's analysis of the creative process of perception begins in the episode's densely packed first paragraph with his isolation of the processes at work in vision (⊜ 3.1–9). Stephen's consideration of the 'ineluctable modality of the visible' – or, as he says later, 'Space: what you damn well have to see.' (9.86) – serves to draw the reader's attention to the impossibility of separating the sense of sight from the processes of thought: that which is seen is necessarily 'thought through my eyes' (3.1–2). If sight is always a form of quasi-creative thought, then the act of seeing can thus be understood as a form of reading and writing that is bound up with a world of created arte-facts – artistic works which bear signatures: 'Signatures of all things I am here to read, seaspawn and seawrack, the nearing tide, that rusty boot. Snotgreen, bluesilver, rust: coloured signs' (3.2–4). In other words, Stephen conceives of the world as something written, a sort of text wherein things become visible as signatures, words or signs that are legible, an idea he returns to later: 'These heavy sands are language tide and wind have silted here' (3.288–9). Stephen then goes on to consider how the coloured signs of the world-writing relate to what Aristotle (who is obliquely mentioned in terms of mediaeval guesswork about his life[14]) in *On the Senses* calls the 'diaphane'. Usually translated as 'the Translucent', the diaphane is that which for Aristotle gives something its transparent quality. Although it is most obvious in air and water, the Translucent is nevertheless found in greater or lesser degrees in other bodies or things: for example, when a banknote is held up to the light, it reveals a watermark, the ink on its other side, etc.; it is thus possible to see through the banknote to the extent that the diaphane is found in it. In *On the Senses*, Aristotle also briefly considers colour as that which marks the limits of the Translucent in bodies or objects because it makes them opaque or adiaphanous. It is on this point that Stephen questions if colour alone is sufficient to account for seeing a particular thing. Aristotle, he thinks momentarily, seems to have been aware of objects prior to noticing their colour. However, Stephen is forced away from a read-ing of Aristotle that relies on a hard and fast limit between the object and its surroundings; he recalls that Aristotle allows the diaphane to penetrate the object: in *On the Senses*, Aristotle concludes that because the air or the sea can, just like colour, look different depend-ing on the position of the observer, it is the diaphane, the Translucent, that – depending on the degree of it contained in a particular object – allows that object to be seen as colourful. Taken together, Stephen's thoughts on the visual open the world up as a text written with colourful signs, the appearance of which is dependent upon the posi-tion of a neo-Aristotelian observer who sees the limit between a col-oured object and the Translucent that surrounds it as permeable, something that Stephen illustrates by playfully describing how such an observer would differentiate between a gate and a door (3.8–9).

If the first paragraph of Stephen's walk seems designed to draw the reader's attention to the coloured writing of the world-text, then the second paragraph – in which he closes his eyes – serves to draw the reader's attention to the world-text's speech (☰ 3.10–24). As Stephen walks through the world-text with his eyes closed, he becomes aware of his existence as movement in space-time – 'I am, a stride at a time. A very short space of time through very short times of space' (3.11–12) – which then reminds him of the distinction, drawn by the German dramatist Gotthold Lessing (1729–1781), between the *Nacheinander* (German, one after another) and the *Nebeinander* (German, side by side) in his *Laocoön* (1766). For Lessing, each realm had an art that was appropriate to it: the art of the realm of the *Nacheinander* was poetry, the events of which unfold successively in time, while the art of the realm of the *Nebeinander* was painting, where action is spaced out and captured all at once. However, Stephen, insofar as he thinks of his existence in terms of movement in space-time, implicitly rejects Lessing's distinction: the realms of poetry and painting are not so easily separated. Stephen, his eyes still closed, his feet clad in Mulligan's borrowed boots, then imagines himself blind, using his walking stick to tap the solid earth, which he imagines to have been made by an artist who is a combination of Plato's Demiurge and Los, Blake's allegorical figure for the creative imagination in 'The Book of Los' (1795). As he makes his way along the strand, Stephen starts to become attuned to a peculiarly rhythmic – and non-human – language that is produced by the interaction of his existence as movement in space-time with the crunchy surface of the world-text – 'Crush, crack, crick, crick' (3.19). It seems that as Stephen walks through the world-text, he is effectively reading, hearing and composing this peculiar language; what is particularly striking about this peculiar, rhythmic more-than-human language is not simply that it remains at once visual and aural, but that it seems to precede the language of the intelligible: 'Rhythm begins, you see. I hear. A catalectic tetrameter of iambs marching' (3.23–4).[15]

This peculiar rhythmic language produces certain disruptions in its reader-hearer-composer: as the artist walks through the world-text listening to the peculiarly rhythmic and more-than-human language it produces, he begins to 'disintegrate' – that is, to talk to himself as if he were already someone else, another (3.25–8). The disintegration of the artist can be read as the logical outcome of an interior monologue such as Stephen's that is composed of a welter of allusions to other authors and their words. These other authors have already 'split' the artist into a glittering mosaic of shards. This is also a logical counterpart to the cracks that split the reflective surface of *Ulysses*. In such an artistic space-time, the notion of a unitary self cannot help but disintegrate in the formulation of a new Irish art.[16] In other words, episode 3 thus makes explicit a tendency that has formed part of Stephen's interior monologue since the first episode: the artist is never simply or completely himself and the interior monologue is already an interior dialogue with others and other parts of the self. There is always the necessary and inescapable clamour of others.

If the artist is effectively composed of others – other artists, other philosophers, their words, their works, etc. – then the question of

the artist's parentage starts to become more and more pressing.[17]
The question of parentage erupts into the text when Stephen, just
after he has been listening to the peculiar rhythmic language of the
world-text, notices two old women carefully making their way down
onto the beach near him. As he watches them, Stephen imagines
that they are midwives on their way to bury a 'misbirth' (📖 3.35–50).
In this passage, Stephen, just as he contemplated the nightmare of
history in 'Nestor', now contemplates the problems thrown up by
the tensions between his biological origins and Catholic doctrine. By
imagining his bellybutton as the mouthpiece of a telephone that
could theoretically be used to call any of one's ancestors up to and
including the first bellybuttonless humans, Adam and Eve in the
garden of Eden, Stephen imagines himself as a link in an ancient
chain of flesh, the other links of which remain capable of having
a conversation with him. However, once this playful image of the
flesh-chain of chatty ancestors is linked to Catholic doctrine, it
takes on a suffocating aspect: since, according to Aquinas's *Summa
Theologica*, God does not think or conceive in terms of time, that
which he conceives of must be thought of as a sort of '*lex eterna*'
or eternal law (3.48): what has not yet come into existence for us
already necessarily exists for God and has already done so for eternity (3.47–8). When he applies this *lex eterna* to the circumstances of
his conception, Stephen sees that it strips the flesh-chain of all desire:
his parents – from an eternity before they were even born – cannot
have had any desire or choice in making him since they were simply
carrying out what God had foreseen for eternity. Stephen then wonders if the deterministic and desireless *lex eterna* is not actually the
'divine substance' that would account for the consubstantiality –
being of the same substance – of God and his sin Jesus – who was,
unlike Stephen, 'begotten, but not made' according to the Nicene
Creed (3.50).

As Stephen continues his walk, he returns to the notion that he
is not one but rather composed of a multitude within: the blood of
the Irish who first interacted and interbred with those they called the
'Lochlanns' or 'lake-dwellers' – the Norsemen (3.300–9). Here, once
again employing the rhetorical technique of composition of place
that he learned from the Jesuits in *Portrait*, Stephen forges for himself
an ancestry wherein the artist becomes a receptacle for the blood and
lusts of the multitudes that still course through him. In doing this,

Stephen, who, as we have seen over and over again, is already so filled with the thoughts of others, now uses his artistic skill to fill himself with the blood and lusts of others, thereby restoring the blood, lust and desire to the flesh-chain that the *lex eterna* threatened to drain from it.

Later in the episode, as Stephen watches some cocklepicking gypsies, the blood and lust of artistic creation return to usher back in the more-than-human rhythmic speech of the world-text which now echoes the rush of blood and lust coursing through him, compelling him to write a fragment of poem (☰ 3.397–405). The poem Stephen writes here is itself, appropriately enough, an echo of 'My Grief on the Sea', a poem translated from Irish by Douglas Hyde (1860–1949).[18] What Stephen writes is thus a sort of 'ancestral echo' – he becomes a conduit for the other voices in his blood – which is itself an echo of the more-than-human rhythmic speech of the world-text, which has now expanded to engulf the Solar System itself (3.403). Given all this, it is not surprising that Stephen's ancestral echo once more attunes him to the resurgence of the rhythmic language of the world-text as he urinates into the sea producing a 'wavespeech' that unites the sea with his urine (3.453–69). The 'fourworded wavespeech: seesoo, hrss, rsseeiss, ooos' (3.456–7) that Stephen's urine produces is thus the rhythmic 'speech' of the artist's bodily interaction with the world-text; at the same time, Stephen underlines the endless quality of the rhythmic movement of the world-text: it outlasts the artist, holding itself beyond his will. The artist cannot force this 'speech'; instead, he must 'piss' into it and listen to its non-human replies. Stephen says that this speech was heard by Saint Ambrose (c. 340–97), an early church father noted for his compositions of church music, who said that *'diebus ac noctibus iniurias patiens ingemiscit'* – 'day and night it [creation] groans over wrongs' (3.466). The language of the world-text is thus not 'happy'; to want it to be happy would be to impose a 'humanity' on that which is other than and more than human and not subject to its will; to call it melancholy would risk the same thing. The more-than-human language of the world-text does not have a specific goal or end: it endlessly furls and unfurls, ceaselessly moving hither and thither like the tide.[19]

As if to underline the non-humancentric aspect of this language and its relative indifference to man, Stephen once again returns in his imagination to another figure that has been bothering him all morning – the drowned man first mentioned in the text at 1.673–7 and whose fate echoed the poem Talbot recites in Stephen's class at 2.64–6. The drowned man then merges with Stephen's mother to become another figure of guilt for Stephen after he admits to himself that he probably would not be able to save him, just as he was unable to save his mother from cancer (3.327–30). Some 140 lines later, the drowned man rises once more to the surface of Stephen's thoughts when he imagines, recalling a snippet of Ariel's song for Alonso from *The Tempest* (I.ii.397–403), the decomposing corpse being pulled from the water (☙ 3.476–81). In imagining the recovery of his body in this way, Stephen views the drowned man as a mortal castrated father who, by having his penis nibbled off by 'minnows', is already in the process of becoming a fish and, since the fish – α – is also a symbol of Christ, (a) God (3.477). In other words, it would seem that (a) man can only enter into the endlessly Protean rhythmic cycle of the world-text insofar as he is a castrated mortal who is always in the process of becoming something other than himself – God, fish, barnacle goose, etc. – and is always 'food' for the next cycle of the living which devours the 'urinous offal' (3.480) of the dead multitudes that made up the previous cycle of life. By ingesting these dead, by breathing their dead breaths (3.479), the living incorporate them, keeping them both alive and dead, keeping their words and lusts living on in the blood. As Gilbert points out on page 128 of his study of *Ulysses*, this cycle can be read as a 'variant of the kabalistic [*sic*] axiom of metempsychosis', wherein 'a stone becomes a plant, a plant an animal, an animal a man, a man a spirit, and a spirit a god'.[20] In this ceaseless flow of transformation, pinning down something's essence or soul becomes rather difficult, a situation that, as 'Proteus' draws to its close, *Ulysses* underlines by staging its own parodic act of metempsychosis: Stephen, who forgot at the end of 'Telemachus' to take back his handkerchief from Mulligan, finds himself with a lump of sea-green snot on his finger: 'He laid the dry snot picked from his nostril on a ledge of rock, carefully. For the rest let look who will' (3.500–1). And with that, Stephen's body, in yet another parallel with Telemachus who also drops out of the *Odyssey* from Book V to XIV, vanishes for a time from the pages of *Ulysses*, leaving behind only a sea-snot-soul clinging precariously to a rock. In so doing, he makes way for the book's new protagonist – Mr Leopold Bloom.

Episode 4: Calypso
Scene: Chez Bloom – 7 Eccles Street
Hour: 8 a.m.
Organ: Kidney
Art: Economics
Technique/Style: Narrative (mature)

Book V of the *Odyssey* opens to find Odysseus, the father of Telemachus, who has spent the last seven years on the island of Ogygia, still under the power of the goddess Calypso (whose name means 'the Concealer'). Calypso forces Odysseus to sleep in her bed every night, but he longs to return home to Ithaca. After Athena intercedes with Zeus on Odysseus's behalf, Zeus instructs Calypso to release him from her spell. Once free, Athena bestows on Odysseus the gift of self-possession, and he finally sets out for home.

In *Ulysses*, 'Calypso' – which is also the first episode in part II – goes a long way towards creating the book's peculiar structure by concealing what has come before: 'Calypso' effectively 'conceals' Stephen as the book's protagonist by introducing the reader into the interior monologue of Mr Leopold Bloom. 'Calypso' also conceals the first three or four hours of 16 June 1904 that the reader has spent in Stephen's company: the episode begins 8 a.m. This shift in time and space and introduces a certain idea of simultaneity into the text: at the same time that the reader follows Mr Bloom as he potters about on the Northside of Dublin City, Stephen emerges, looking displeased and sleepy onto the roof of Buck Mulligan's Martello Tower on the Southside. Read thus, 'Calypso' effectively 'restarts' the book, fragmenting the narrative's 'progress' by introducing an odd temporal and spatial structure. *Ulysses* is thus a book that the reader can only read by doubling back, by experiencing a double-start that not only conceals but also, as I will suggest below, marks an interesting shift in perspective – in the very notion of perspective.

Mr Bloom, who happens to be of Jewish extraction – I will come back to this – sells advertising space in newspapers for a living, and is married to Marion (Molly) Bloom, a professional singer. The Blooms had two children: a 15-year-old daughter, Milly, who works as a photographer's assistant in Mullingar, a town in County Westmeath, and a son, Rudy, born 11 years earlier, but who only survived 11 days. As the episode opens, Mr Bloom, who 'ate with relish the inner organs of beasts and fowls' (4.1), is preparing breakfast for himself and his wife. Hunger has put kidneys 'in his mind' (4.6); Mr Bloom thus seems immune to a Cartesian mind/body split. Mr Bloom, we also learn, is particularly fond of kidneys because they 'gave to his palate a fine tang of faintly scented urine' (4.5). Mr Bloom's taste for urine scented inner organs – although it may seem very odd – puts him at once in contact with Stephen's reading of the world-text in which he, as a living being, metempsychotically 'devour[s] a urinous offal from all dead' (3.479–80). Thus, what could have appeared as a simple 'quirk' of Mr Bloom's, in fact puts him squarely in the world-text Stephen has been reading in 'Proteus'.

After checking his pockets for his latchkey – 'Not there' – and his potato – 'I have' (4.72–3), Mr Bloom pulls the halldoor to and sets off to the butcher to buy his kidney; as he does so, the book introduces us to his interior monologue, which is on the whole easier to follow than Stephen's simply because Mr Bloom is not a young, alienated and erudite aspiring artist who grapples with politics, history and ancestry in an effort to formulate a theory of Irish art. His thoughts are consumed with practical observations, puzzles and questions about the world. For example, he wonders if the black clothes he wears for Patrick Dignam's funeral will make him feel the heat more (4.78–81) and speculates on how Irish publicans make their money (4.126–35). Mr Bloom is also afraid of growing old, a fear that he has a tendency to ward off by thinking of his wife's warm flesh (4.218–42).

On his return home from the butcher, Mr Bloom picks up the morning post: a letter from Milly to her father and a card to her mother, and a second letter addressed to 'Mrs Marion Bloom' – not 'Mrs Leopold Bloom', which would have been in proper keeping with the etiquette of addressing a married woman in 1904 Dublin – in the distinctive handwriting of Hugh (Blazes) Boylan, who is organizing Molly's next singing tour. Shortly after bringing his wife her letter and card, and just after he has put the kidney on the pan to fry, Mr Bloom returns to the bedroom with her breakfast and, catching a glimpse of the opened letter poorly concealed under her pillow, is unable, not unlike Odysseus, to leave Calypso's room. Instead, in an almost unconscious reaction to feeling threatened by Boylan's letter, Mr Bloom stays to straighten over the bed with his wife still in it. Molly uses this opportunity to ask her husband a question about a difficult word she encountered while reading *Ruby: Pride of the Ring*: 'metempsychosis' (4.331–43). Here, Molly draws Mr Bloom's attention to precisely the word that best described Stephen's contemplation of the writing of the world-text at the end of 'Proteus' – 'metempsychosis' – placing it squarely before the reader, and setting the stage for *Ulysses*'s second scene of instruction in its first fifty-odd pages.

Molly's lesson in philology, just like Sargent's algebra lesson in 'Nestor', serves to guide the reader of *Ulysses* in coming to grips with the new form of Irish art that is taking shape between its covers (☙ 4.361–81). In this passage, Mr Bloom, using the example of *The Bath of the Nymph*, a picture that hangs over the Blooms' bed, does a solid job of explaining metempsychosis as a mystical doctrine common in ancient India and ancient Greece (and taken up again by late nineteenth century theosophists), which held that the soul was eternal and thus would eventually be reborn in another – not necessarily human – body. Mr Bloom's lesson on the word 'metempsychosis' is also tremendously useful in that it helps the reader make sense of the Gilbert schema, where the structural and formal parallels between the episodes and characters of the *Odyssey* and those of *Ulysses* were first published. In other words, Stephen 'becomes' Telemachus and Mr Bloom 'becomes' Ulysses through metempsychosis. However, this is not to suggest that Joyce, Stephen or Mr Bloom – or, for that matter, the text of *Ulysses* – actually believed or believes in the concept or doctrine of metempsychosis: on the contrary, since Odysseus/Ulysses, Mr Bloom and Stephen are all characters in texts, metempsychosis points to an intertextual relationship; that is, a relationship between different texts or books.

It is also possible to see in Mr Bloom's lesson on metempsychosis a shift away from the doctrine of the soul's passage into another body to one that has more in common with the 'kabalistic variant' of metempsychosis sketched by Stephen at the end of 'Proteus'. According to Gilbert, in kabalistic metempsychosis, 'a stone becomes a plant, a plant an animal, an animal a man, a man a spirit, and a spirit a god' (168). The similarity between Stephen's and Mr Bloom's conceptions of metempsychosis becomes even clearer through a brief consideration of the example that Mr Bloom uses to illustrate the doctrine: the picture of *The Bath of the Nymph* which hangs over the Blooms' bed. A nymph – from the Greek νύμφη, which also means 'bride' and 'veiled' – was the personification of a certain natural location or feature, such as a tree or a river. It is hard to reconcile the figure of the nymph with a doctrine that insists on holding onto the idea of an eternal soul that is transferred from body to body. Further, Mr Bloom's definition of metempsychosis – that 'we all lived before on the earth thousands of years ago or some other planet' (4.363–4) – looks remarkably similar in scope to Stephen's poetic response to the language of a world-text that resonates with the blaze and roar of 'cataractic planets' (3.401–4). It is by going back to the previous episodes – that is by following the double start of *Ulysses*'s own trajectory – that these similarities emerge. Once this similarity is spotted, it also becomes apparent that Mr Bloom offers a different perspective on the language of the world-text that Stephen contemplates in 'Proteus'. This shift in perspective becomes especially 'Bloomian' when Mr Bloom solves the puzzle of where the picture of the nymph came from (free with *Photo Bits*, a 'photography magazine' that was filled with images bordering on soft-porn), notes how much the frame cost him (three shillings and six pence [4.371–2]) and asserts the central place Molly has in his thoughts (she wanted it over the bed and it reminds Mr Bloom of a younger, slimmer version of his wife).

After Molly smells something burning, Mr Bloom runs downstairs to rescue his kidney – 'Done to a turn' (4.391–2). He settles down to breakfast while reading and re-reading Milly's letter. As he reads, he remembers that Milly turned 15 the day before and that Rudy would have been 11 had he lived (4.415–20). He next begins to worry about Milly because of her awakening sexuality (4.428–37) and her interest in a boy – Alec Bannon, the same one Mulligan mentions receiving a card from at 1.684 – who sings a song 'about those seaside girls' (4.409). It is this detail that triggers a 'soft qualm of regret' in Mr Bloom: that song just happens to be Blazes Boylan's song. His recollection of Boylan – and his impending visit to Molly – paralyses Mr Bloom once more (4.447–50). Here, the reader gets his/her first solid clue that Molly and Blazes Boylan are perhaps planning something behind Mr Bloom's back.

This qualm quickly turns into a 'gentle loosening of his bowels' (4.460), so Mr Bloom heads to the 'jakes' – the toilet at the end of the garden – with a copy of *Titbits* magazine because he 'liked to read at stool' (4.465). If Stephen is a reader of the peculiar rhythm of the world-text, so too is Mr Bloom. As he reads the prize titbit, *Matcham's Masterstroke* (≊ 4.500–40), Mr Bloom playfully, pleasurably, allows his own digestive, excretory rhythms – aided by a tablet of cascara sagrada, a laxative made from the bark of the buckthorn tree – to interact with the rhythm of the text he reads, 'yielding but resisting' until he reaches the middle of the second column of text. In other words, Mr Bloom's method of reading suggests that there is a continuity of bodily and textual rhythms, just as Stephen saw the rhythmic continuity of the world-text and his existence-as-rhythmic-movement through it: *Ulysses* thus seems to be a text that invites the reader to erase the hard oppositions of world/text and body/text. And, as if to underline the continuity between the rhythms of text and the rhythms of the body, Mr Bloom unceremoniously wipes his arse with the page he has just read, writing a short, shitty text of his own.[21]

Episode 5: The Lotus Eaters
Scene: The Bath
Hour: 10 a.m.
Organ: Genitals
Art: Botany, chemistry
Technique/Style: Narcissism

In Book VI of the *Odyssey*, Odysseus, after escaping from Calypso's island, winds up on Scheria, where he is entertained at King Alcinous's court. He reveals himself to the king in Book IX, after which he begins to tell the story of his adventures. One of his stories recounts how he and his men were forced by a storm to the land of the Lotus Eaters, where some of his men ate the lotus flower, succumbed to its narcotic power and began to forget about returning home. After forcing the drugged men back onto his ship, Odysseus quickly sets sail. In *Ulysses* the narcotic theme winds its way through the text of episode 5, which finds Mr Bloom, who now brandishes a rolled up newspaper, speculating variously on how the summer heat in Dublin and the climate in other exotic locations produces lethargy, how army training hypnotizes soldiers and – channelling Marx – how organized religions act as a narcotic on the minds of the faithful.

After picking up a letter sent to him under his flowery pseudonym, 'Henry Flower Esq', from his post office box on Westland Row (5.54–66), Mr Bloom runs into an acquaintance named M'Coy. The letter (5.241–59) turns out to be part of an ongoing illicit correspondence Mr Bloom has been conducting with a woman named Martha Clifford. Their correspondence consists in Mr Bloom writing – and thus teaching – Martha certain words, which in turn causes her to repeatedly threaten to 'punish' Mr Bloom for being a 'naughty boy': something he clearly seems to enjoy. Martha's letter contains an interesting typo: she mistypes the word 'word' as 'world' (5.245), a 'mistake' that serves to underline once more the continuity between world and text seen in the previous episodes.

After discreetly tearing up the letter's envelope, Mr Bloom, enticed by the prospect of some cool air, enters All Hallows church, also on Westland Row. He arrives just in time to see the Eucharist being distributed to a congregation of women (≋ 5.344–52). As Mr Bloom, who is clearly not a practicing Catholic, watches the women take the Eucharist, he speculates on the narcotic effect of religion by wondering if the pre-Vatican II-use of Latin during the mass is not done to 'stupefy' the communicants before they close their eyes and eat the corpse of Christ (5.350–1). Once again, it is easy to read here in Mr Bloom's thoughts an echo of Stephen's attempt to close his eyes to hear the rhythm of the language of the world-text on Sandymount Strand. In a further echo of Stephen's ruminations on the metempsychotic transformations of man, fish, Christ and how the living devour the dead, Mr Bloom reads communion as a scene in which the communicants eat the Christ-corpse-god and suggests that Christians have more in common with cannibals than they might at first imagine: 'Rum idea: eating bits of a corpse. Why the cannibals cotton to it' (5.352).

After he leaves the church, Mr Bloom remembers that he has to pick up some lotion for Molly at Sweny's, the chemist. While there he purchases himself a cake of lemon soap with which to bathe before he joins Dignam's funeral. Upon leaving the chemist he meets another acquaintance, Bantam Lyons, who wants to check Mr Bloom's newspaper for the horseracing results (5.520–41). Mr Bloom twice tells Lyons to keep the paper because he 'was just going to throw it away' (5.534; 537–8). Lyons, evidently hearing something else, gives it back to Mr Bloom and runs off. Mr Bloom continues on his way towards the Leinster Street Turkish and Warm Baths; passing the gates of Trinity College, he notices a poster for the college sports day: 'Damn bad ad. Now if they had made it round like a wheel. Then the spokes: sports, sports, sports: and the hub big: college. Something to catch the eye' (5.552–4). Here the reader learns something more about how Mr Bloom reads: as his idea for a circular poster with radiating lines of text mimicking the shape of a bicycle wheel makes clear, Mr Bloom is capable of writing and reading text in a non-linear fashion. Perhaps with the circularity of the wheel in mind, Mr Bloom then echoes Stephen's notion about the endlessly cyclical watery flow of creation, before foreseeing his body transformed into the Eucharist through an echo of Jesus' words at the last supper – themselves taken from St Paul's *First Epistle to the Corinthians* – 'This is my body which is for you' (🕮 5.563–72). In his vision of himself, Mr Bloom's penis, not unlike the drowned man's penis in Stephen's image, undergoes something of a transformation once it is immersed in the everflowing 'stream of life' (5.563–4); however, instead of becoming a fish, Mr Bloom's penis becomes, perhaps appropriately given his name, a flower.

Episode 6: Hades
Scene: Glasnevin Cemetery
Hour: 11 a.m.
Organ: Heart
Art: Religion
Technique/Style: Incubism

In Book XI of the *Odyssey*, Odysseus descends into Hades, the world of the dead, to consult the shade of Tiresias, the blind prophet, before continuing his journey to Ithaca. Tiresias tells Odysseus that it is Poseidon, god of the sea and earthquakes, who has been hampering his efforts to get home. He also tells the traveller that his men must not harm the cattle of the sun-god; if they do so, they will be killed, Odysseus' difficulties in getting home will increase, and, once he finally gets home, he will find his palace overrun with usurpers.

Mr Bloom, refreshed after his bath, steps aboard the funeral carriage that will convey him and his travelling companions (Stephen's father, Simon Dedalus, Jack Power and Martin Cunningham, who both appeared as characters in the short story 'Grace' in *Dubliners*) to the land of the dead – Glasnevin Cemetery on Dublin's Northside – for the interment of Patrick Dignam. As the carriage sets off, Mr Bloom sees Stephen Dedalus – doubtless on his way towards Sandymount Strand to begin reading the world-text – for the first time that day and notices that he, like himself, is 'clad in mourning' (6.40); Mr Bloom tries unsuccessfully to point him out to Mr Dedalus. This is the first hint in the text that Stephen has two fathers: a biological one whose resemblance to him causes him some anxiety in 'Proteus' (3.45–50) and who now fails to recognize him, and a spiritual one, also clad in mourning, and who lost another son 11 years earlier, aged 11 days.

Mr Bloom's travelling companions pass their journey by indulging in gossip about acquaintances, the deaths of children, suicide and casual anti-Semitism; Mr Bloom, who is of Jewish extraction, has lost an infant son and whose father committed suicide (6.343–65), understandably divides his time between looking out the carriage window and looking at his newspaper. The conversation in the carriage thus underlines Mr Bloom's alienation; this allies him with Stephen who, as the first three episodes illustrate is alienated socially, intellectually, politically and artistically.

Once Dignam is interred, Mr Bloom, having cast the same skeptical eye over the graveside ritual he cast over communion in the previous episode, ends up in conversation with Tom Kernan, yet another character from 'Grace'. Mr Kernan, apparently still grappling with his conversion to Catholicism, states his preference for the impressive simplicity of the Protestant Church of Ireland service, focusing in particular on how the phrase 'I am the resurrection and the life' touches a man's 'inmost heart' (6.670). Mr Bloom's interior monologue on the heart in response to Mr Kernan's pronouncement (≋ 6.669–82) neatly illustrates how his playful pragmatism neatly punctures the façade of po-faced piety: Mr Bloom jokingly imagines – after John 6.40 – that on the occasion of the Resurrection and Last Judgment, when the dead will supposedly be raised in the flesh, the zombified corpses will be searching about for their 'rusty old pumps' and other odds and ends. Mr Bloom's joke also opens up an interesting continuity between the human body and machines and mechanical devices. The continuity of the mechanical and the living that Mr Bloom points to here can be read both as an echo and expansion of Stephen's contemplation of the place of man in the world-text. As I suggested above, Stephen's formulation of the world-text cannot be reduced to exclusively human terms of reference: as I also argued above, since both Stephen and Mr Bloom see man's place in the world-text as that of a mortal component caught in the flow of the world-text, both effectively deny the idea of an eternal life – and therefore the metaphysical conception of the human soul. At the same time, Mr Bloom could be said here to expand and modernize not only Stephen's view of the world-text, but also his own conception of the process of metempsychosis seen in episode 4, by including machines and mechanical devices. And, given his predilection for machines, it would seem that Mr Bloom is perhaps more of a Daedalus than Simon Dedalus.

After noticing and wondering about a mysterious 'lankylooking galoot' 'in a macintosh' (6.805–6) – the identity of whom is a famous unsolved puzzle in the text – and giving his name to the newspaper reporter covering the funeral, Joe Hynes (who is also a character in the *Dubliners* short story 'Ivy Day in the Committee Room'), Mr Bloom's fascination with the continuity of humanity and machines resurfaces when he imagines using a particular mechanical device – a gramophone – as a way of remembering and extending human 'life': 'After dinner on a Sunday. Put on poor old greatgrandfather. Kraahraark! Hellohellohello amawfullyglad kraark awfullygladaseeagain hellohello amawf krpthsth' (6.964–6). Here, the gramophone acts – in much the same way as the camera does (6.966–7) – as a technological device that makes it possible to contact the departed's 'soul'; the disc on which the voice is stored is the bit of the individual that 'survives' death. These devices can be understood to act as types of writing devices that can then be used to repeatedly inscribe the dead in the memory of the living. In other words, technological devices such as the gramophone or the camera would signal yet another way in which the dead become something other than what they were and are incorporated into the living. The gramophone would thus be an integral part of the metempsychotic flow of the world-text since it is through this device that man is on his way to becoming (a) machine.

As if to underline the connection between the gramophone and the metempsychotic flow of the world-text, Mr Bloom uses the occasion of seeing a large grey rat scurrying between the graves to recall (note especially the recurrence of the image of the 'saltwhite corpse' in both interior monologues which are also taking place at approximately the same time in the text) Stephen's thoughts on Sandymount Strand (⥱ 6.979–1005). Here, Mr Bloom imagines a number of other things – in addition to a machine or part of a mechanical device – that mortal man can become in death: a rat, a bird, quicklime, a fish, fire, earth, maggots, etc. As he catalogues these living, dead, organic and inorganic possibilities, Mr Bloom simultaneously expands his ruminations on the Eucharist and corpse-eating begun in episode 5 to include these different forms of consuming the dead, going so far as to include cheese – 'corpse of milk' – in his catalogues of corpses (6.982). Like Stephen – who argues with his mother for the right to live in 'Telemachus': 'Ghoul! Chewer of corpses! No, mother! Let me be and let me live'. (1.278–9) – Mr Bloom wants to be counted as one of the living (6.1003–5), the ones doing the corpse-eating. Having passed through the underworld and communed with the dead,

Mr Bloom passes back through the cemetery gates, re-entering the realm of the living where the wind-god, 'Aeolus', awaits.

Episode 7: Aeolus
Scene: The Offices of the *Evening Telegraph* and the *Freeman's Journal*
Hour: 12 noon
Organ: Lungs
Art: Rhetoric
Technique/Style: Enthymemic[22]

In Book X of the *Odyssey*, Odysseus, after tangling with the Cyclops, reaches the shores of Aeolia, ruled by Aeolus, the god of wind. Aeolus helps Odysseus by confining all the unfavourable winds in a bag, which Odysseus stows on his ship. Within sight of Ithaca, Odysseus's men, suspecting that there is treasure in the bag, open it and the unfavourable winds blow them back to Aeolia. Aeolus refuses to help them again. Episode 7 of *Ulysses* follows Mr Bloom to the offices of the *Freeman's Journal*, one of the newspapers that he sells advertising for. Joyce's Homeric parallel thus appears to suggest that like Aeolus, journalism has a certain amount of control over the winds of public opinion. While Mr Bloom goes about his business, other characters – Simon Dedalus, Ned Lambert, Professor MacHugh, J.J. O'Molloy, Mr O'Madden Burke, Myles Crawford, editor of the *Freeman's Journal* and Stephen, who faithfully delivers Mr Deasy's letter on foot and mouth disease – drift in and out of the newspaper offices. Mr Bloom's and Stephen's paths thus cross for the second time, and the reader is treated to snippets of their interior monologues amid the din of machines and debates on Irish politics and culture.

'Aeolus' ushers a linguistic and textual playfulness into the text of *Ulysses*. This is done in two ways: first, the text is punctuated by lines of text in capital letters – for example, 'GENTLEMEN OF THE PRESS' (7.20) – that, appropriately enough, typographically mimic the sort of headlines one would find in a newspaper; second, since the art of the episode is, according to the Gilbert schema, 'rhetoric', the text employs well over a hundred rhetorical techniques.[23] Taken together, this episode's typographical mimicry and attention to rhetorical techniques signal what might be called a 'thickening' of language in *Ulysses*. This thickening of language also foregrounds the book's preoccupation with something other than simply presenting a character or unfolding a plot: it calls attention to the playful textuality of *Ulysses* itself. Thickened language, insofar as it distorts the simple reflection of reality, can thus be read as producing yet more cracks in the series of cracks that have split the reflective surface of the book since episode 1. The difference is that in 'Aeolus' these fractures now draw attention to the book as a typographically and semantically playful text that is itself repeatedly criss-crossed by all sorts of routes and lines of transport and telecommunications – tramlines, telephones and postal routes.

As the episode begins, Mr Bloom is talking to Red Murray, a fellow newspaper employee, trying to get a copy of an advertisement that he wants to place in the *Evening Telegraph* for one of his clients, Mr Alexander Keyes: 'Red Murray's long shears sliced out the advertisement from the newspaper in four clean strokes. Scissors and paste' (7.31–2). This scene is interesting because it neatly introduces the motif of cutting and pasting, which itself succinctly names what the text of *Ulysses* is doing when it allows the faux-newspaper headlines to interrupt the narrative. The ad Mr Bloom wants a copy of is also interesting because it underlines semantic playfulness in the text, something that becomes clear once Mr Bloom speaks to the print manager in the section headed 'HOUSE OF KEY(E)S' (≋ 7.141–51). The Keyes ad introduces advertising into the text as a form of composition in which visual and lexical playfulness can take place: the crossed keys in the ad are a visual pun on the name of the client, Keyes. At the same time, the ad is also explicitly political because the phrase, 'the House of Keyes' deliberately invokes the Manx parliament, which was known as the House of Keys, and which – unlike Ireland at the time – enjoyed a limited form of 'home rule' (7.150).

The reader is thus introduced to a form of 'cut and paste' textual pun-play – in the form of advertising – that echoes through Mr Bloom's thoughts in the section headed 'ORTHOGRAPHICAL' when he remembers that Martin Cunningham forgot to give his usual 'spellingbee conundrum' to his fellow mourners (≋ 7.164–70). Mr Cunningham's spelling test, which revolves around words that playfully echo other words – pealed, peeled, pear, pair, symmetry, cemetery, etc. – further underlines the text's linguistic playfulness.[24] This textual exuberance, which can now be thought of as a pun-like system of echoes that bounce back and forth between similar sounding words, is then connected by Mr Bloom to the language of the world-text wherein machinery and mechanical devices do their 'level best to speak' (7.176). Here, machines and mechanical devices now get to speak in their 'own' voices: 'Sllt' (7.174–7). The printing machines – which, interestingly enough, are also recording devices akin to the gramophone and the camera – thus partake in the world-text by producing text.

These printing machines are not passive, however: they also introduce a different way of reading and writing into the text of *Ulysses*. These machines require readers who are able to read not only according to the demands of Western European Christian textual traditions, but also according to what Mr Bloom, given his heritage, sees as Jewish textual traditions:

> He stayed in his walk to watch a typesetter neatly distributing type. Reads it backwards first. Quickly he does it. Must require some practice that. mangiD kcirtaP. Poor papa with his hagadah book, reading backwards with his finger to me. Pessach. (7.204–7)

Watching the typesetter read and write 'Patrick Dignam' backwards reminds Mr Bloom of his father reading to him in Hebrew the story of the exodus of the Jews from Egypt during 'Pessach', or Passover. If the reader could be said to learn from Stephen in 'Nestor' that to read like Moses Maimonides or Averroes – that is, to read as Jew or a Muslim – is to read 'algebraically', using their 'dark' 'mocking mirrors', then the reader could now be said to learn from Mr Bloom that one must read text kinetically – as 'Jew' and 'Gentile' – backwards and forwards – a point underscored by two famous palindromes which appear later in the episode, 'Madam, I'm Adam. And Able was I ere I saw Elba' (7.683), and the repeated references to the to-and-fro of telephone, mail and tramlines throughout the episode.[25] This 'zigzagging' mode of reading fits perfectly with a book that starts twice, a beginning that invites its reader to look for symmetries, doubles, correspondences, puns and echoes by juxtaposing snippets of the text with each other: in other words, the reader reads *Ulysses* playfully by metaphorically 'cutting and pasting' its text. And it is cutting and pasting that makes it possible to see that when Mr Bloom recalls the Passover chant that looks forward to the day when God comes to right the wrongs done to the people of Israel, he is basically restating both his and Stephen's reading of the world-text as the ebb and flow of life and death in which everybody is 'eating everyone else. That's what life is after all' (7.210–14). It is also worth noting here that

Mr Bloom expresses a certain scepticism regarding the very same concept – 'Justice' – that Stephen singles out for criticism as one of those 'big words [. . .] which make us so unhappy' (2.264).

If, as I have been suggesting, 'Aeolus' teaches the reader to read *Ulysses* playfully by cutting and pasting and going back and forth looking for puns, echoes and correspondences, then it is perhaps not surprising that the same episode also introduces a way of reading that treats text itself as a series of 'locations' or 'places' that can then be used to weave a narrative. This mode of reading is introduced later in episode 7 when Myles Crawford, the editor of the newspaper, tells the story of how, in 1882 the journalist Ignatius Gallaher (also a character in the *Dubliners* short story 'A Little Cloud'), managed to send by cable details of two murders that took place in the Phoenix Park in Dublin to the *New York World*. Because the killings were political in nature – they were carried out by an Irish Nationalist group known as the Invincibles and the victims were key administrators of British rule in Ireland – they attracted international attention. According to Crawford, whose knowledge of the exact particulars of the now 22-year-old murders is perhaps a little sketchy (he gets the year wrong, etc.), Gallaher used certain letters from a newspaper ad for Bransome's coffee as a sort of coded map on which he could locate key sites – viceregal lodge, parkgate, Inchicore, etc. – for the American journalist who had his own copy of the ad:

– B is parkgate. Good.
  His finger leaped and struck point after point, vibrating.
– T is viceregal lodge. C is where murder took place. K is Knockmaroon gate. [. . .]
– Hello? Evening Telegraph here. Hello? . . . Who's there? . . . Yes . . . Yes . . . Yes.
– F to P is the route Skin-the-Goat drove the car for an alibi, Inchicore, Roundtown, Windy Arbour, Palmerston Park, Ranelagh. F. A. B. P. Got that? X is Davy's publichouse in upper Leeson street. (7.659–69)

In Crawford's demonstration, which is interrupted by Mr Bloom's phone call, the ad acts as a coded map that makes it possible for someone who – for reasons of time or space – could not have witnessed a particular event to map it and reconstruct it. And in an episode that seems so keen to introduce textual playfulness and the kinetic method of reading it demands of the reader, Crawford's 'map' becomes a site worthy of attention for a number of reasons. First, Crawford's 'ad-map' demands that the reader read not just from side to side, but also up and down. Second, the choice of a newspaper ad serves to underscore the continuity between reading the ad-map and the playful punning style found in Mr Bloom's 'House of Keyes' ad. Third, the ad-map makes it clear that not only can one text – the coffee ad – be used to map or recreate another – the newspaper story about the Phoenix Park murders – but that the text used need not have anything to do with what it codes or decodes: Crawford demonstrates that specific textual locations – letters like F. A. B. P. and X, for example – can be arbitrarily isolated and imbued with meaning – used as points or places that can then be used to tell another story. Not only does this introduce a certain notion of the arbitrariness of signs and letters into the text, but it can also be read as a revealing clue to the extra-textual relationship between the text of *Ulysses* and Homer's *Odyssey* that does not have to rely upon actually believing in an occult doctrine like metempsychosis. Fourth, the ad-map makes clear that text is something that can be used to overcome distances in time, space and nationality when used in conjunction with communications technology. Crawford's demonstration thus introduces a level of formal and stylistic complexity into the text that ties together the issues of advertising, cutting and pasting, puns, playfulness, the place of technology and (en)coding.

Episode 7 ends with the editor and the others leaving to go to the pub for a lunchtime drink, with Stephen telling the group his 'parable' about two old women who buy plums and go to visit Nelson's Pillar, a monument dedicated to Admiral Lord Nelson (1758–1805), then located on Sackville (now O'Connell) Street in the centre of Dublin. As they leave, Mr Bloom, who is not invited, and who does not get the answer he wanted from the editor of the paper regarding the placement of the ad, observes Stephen's clothing with interest, particularly his new boots. However, as I have been suggesting, the text of episode 7 is perhaps less notable for its reintroduction of familiar characters, and more for its repeated interruptions of the narrative. These interruptions have been seen by some Joyceans as the work of a mysterious figure, which is neither a character (because it is not caught in or subject to the 'action' of the narrative) nor the book's narrator. This figure has come to be known as 'the Arranger'.[26] The Arranger's work takes place on the formal and stylistic level of the text, punctuating it with cut and pasted headlines that comment on the narrative and direct the reader's attention to the textual surface of *Ulysses*.[27] This is not to say however, that the Arranger only shows up in 'Aeolus'; as I suggested above, it is possible to discern this figure's work in the mysterious word 'Chrysostomos' or the scene of Clive Kempthorpe's 'debagging' in episode 1. On this reading, the Arranger – there is nothing to assure us of its gender – appears to have been 'in' the text all along even though it only erupts into 'full view' in episode 7. The Arranger's appearance in 'Aeolus' also foreshadows a certain displacement of Mr Bloom and 'realism' in the text. This displacement is heralded by the reader's getting to see events that take place outside Mr Bloom's point of view, despite having spent the previous four episodes so close to him.[28] Mr Bloom, like Stephen, does not disappear entirely; however, even though the Arranger recedes for the most part from episode 8, it reappears with some vigour towards the end of episode 9 and plays an increasingly dominant role for the remainder of the book as Mr Bloom and Stephen seem to fade. This is not to suggest that the Arranger marks a complete break with what has come before; on the contrary, insofar as it plays a role in disturbing the reflective surface of the text, the Arranger is yet another manifestation of Irish art.

Episode 8: The Lestrygonians
Scene: The Lunch at Davy Byrne's Pub
Hour: 1 p.m.
Organ: Oesophagus
Art: Architecture
Technique/Style: Peristaltic

In Book X of the *Odyssey*, Odysseus recounts his misadventures at the hands of Aeolus. After they are blown back from Ithaca by Aeolus's wind, Odysseus and his crew reach the island of the Lestrygonians. All ships – except Odysseus's which remains in more open water – drop anchor in a bay ringed in by a high cliff. An exploration party from the ships anchored in the bay is lured ashore by a young girl whom they follow to the hall of Antiphates, the king of the Lestrygonians. The king – a giant and a cannibal – eats one of the party before leading his men in the destruction of all the other ships anchored in the bay. Only Odysseus and his crew escape to Circe's island.

Reading episode 8 the reader notices the absence of the newspaper headlines that broke up the text of episode 7. It is now getting on for lunchtime and Mr Bloom, after his less than successful trip to the newspaper offices, starts to notice food all about him. He heads south of the River Liffey encountering a young man handing out 'throwa-ways' – religious flyers – that apocalyptically preach the necessity of blood sacrifice and announce the imminent return of Elijah (8.1–20). This leads Mr Bloom to ponder briefly the crossovers of advertising and religion before he notices how undernourished one of the Dedalus daughters – Dilly – looks as she stands outside Dillon's auc-tionrooms (8.27–9). As he crosses the Liffey, Mr Bloom tosses the throwaway into the waters and notices the seagulls, which he then decides to treat to two Banbury cakes purchased from a nearby street vendor. As he watches the gulls devour their treat over the river, he contemplates how that which eats tends to absorb certain character-istics of that which it eats (❦ 8.88–96). While gazing at the river, Mr Bloom notices a small boat with an advertisement for Kino's trousers – '11/' (8.91) – noting that 'All kinds of places are good for ads' (8.95–6). Mr Bloom's thoughts as he looks at the boat moving on the water's surface not only recall his thoughts from 'The Lotus Eaters' on the stream of life, where things can take on the appear-ances of other things, but also his continuing interest in the art of advertising. And it is these thoughts on advertising that once again echo Stephen's earlier contemplation of the shifting world-text on Sandymount strand insofar as advertisements transform the surface of the world – for example, a boat or a wall – into a potentially infi-nite series of mobile texts that demand to be read.

Mr Bloom's contemplation of a shifting world-text gives way to his noting for the reader the peculiarity of telling the time in Dublin, which in turn reminds him of a word that will – like Molly's 'metem-psychosis' – bother him for the rest of the day – 'parallax' (❦ 8.109–13). Mr Bloom's chain of thoughts here requires a little unpacking: in the days before local Dublin time was synchronized with Greenwich Mean Time (GMT), the timeball – which was located on the roof of the ballastoffice building at the southern end of O'Connell bridge in Dublin – was a device that consisted of a ball on a pole. The ball dropped to signal 1 p.m. GMT for the benefit of local shipping traffic. Local Dublin time – the 'Dunsink time' Mr Bloom refers to – was 25 minutes behind GMT. Given all this, it appears that Mr Bloom is in error in supposing that it is after 1 p.m.: it is actually sometime after 12.35 Dunsink time, not after 1 p.m. The time*ball* reminds Mr Bloom of the English astronomer royal, Sir Robert Ball (1840–1913), whose book, *The Story of the Heavens* (1885), Mr Bloom has in his home library (17.1373). Parallax – the word Mr Bloom has trouble with – is a common phenomenon in astronomy: it names the apparent change in the position or direction of an object when it is observed from two different points of view. For example, a star may be seen to have changed its position with respect to other heavenly objects when observed from two different points in space in the earth's orbit around the sun.

Sometime later in the episode, Mr Bloom's thoughts return to the timeball (8.571–8). This time, however, Mr Bloom approaches the timeball from a different mental perspective, which changes his perception of it: this change in perspective allows him to correct his earlier mistake regarding the timeball's relation to Dunsink time and GMT. He then imagines the best way of approaching the director of the observatory at Dunsink – the Irish astronomer royal, Charles Jasper Joly (1864–1906) – in order to get an answer to his question regarding the definition of parallax. The irony here is that Mr Bloom has unconsciously enacted a practical and earthly form of parallax despite the fact that he fails to grasp the concept consciously: 'Ah. His hand fell to his side again. Never know anything about it. Waste of time' (8.579–81). Parallax in the text thus becomes something of a general principle: it is discenible in the shift from thought to thought, between unconsciousness and consciousness, from character inside the text to the reader outside it. In other words, parallax in *Ulysses* is no longer simply confined to apparent changes brought about by different physical points of observation.

If parallax can include unconscious movements or gestures, then it can also include moods, bodily desires and needs: these parallactic shifts recreate both the world and the text of the world around Mr Bloom as he walks through Dublin. The ability of parallax to rearrange the text of the world is powerfully illustrated when Mr Bloom observes a group of men wearing sandwich boards advertising Wisdom Hely's – a Dublin-based firm of stationers and printers that he used to work for – as they parade down the street: 'He read the scarlet letters on their five tall white hats: H. E. L. Y. S. Wisdom Hely's. Y lagging behind drew a chunk of bread from under his foreboard, crammed it into his mouth and munched as he walked. Our staple food' (8.125–8). Here, amidst delightful wordplay – a hungry sandwichman advertising a stationers eats a piece of bread, a staple food – Mr Bloom notices how a bodily need – hunger – disrupts and rearranges the linear surface of the world-text: 'Y' loses his place because he is hungry. Read thus, hunger becomes a force that parallactically rearranges linear text, producing a different arrangement of a phenomenon, a different perspective: here the text offers additional textual evidence for Mr Bloom's ability to read in a nonlinear fashion – an ability that became noticeable at the end of episode 5. At the same time, the scene Mr Bloom observes here also begins to erode the hard-and-fast distinction between bodies and text. In short, the scene suggests that a hungry text-body makes for a mobile and moving text, a text that remains open to disruption by what goes into it.

Soon after his encounter with the sandwichmen, Mr Bloom meets and converses with Mrs Breen – a former flame of his – who informs him of, among other things, Mrs Mina Purefoy, who has been in labour for the last three days (the birth of baby Purefoy will play a major role later in episode 14). After taking his leave of Mrs Breen, Mr Bloom continues on his journey, passing by the offices of the *Irish Times* newspaper, which prompts him to recall the ad he placed there – 'Wanted, smart lady typist to aid in literary work' (8.326–7) – which elicited 44 replies, one of which was from Martha Clifford. He then recalls snippets from Martha's latest task (8.327–33). Mr Bloom continues walking towards Grafton Street where he passes, dallying, the windows of Brown Thomas, an upscale department store. He notices the silk petticoats and stockings which immediately transforms Dublin into a version of the far east, setting off a chain of association that ends for him in a fusion of hunger and sexual desire: 'With hungered flesh obscurely, he mutely craved to adore' (8.638–9). With his appetites aroused, Mr Bloom steps into the Burton restaurant on Duke Street but is disappointed to find only 'Men, men, men' (8.653) and his desires give way to horror as he regards the frenzied male orgy of eating: 'Gulp. Grub. Gulp. Gobstuff. [. . .] Eat or be eaten. Kill! Kill!' (8.701–3). He crosses the road to Davy Byrne's – deeming it a 'Moral pub' (8.732) – where he ponders cannibalism, prompted by his recollection of the newspaper ad for 'Plumtree's potted meat', which was placed under Dignam's obituary notice. Mr Bloom then indulges in racist speculation on how the wives of a cannibal chief who has eaten the sexual organs of their potted-meat victims look forward to reaping the benefits of his meal. The virile chief's enhanced performance transforms the once incomplete home into an abode of bliss (8.741–50). Sex and hunger are never too far apart for Mr Bloom.

Mr Bloom, engaging in half-hearted conversation with Nosy Flynn, one of the pub's regulars, surveys his options before eventually ordering one of the most famous light lunches in literature: a glass of Burgundy and a gorgonzola cheese sandwich, which he cuts into strips and studs with yellow mustard. As Mr Bloom eats – savouring the 'feety savour of green cheese' (8.819) – and tastes the French sun in his Burgundy, his feelings of desire rekindle, and he is transported back to the day he spent with Molly on Howth Head (🥄 8.913–32). Mr Bloom once again enacts parallax here: he notes the shift in the 'me' from that day on Howth Head to the 'me' that stands in Davy Byrne's. As he gazes at the bar, he boils beauty down to one word: 'curves' (8.920). These curves then link to the frozen curves of naked statues of goddesses held in the museum, who deny no man a look (8.922–3). He imagines a statue coming alive – like the statue of Galatea did after its sculptor Pygmalion prayed to Aphrodite – and addressing a human. Mr Bloom contrasts these immortal bodies with the human ones that have two holes – a mouth and an anus – before realizing he has never actually checked to see if they have anuses. He thus resolves to do some discreet research when he visits the library to track down a copy of the Keyes ad (8.929–32).

Before Mr Bloom leaves Davy Byrne's he goes to relieve himself. While he is away from the bar, Bantam Lyons, the man he met in episode 5, and a group of drinking companions enter the pub. Mr Bloom leaves without seeing him, but Lyons tells the group that Mr Bloom has given him a tip for the Gold Cup horse race (8.1006–25). As he heads towards the library, Mr Bloom catches sight of Blazes Boylan's straw hat and tan shoes; after a second of panic, he swerves into the museum where he can pursue his research on the anatomical correctness of the statues of goddesses.

Episode 9: Scylla and Charybdis
Scene: The National Library of Ireland, Kildare Street, Dublin
Hour: 2.00 p.m.
Organ: Brain
Art: Literature
Technique/Style: Dialectic

In Book XII of the *Odyssey*, Ulysses and his men come back from the underworld and return to Circe's island to bury a dead comrade at his request. Circe gives Odysseus sailing directions and offers him a choice of routes: one passes the Wandering Rocks, which entails certain death, and the other passes between Scylla, a six-headed beast, and Charybdis, a whirlpool. Odysseus opts for the second route, passing close to Scylla who attacks his ship and kills six of his men.

Episode 9 of *Ulysses* takes place in the National Library of Ireland on Kildare Street in Dublin. The episode is centred on Stephen and his theory of fatherhood and authorship in Shakespeare – the 'algebra' that Buck Mulligan refers to in episode 1: 'He proves by algebra that Hamlet's grandson is Shakespeare's grandfather and that he himself is the ghost of his own father' (1.555–7). Stephen, who has been struggling with the notion of his biological origins and his role as an artist since the beginning of the book, treats Shakespeare's writings as code-texts – more complex than certainly, but not completely unlike Myles Crawford's demonstration with the Bransome coffee ad in 'Aeolus' – on which he maps the questions and feelings that have been preoccupying him all day. Stephen's theorizing takes place in dialectical fashion with an informal audience made up of librarians and luminaries from Dublin's writing scene: A.E. (George Russell, 1867–1935) the poet, John Eglinton (the pseudonym of the essayist William Magee, 1868–1961) and two librarians, Mr Lyster and Mr Best. The group is later joined by Buck Mulligan, and is interrupted briefly by 'a bowing dark figure' (9.602–3) – Mr Bloom, who is looking for another copy of the Key(e)s ad. Because the language of this episode is thickened with hundreds of citations of, and allusions to, almost all of Shakespeare's writings, there are far too many to keep track of in the following necessarily brief discussion; once again, Gifford will prove to be a reliable enough guide.

The discussion of Shakespeare twists and turns through many of the fashionable and unfashionable theories about Shakespeare's life and how it may or may not have influenced his writing. Stephen devotes a great deal of his first part of his theory to reading *Hamlet* as a text that encodes Shakespeare's coded attempt to tell of his sexual betrayal at the hands of his wife, Ann Hathaway (9.147–80). Ann, who was eight years his senior and seduced him at the age of eighteen (9.450–81), cuckolded him with his brother, Edmund (9.983–1015). Stephen thus sees Shakespeare's writings as an attempt – 'an old dog licking an old sore' (9.475–6) – to heal the unhealable sexual wounds inflicted by Ann. According to Stephen, Ann's infidelity allows for the possibility of the usurper to reproduce himself, and the trace of a usurper produces an intolerable rupture in the artistic ego: 'His own image to a man with that queer thing genius is the standard of all experience, material and moral. Such an appeal will touch him. The images of other males of his blood will repel him. He will see in them grotesque attempts of nature to foretell or to repeat himself' (9.432–5). Shakespeare, according to Stephen, must be able to see his face mirrored in his bloodlines, his creation and his world: if, like Wilde's Caliban, he cannot with certitude see his face in that glass, he is repulsed and wounded. The sexual wound inflicted on Shakespeare is thus also an ego-wound: it suggests also that 'fatherhood' itself is vulnerable to the mother – in the end, it has only her word that she has been faithful.

However, even if *Hamlet* reveals its inherent vulnerability, father-hood nevertheless remains 'a necessary evil' (9.828). Saying these words, Stephen thinks of the chasm that separates him from his own father, who 'does not know me' (9.827). Stephen goes on to link the vulnerability, uncertainty and necessary evil of fatherhood with the 'mystical estate' of 'apostolic succession' (❦ 9.837–45). 'Apostolic succession' – the apparently uninterrupted descent from Jesus's apostles to ordained bishops in the Catholic Church – is a 'mystical' attempt to combat the uncertainty of the 'void' of fatherhood.[29] As a solution, however, it does little to reduce incertitude because, inso-far as it is a mystical descent, it is subject to faith, not knowledge; it thus remains 'unknown' – in the sense of unknowable – to man. Thus, paternity remains akin to a 'fiction', which Stephen here contrasts with the 'truth' of *amor matris* – both the love of the child for its mother and the mother for the child (9.842–3). Through this contrast Stephen appears to imply that every father simply has to believe the mother when she says that a child is his.[30] Stephen further underscores the weakness of fatherhood by conceiving of the relation between father and son as one that is subject to ugliness, pain, jeal-ousy and rivalry (9.854–9).

Given his view of the sorry state of fatherhood, it is perhaps not surprising that Stephen sees in Shakespeare a coded attempt – not unlike that of the Catholic Church – to combat its vulnerability. Thus he reads Shakespeare, or those believed to be responsible for writing 'Shakespeare's' work – 'Rutlandbaconsouthamptonshakespeare'[31] – through the lens of an uneasy mixture of the Scholastic logic of Aquinas, Sabellius (fl. ca. 215) and artistic creation (❦ 9.862–71). In this complex passage, Stephen upholds both Sabellius's heretical posi-tion – that the Father was Himself His Own Son – and Aquinas' logi-cal refutation of his position – how can there be a father without a son and vice versa? – to suggest that the Shakespeare who wrote *Hamlet*, was neither a father because his son, Hamnet, had died at age 11 nor a son because his father was dead. Stephen thus frees Shakespeare of the uncertainty of fatherhood, imagining him instead to be – in an echo of his own artistic credo at the end of *Portrait* – the artist-father 'of all his race'. Once Shakespeare is the father of all his race, he is the father of everyone – from his own grandfather to his neverborn grandson. In this way, Shakespeare can make the son 'consubstantial with the father' (9.481) and approximate God's relation with his son. His artistic ego knows no threat because he is the father of all, and all are his sons reflecting him back to himself. In other words, Shakespeare, just like the Roman Catholic Church, writes in order to restore himself by writing the need for women and the uncertainty of fatherhood out of the equation.

It is this form of artistic 'fatherhood' – which, somewhat paradoxically, remains fatherhood – that holds out the possibility of covering over the wounds caused by sex, turning them into the internal wounds of an artist in conflict with himself: as father of his race, Shakespeare is, as John Eglinton puts it referring to *Hamlet*, 'the ghost and the prince. He is all in all', a sentiment that Stephen concurs with (⏧ 9.1018–24). However, if, as Stephen suggests to Eglinton, the Shakespeare of *Othello* remains both 'bawd' and 'cuckold', then his creation differs somewhat from that of the '*dio boia*' (9.1049) – Stephen uses the Italian for 'hangman god' to refer to the Catholic God – because 'bawd' and 'cuckold' remain the only parts of his creation in which he cannot be found (⏧ 9.1040–52). The hangman god is not 'in' the bawd and the cuckold, according to Stephen, because there is no need for them in the economy of Heaven, where the pain of sex ceases and its wounds heal because man becomes – in an echo of Jesus' words in Matthew 22.30 – an androgynous angel, married to himself. This heaven stands in contrast to Shakespeare's creation in which the wounds of sex and betrayal become the internalized goading and suffering of the artist-father. However, on closer inspection, the creation of Shakespeare and the creation of the 'hangman god' share some common ground. First, the creation of both is seen by Stephen as something essentially written: Stephen notes in passing the logical inconsistency in the 'folio' of the world as it appears in Genesis. Second, it is impossible for either God or Shakespeare to meet another – that is, someone who or something that is truly another – in their creation since they only ever meet themselves.

Thus, despite the presence of the bawd and the cuckold in his art, Shakespeare – the artist-father of all his race – still only sees his reflection reflected back by his creation: and, since he sees only himself in everything, he too has thus assured himself a theologically perfect bloodline. And, when Stephen attempts – citing the work of the Belgian symbolist poet and dramatist Maurice Maeterlinck (1862–1949) – to generalize this essentially narcissistic structure of God-like creation to everyone – 'We walk through ourselves, meeting robbers, ghosts, giants, old men, young men, wives, widows, brothers-in-love, but always meeting ourselves' (9.1044–6) – he ends up conceiving of all human identity in an essentially theological way. Thus, 'we' also find it impossible to meet with another that is not already ourselves. Stephen is thus still caught between two models of creation that never stop being theological, narcissistic and male, caught between the Scylla and Charybdis of the two by now familiar masters of the aspiring Irish artist: one English – Shakespeare – and one Roman – the Catholic Church.

That being said, it is perhaps the maleness and the narcissism of these creative artist-fathers that ultimately prevents Stephen – who notes that women teach men about dialectic and 'how to brings thoughts into the world' (9.235–7) – from believing in this theory of creation when pressed by Eglinton (9.1064–7). Stephen's lack of belief also places him beyond the 'ego' and the 'egomen' (Latin, 'I on the one hand'): 'I believe, O Lord, help my unbelief. That is, help me to believe or help me to unbelieve? Who helps to believe? Egomen. Who to unbelieve? Other chap' (9.1078–80). This 'other chap' is not of the 'I' or the 'ego'. The 'other chap' who prevents belief gestures beyond narcissistic and theological models of creation. Nevertheless, this 'other chap' is not simply 'male' since it can be associated with the place of the cuckold and the bawd in Stephen's reading of Shakespeare. If Stephen seemed to prefer Shakespeare's creation over God's then it is perhaps because Shakespeare's creation – unlike the hangman god's – keeps a place for the wounds of sex and sexual difference through its regard for the figures of the cuckold and the bawd. The bawd and the cuckold however, are not containable by Shakespeare's creation, even though they may find a place there: this is because it is the bawd who, according to Stephen, remains capable of cracking the reflective surface of the mirror-creation wherein the artist-father-creator would ordinarily see only himself. Through her unfaithful actions, the bawd disrupts the artist-father-creator's attempt to secure himself the perfect bloodline by allowing into his creation the bastard who brings with him the repulsive images of those 'others' that wound him (9.432–5). Further, the bastard cleft in the mirrored surface of the cuckolded artist-father-creator's creation also means that this creation no longer serenely reflects the artist-father-creator's 'race': through this cleft, something dark, algebraic – Jewish, Arabic – enters that creation. And it is surely no accident that as Stephen and Mulligan pass through the doorway of the library, just such a dark figure passes between them – 'The wandering Jew, Buck Mulligan whispered with clown's awe. Did you see his eye? He looked upon you to lust after you' (9.1209–10): that figure is Mr Bloom, a 'Jew' who is only an hour or two away from being cuckolded by a bawd and who himself will become a woman in 'Circe'.

Episode 10: The Wandering Rocks
Scene: The Streets of Dublin
Hour: 3 p.m.
Organ: Blood
Art: Mechanics
Technique/Style: Labyrinth

This episode marks the mid-point of *Ulysses*. The structure of the episode is unusual in a number of respects: the text is made up of individual vignettes – 19 in all – which are typographically separated from each other in the Gabler and 1922 editions by three asterisks (* * *) in the centre of the page. Certain of these vignettes centre on characters familiar to the reader – Mr Bloom (10.585–641), Stephen (10.800–80), Mr Dedalus (10.882–954) – while others deal with characters barely even glimpsed in the text – Master Patrick Dignam, son of Paddy Dignam (10.1122–74), Tom Rochford, an inventor (10.465–583), Ned Lambert, a travelling salesman (10.398–463), Katey, Boody and Maggy Dedalus, three of Stephen's sisters (10.258–97). Some characters, such as Stephen and Mr Dedalus also appear as the focus of more than one vignette. At various points in the episode, snippets from certain vignettes appear in other vignettes, a structure that suggests that the vignettes fit together like the teeth in meshing gears or cogs. At the same time, the dynamically interlocked structure of the episode gives it a synchronized structure: all of the events in these vignettes seem to be unfolding simultaneously. The episode is also

framed by the journeys of two figures of authority: one ecclesiastical –
the very reverend John Conmee S J, rector of Clongowes when
Stephen was a young student there and later prefect of studies at
Belvedere College, when Stephen was a student there (10.1–205) –
and the other civic – William Humble, earl of Dudley (1866–1932),
the lord lieutenant of Ireland (10.1176–282). The episode is also unusual in that there is no direct Homeric parallel: in Book XII of the
Odyssey, Odysseus, heeding Circe's advice, decides to try his luck
with Scylla and Charybdis rather than risk the Wandering Rocks –
shifting hazards that cause the seas to boil.[32]

In what follows, I will focus on just one vignette from episode 10:
vignette 7, which deals briefly with Miss Dunne, Blazes Boylan's
secretary (☙ 10.357–97). In particular, I am interested in how the
vignette meshes with other vignettes, a process I will highlight by
placing the interlocking words in **bold**.

Vignette 7 begins with Miss Dunne hiding her copy of *The Woman
in White* – the 1860 mystery novel by Wilkie Collins (1824–1889) –
and wondering if an unnamed 'he' is in love with someone named
'Marion'.[33] As she begins rolling a sheet of paper into her typewriter,
her vignette is interrupted by a sentence that seems to bear no relation to it: '**The disk shot down the groove, wobbled a while, ceased and
ogled them: six**' (10.373–4). This sentence later appears almost verba-
tim in vignette 9 where Tom Rochford shows off a device he has
created using numbered disks to indicate to those arriving late to a
music hall show what act is on stage at any given moment, and what
acts have already finished: '**He slid it into the left slot for them. It shot
down the groove, wobbled a while, ceased, ogling them: six**' (10.468–9).
Miss Dunne's vignette resumes until another unrelated sentence
interrupts it again: '**Five tallwhitehatted sandwichmen between
Monypeny's corner and the slab where Wolfe Tone's statue was not,
eeled themselves turning H. E. L. Y'S and plodded back as they had
come**' (10.377–89). This interruption not only reintroduces the sandwichmen from episode 8, but is also a recollection of their reappearance in vignette 5, where Miss Dunne's employer, Blazes Boylan, is
selecting fruit to send as a present to Molly Bloom: '**H. E. L. Y'S filed
before him, tallwhitehatted, past Tangier lane, plodding towards their
goal**' (10.310–11). Miss Dunne's next interruption is narrative based –
'**The telephone rang rudely by her ear**' (10.388) – which neatly serves to
underline the importance of interruption in the episode by drawing

the reader's attention to yet another form of it. The caller is Boylan who phones his office for messages just after he finishes flirting with the girl behind the counter in the fruitshop in vignette 5: '**May I say a word to your telephone, missy? he asked roguishly**' (10.336). Miss Dunne informs Boylan that a Mr Lenehan will meet him at four in the Ormond Hotel, an appointment for which Lenehan takes his leave of Tom Rochford in vignette 9 (10.490). As he leaves, Rochford is keen for Lenehan to keep his promise of mentioning the invention to Boylan, who, it will be recalled from episode 4, is a concert pro-moter (10.481–6).

As I mentioned above, the interruptions in this episode can be understood to lend it an air of synchronicity: events that take place at different points in the episode occur at the same time as the others. This textual technique is a sort of cubism in words insofar as it puts the reader in a position to 'see' different parts of the episode at once. At the same time, these interruptions also reinforce a non-linear form of reading in the text, a form of reading that has already been associ-ated with advertising (recall Mr Bloom's thoughts and observations in 'The Lotus Eaters' and 'Lestrygonians' and the reconstruction of Ignatius Gallaher's use of the coffee ad in 'Aeolus') and Mr Bloom's struggle with the concept of parallax in 'Lestrygonians'. In 'The Wandering Rocks', however, it would appear that *Ulysses* exceeds its textual boundaries and reaches out to envelop the reader: that is, the characters 'in' the text are no longer the only ones whom the text expects to read non-linearly. In other words, the reader – if s/he wants to come to grips with these textual interruptions – is now expected to mimic Mr Bloom and advertising by reading in a non-linear fashion, shuttling back and forth across the text. And, since 'The Wandering Rocks' demands the reader's knowledge of previous episodes in the text – pertaining to Boylan's livelihood, Molly's appoinment, Mr Bloom's illicit correspondence, for example – the reader is also expected to shuttle back and forth through all the episodes of the text to date: indeed, the reader's performance of this shuttling motion will be demanded more and more frequently as the text advances. In many ways, to read thus is also to read parallactically: in order to compare the echoing shards of other vignettes or episodes in the vignette or episode being read, the reader must necessarily consider those shards from a number of – potentially infinite – different points of view. The form of reiterative non-linear reading that the text demands of its reader in 'The Wandering Rocks' is thus yet another instance of *Ulysses* breaking the reflective surface of its text by instructing the reader in how to read – self-reflexively, non-linearly – that fractured text.

CHAPTER FOUR

READING *ULYSSES* II: FROM 'SIRENS' TO 'PENELOPE'

As mentioned in the previous chapter, 'The Wandering Rocks' marks something of a midpoint in the text of *Ulysses*. Episode 11, 'Sirens', introduces what is widely regarded as the text's formally 'experimental' or 'innovative' episodes – 11–18. These episodes are marked by a series of episode-by-episode shifts in the technique or style of the narrative. These shifts produce two major displacements in the text: first, the interior monologue and the omniscient third-person narrator that have been the major hallmarks of the text thus far are displaced; second, the displacement of the interior monologue and the omniscient narrator, which have been so instrumental in creating the concrete 'realism' of the narrative – that is, the level of narrative on which Stephen and Mr Bloom go about their daily business interacting with acquaintances and colleagues as they move about Dublin city – produces a parallel displacement of realism. This displacement of a concern with realistically mirroring the real world and the movement towards shifting narrative styles that serve to direct the reader's attention to the playful surface of the book's text, should, of course, come as no surprise to a reader who has made it through episode 10. As I have tried to point out in the preceding chapter, *Ulysses* frequently disrupts the notion that a text's job is to reflect serenely something called 'reality'. However, if there is a major difference between episodes 1–10 and episodes 11–18, it perhaps lies in the fact that the reader can no longer ignore the text's shift away from realism. This is not to say, however, that the interior monologue ceases to play a role in the remainder of the text or that the level of narrative reality in the book simply drops away: elements of both remain. However, the reader should not spend his or her energy trying to 'read through' the turbulence of these stylistic shifts in an effort to seek and dig out a level of reassuring realism or reality similar to that which the text has skilfully presented hitherto: to read thus would be to miss too much – if not all – of the humour and playfulness of the text. For that reason alone, the reader is perhaps better off sticking closer to the textual surface of the text. Finally, the text's playful deployment of these shifting styles of narrative in the final eight episodes also serves to remind the reader that the overwhelming 'reality' brought to the text by the interior monologue and the omniscient narrator is itself a style, a style that episodes 11–18 reposition as just one possible style or mode of writing among a vast array of other possible styles.

Episode 11: Sirens
Scene: The Bar and Restaurant of the Ormond Hotel
Hour: 4 p.m.
Organ: Ear
Art: Music
Technique/Style: Fugue

In Book XII of the *Odyssey*, Circe warns Odysseus about the two singing Sirens he must pass on his journey away from her island. The Sirens' song is so potent, she warns, that it is capable of causing passing sailors to lose their minds and be dashed on the rocks of their island. She says that if he wants to hear their song, he must block his men's ears with wax and have himself tied to the mast of his ship; on no account must his men untie him. Odysseus follows Circe's instructions, and he gets to hear the Sirens' song of false pleasure and prophecy, before sailing on to the passage between Scylla and Charybdis.

Episode 11 of *Ulysses* begins with what at first or second glance appears to be 63 fragmentary shards of text that bear no logical or meaningful connection to each other (❦ 11.1–63). These lines contain fragments of sentences and words, some of which – 'A jumping rose on satiny breast of satin, rose of Castile' (11.08) – are more recognizable as belonging to the English language than others – 'Rrrpr. Kraa. Kraandl' (11.60). It is easy to imagine that the opening lines of episode 11 would be bewildering for a reader who has not had to negotiate the labyrinth of episode 10 and the splinters of textual fragments that fractured its narrative surface. Such a reader might suspect that the impressionistic flurry of snipped sounds that constitutes the opening of episode 11 could – with a little vigilance and patience – be found in a similar but different form elsewhere in the episode. Such a suspicion would pay off because each of these sixty-three lines – except for 'Begin!' (11.63) – is repeated in an easily recognizable form at various points throughout the rest of the episode: for instance, the first shard of text – '**Bronze by gold heard the hoofirons, steelyringing**' (11.01) – is echoed in the very first lines of the 'main body' of the episode's text: '**Bronze by gold**, miss Douce's head by miss Kennedy's head, over the crossblind of the Ormond bar **heard the viceregal hoofs go by, ringing steel**' (11.64–5).[1] In other words, the mode of reading the reader learns in episode 10 is immediately put to the test in 'Sirens'. It would thus appear that the text of *Ulysses* wants to play a sort of game with the reader: in this textual game, the reader, when confronted with something that at first does not appear to 'fit' the narrative or that does not seem to 'make sense', is expected to look to other parts of the text in order to solve the enigma.[2] This textual game – as I will suggest below – also involves a ratcheting up of the text's own awareness of itself as (a) text.

The opening lines of the main body of the text (11.64–79) also neatly and explicitly introduce the critical role music plays in this episode: the barmaids, Miss Douce and Miss Kennedy, are the avatars of the Homeric Sirens whose seductive song is lethal to unsuspecting males – 'He's killed looking back' (11.77). The centrality of music in this episode has led many Joyceans to hear the opening 63 fragmented lines of text as a sort of musical prelude or overture that introduces to the reader – in an astoundingly efficient fashion – the key notes, motifs and themes that recur throughout the main body of the episode.

The action of episode 11 is fairly simple: Mr Bloom, feeling hungry and somewhat depressed because it is fast approaching 4 o'clock – the time Boylan and Molly are scheduled to meet – gets an appropriately melancholy theme 'Bloom. Old Bloom. **Blue Bloom is on the** rye' (11.230–1 and 11.6). He stops off at Daly's, a stationery shop on Ormond Quay Upper, in order to buy some writing paper for his reply to Martha Clifford's letter. While in the shop, Mr Bloom, for the third time that day, sees Blazes Boylan pass by on his jingle – a two-wheeled jaunting car drawn by a horse – a contraption that underscores Boylan's theme in the episode: '**Jingling** on supple rubbers it **jaunted** from the bridge to Ormond quay' (11.304–5 and 11.15). There is thus a clear contrast in the episode between Boylan's jaunty theme with Mr Bloom's melancholy one: 'Jingle. Bloo' (11.19). Boylan stops his jingle outside the Ormond hotel to keep his appointment with Lenehan and Mr Bloom leaves Daly's to see what Boylan is up to. As he approaches the parked jingle warily, Mr Bloom is saluted by Richie Goulding – Stephen's uncle on his mother's side – whom he joins for lunch in the hotel, so as to keep an eye on Boylan's movements. While Mr Bloom and Richie Goulding are seated in the dining room, Boylan – in the company of Simon Dedalus and Lenehan – begins to flirt openly with Miss Douce in the bar. Boylan, his sexual appetite whetted, is now 'Boylan with impatience' (11.426) in anticipation of his assignation with Molly and he abruptly makes to leave the bar. Lenehan, discommoded, pointedly asks if Boylan's rush is due to his having an erection: 'Got **the horn** or what?' (11.432 and 11.23). Lenehan's question to Boylan echoes throughout the rest of the episode, and Mr Bloom just catches the sound of the jingle as it leaves for 7, Eccles Street. Mr Bloom has thus – somewhat masochistically – just watched the man who will cuckold him actually leave to commit the act. As Lenehan and Boylan leave, Simon Dedalus is joined by Fr Cowley and Ben Dollard. For the remainder of the episode, Mr Bloom eats melancholically in the company of Richie Goulding, his thoughts dwelling on the sorry state of his marriage and subject to influence by the songs the three men in the bar sing and play – 'Love and War' by T Cooke,[3] 'M'appari' from the 1847 light opera, *Martha* by Friedrich Von Flotow (1812–1883), and the 1845 Irish rebel ballad, 'The Croppy Boy', by William B McBurney – also known as Caroll Malone – (1844–1892).

However, episode 11 does not only send the reader in search of intra-episode echoes or repetitions of text, it also sends the reader in search of echoes and repetitions from elsewhere in the book. In doing so, the text makes clear that each echo can be read as an instance of the text knowingly citing itself. For example, just as Mr Bloom and Richie Goulding are served their dinner by Pat the deaf waiter, there occurs an explicit repetition of the opening lines of 'Calypso' – 'Mr Leopold Bloom ate with relish the inner organs of beasts and fowls. He liked thick giblet soup, nutty gizzards, a stuffed roast heart, liverslices fried with crustcrumbs, fried hencods' roes' (4.1–3): 'Pat served, uncovered dishes. Leopold cut liverslices. As said before he ate with relish the inner organs, nutty gizzards, fried cods' roes' (11.519–20). Here *Ulysses* displays something of an 'awareness' of itself as a written thing, as text: indeed, it seems to wink at the reader with its 'As said before'. Because the recurrence of the opening lines of episode 4 takes place in the midst of echoes from the prelude that opens episode 11, it would seem that the reader of episode 11 – who has been encouraged to read in a non-linear fashion by zigzagging back and forth within the episode to track down textual echoes – is now actively encouraged to extend that kinetic and Bloomian mode of reading to not only the previous episodes but the text as a whole. A similar citational echo recurs a few lines later – 'Bloom ate liv as said before' (11.569) – further underscoring both the mode of reading and the book's awareness of its own textuality. The text is thus very much aware of the game of non-linear readerly hide and seek it is playing with its reader.

The importance of music in the text is also underlined as Mr Bloom listens to Simon Dedalus sing Flotow's 'M'appari' – a song with strong associations for Mr Bloom. In the opera, the character named Lionel sings to his lost love, Martha; Lionel's plight thus reflects Mr Bloom's situation with respect to Molly, while the lost love's name reminds him of his naughty letter-writer, Martha Clifford. As he listens to Simon Dedalus, Mr Bloom imagines the song's rhythm as an echo of something that lies 'behind' it (❦ 11.701–9). Although his numerous references to gushes, flows, floods and dilations here seem to make it clear that he is not simply excluding the mechanisms of female arousal and excitement, that which Mr Bloom believes he sees 'behind' words and music as he plays with an elastic band seems to be both phallic and ejaculatory: indeed, the throb that swells to become 'a pulsing proud erect' (11.702) is in fact Mr Bloom's imaginary reconstruction of Blazes Boylan's sexual athleticism with Molly.[4] In other words, what Mr Bloom thinks is 'behind' the music is actually Mr Bloom's imaginary reconstruction of what he thinks Boylan is now doing to Molly in 7, Eccles Street. And, as 'M'appari' reaches its climax – with the line 'Come to me!' – the ejaculatory maleness that Mr Bloom imagines he sees behind words and music is underlined when he, Simon and Lionel become fused together:

Siopold!
Consumed!
Come. (11.752–54)

In other words, the 'something', the 'reality' that Mr Bloom imagines to lie behind music and words appears to be the insistent, male, rhythmic, animalistic – the words 'tup', 'tep' and 'tip' (11.706–9) all mean to copulate like animals – throb of sex.

However, one might wonder here if the sheer maleness of the musical orgy in the Ormond is not, ironically, the false lure of a Siren song. It seems reductive – and simply phallocentric – to say that music and words are themselves merely the rhythmic echoes of the male experience of sex. This is perhaps why, as if to contrast with this phallic male Siren song, the reader is treated to a short unseen private musical performance outside the Ormond hotel, in which Mr Bloom plays a role. This performance takes place just as the 'blind stripling' – the piano-tuner whom Mr Bloom helped across the road some hours before (8.1075–113) and whose return has been heralded throughout episode 11 by the insistent 'taps' of his cane – re-enters the bar to retrieve his tuning-fork, which someone was playing with earlier in the bar (11.313–16):

> Tip. An unseeing stripling stood in the door. He saw not bronze. He saw not gold. Nor Ben nor Bob nor Tom nor Si nor George nor tanks nor Richie nor Pat. Hee hee hee hee. He did not see.
>
> Seabloom, greaseabloom viewed last words. Softly. *When my country takes her place among.*
> **Prrprr.**
> Must be the bur.
> **Fff! Oo. Rrpr.**
> *Nations of the earth.* No-one behind. She's passed. *Then and not till then.* Tram kran kran kran. Good oppor. Coming. Krandlkrankran. I'm sure it's the burgund. Yes. One, two. *Let my epitaph be.* Kraaaaaa. *Written.*
> *I have.*
> **Pprrpffrrppffff.**
> *Done.* (11.1281–94 and 11.58–62)

None of the Sirens – male or female – actually 'see' Mr Bloom's performance, which consists of his discreet attempt to break wind while reading the last (italicized) words of the Irish rebel leader, Robert Emmet (1778–1803), on a picture in an antiqueshop window. Hampering Mr Bloom's attempts at discretion is the proximity of a prostitute he has had dealings with in the past; aiding those attempts is the loud noise of a tram rumbling by. Mr Bloom's fart thus becomes part of a noisy 'symphony' by entering into a rhythmic relationship with Emmet's words, the movements of the prostitute and the rumbling clanging of the tram. This symphony is essentially a performance of Mr Bloom's speculation that everything can act as an instrument (11.1237–46) – itself an echo of his earlier observation that 'Everything speaks in its own way' (7.177). In addition, this performance also effectively displaces the decidedly phallic music from earlier in the text since it gives a certain privilege to the rhythmic 'music' of the anus which enters into a sort of 'harmony' with the rhythmic movement of modern transportation and the solicitation of sex. Mr Bloom's mini performance also makes it easier to grasp why the text of 'Sirens' seems to delight in using onomatopoeia, chopping up words, fusing the fragments back together in different ways and employing a fluidly shifting syntax in conjunction with obsessively repeated fragments of text: all this chopping, fusing and repeating not only 'thickens up' the book's use of language, but also allows the rhythms of the body and modern life to resound or 'speak' on, in and through its pages.

The deployment of these rhythms and their relationship to language, however, is particularly complex in a text such as *Ulysses*, which, as I have been suggesting, seeks to disrupt the notion of the text as a simple 'reflection' of reality. Useful light can be shed on the complex relations of rhythm and text in 'Sirens' by considering it alongside the 1929 painting *'La trahison des images'* (*'The Treachery of Images'*) by the Belgian surrealist painter René Magritte (1898–1967). Magritte's painting depicts a beautifully rendered image of a pipe with the legend *'Ceci n'est pas une pipe'* ('This is not a pipe') written beneath it. Magritte's painting stages the radical difference between what a viewer of the painting is actually seeing – a series of artfully arranged blotches of pigment – and what the viewer thinks s/he is seeing – a pipe. The closing lines of 'Sirens' cited above can be understood to stage the Joycean version of the radical difference between what is seen and what is not in terms of text with the entrance of the blind piano-tuner, whose cane suddenly makes a sound different to the 'taps' that it has been making throughout the episode: 'Tip. An unseeing stripling stood in the door. He saw not bronze. He saw not gold. Nor Ben nor Bob nor Tom nor Si nor George nor tanks nor Richie nor Pat.' This change in sound seems important: it suggests that the text is here offering the reader something of a 'tip' that appears to be a little cryptic since it is also self-evident: the blind piano-tuner 'sees' nothing. This 'tip' becomes less cryptic if the reader reads it beyond the narrative level: in other words, the blind piano-tuner sees nothing not simply because he is blind, but because there is no 'Ben nor Bob nor Tom nor Si nor George nor tanks nor Richie nor Pat' in the text to be seen. In other words, the text here draws attention to itself *as text* – as something which does not – even when the reader sees it – ever present the reader with 'a picture' that 'looks like' reality. In other words, the text, by calling attention to itself as text, paradoxically prevents the normal or regular functioning of text as the transparent carrier of meaning. The disruption of text is also highlighted by the text's almost manic laughter – 'Hee hee hee hee. He did not see.' This laughter is less the mockery of a disabled individual than a hint to the reader that the text has been playing a sort of a joke on him/her all along: the reader is, in actuality, akin to the blind piano-tuner that enters the Ormond Hotel for the simple reason that neither 'sees' – or, for that matter 'hears' – anything: instead of Magritte's paint, the reader sees only – indeed, has only ever seen – words printed on the page. The result is that the words in 'Sirens' are radically differentiated from the ideas and objects that they would ordinarily represent in 'normally' functioning text. It is these 'broken' words that 'Sirens' chops up, fuses, repeats, etc., using them to draw attention to rhythm in the text, 'behind' which a hearer – just like Mr Bloom – then imaginarily projects 'something': that something may have to do with his/her own bodily drives – defecation, sexual frustration, hunger, etc. – or their preoccupations, worries, fears and so on. These peculiar textual rhythms are thus not the simple reflections of 'real' bodily rhythms; nevertheless, these textual rhythms engage with bodily rhythms – something Mr Bloom has demonstrated since his visit to the jakes in episode 4; these differing rhythms enter into a rhythmic relationship with each other and, in doing so, once more erode the hard-and-fast distinction between world and text. However, as Mr Bloom shows during the final rhythmic symphony, the broken, chopped up and repeated rhythmic language of the text engages not only natural bodily rhythms but also the socio-mechanical rhythms of the modern world, entering into rhythmic – hidden, harmonic, contrapuntal and so on – relations with those as well. These engaging rhythmic relations are possible because rhythm is itself 'no-thing' except the differential relationship – the 'gap' – between two possible things. Through these relations, the body and the modern world, are not so much represented or imitated in *Ulysses*; instead, they, to use a Bloomian phrase, speak musically in and through it.

Episode 12: Cyclops
Scene: Barney Kiernan's Pub, 8–10 Little Britain Street
Hour: 5 p.m.
Organ: Muscle
Art: Politics
Technique/Style: Gigantism

In Book IX of the *Odyssey*, Odysseus recounts his adventures among the Cyclopes – giant, brutish, one-eyed monsters. Odysseus and his landing party become trapped in the cave of Polyphemus, who feasts on two crew members on the first evening and two more on the second. After the second feast, Odysseus decides to act; he gets Polyphemus drunk, telling him that his name is 'Noman', and when the giant falls asleep, he blinds him with a fire-hardened stake. Polyphemus screams that 'Noman' has blinded him; his neighbours, taking him literally, do not offer help. Odysseus and his men then escape the cave by hiding among the giant's sheep. Once at sea, Odysseus, unable to stop himself taunting Polyphemus, reveals his name and nearly has his boat sunk by the giant who throws a huge rock in the direction of the sound. Polyphemus then asks his father, Poseidon, to make Odysseus's journey home miserable.

In 'Cyclops' the reader finds him/herself in the company of a new narrator who remains unnamed throughout the episode. This narrator is, in many ways, a typical Dubliner – grumpy, quickwitted and foulmouthed. He is chatting to a member of the Dublin Metropolitan Police when this epsiode's Homeric parallel pokes hilariously into the text in the form of a chimney sweep's gear that nearly blinds him (☙ 12.1–5). As the opening lines of the episode make clear, the narrative style is markedly different from that of of episode 11: Mr Bloom is nowhere to be seen; gone are the chopped up words and repetitions; gone are the musical overtones. Gone too is Mr Bloom's interior monologue; and when he eventually puts in an appearance, the reader will only get to see him from the point of view of the hostile (he frequently makes anti-Semitic statements), sour (he has nothing good to say about anyone or anything that crosses his path) and (God forgive me!) frequently hilarious nameless narrator.

The Joe Hynes the narrator sees as he turns to curse the sweep is a familiar figure: he is the newspaper reporter that Mr Bloom spoke to briefly at Paddy Dignam's funeral in episode 6 and tried to recover his money from while at the newspaper offices in episode 7. Hynes and the nameless narrator know each other, but obviously have not seen each other in a while: Hynes is not only surprised to see the narrator in the locale (Arbour Hill, just north of the Liffey), but is also unaware of his new line of work – a collector of bad and doubtful debts on the case of a man named Geraghty who has stolen tea and sugar from a merchant named Moses Herzog (❧ 12.23–51). Here, a legal notice – one that doubtless would be quite similar to the one the nameless narrator is trying to serve Geraghty – interrupts the conversation between Joe and the narrator (12.33–51), once again jolting the reader – who should, perhaps, by now be expecting interruptions – out of the 'reality' of the narrative. In all, there are 33 such passages that interrupt the narrative of 'Cyclops', each offering a sort of parodic or mocking commentary on the events being narrated. Even though the style of each interruption varies somewhat – by turns epic, legalistic, journalistic, sensationalist, sentimental, childish and so on – each uses exaggeration to mock or parody the event it comments on. Thus, even though they do not seem to be the work of the nameless narrator, these interruptions – due to their mocking tone – can be said to share his bilious outlook: as a result, they are also frequently hilarious. Nor are these interruptions the work of another fully fledged narrator since they are not sustained throughout the main narrative thread. Further, because they interrupt to paint scenes, as it were, over the top of the main narrative thread, they appear to take place for the benefit – and entertainment – of the reader. As such, they exist on the same narrative plane as the handiwork of the Arranger who punctuated the text of episode 7 with newspaper headlines that grew ever more overblown and parodic as the episode progressed. Finally, it should be noted that episode 12's interruptions differ from the interruptions that occur in episodes 10 and 11 insofar as they are not echoes of other parts of the text.

The action that occurs in the main narrative thread of 'Cyclops' is at first fairly simple: Joe and the nameless narrator head to Barney Kiernan's pub – 8–10 Little Britain Street – where their paths cross with a number of characters: 'the citizen', a hard-drinking and ill-tempered Cyclops of an Irish nationalist; his fearsome hound, Garryowen; Bob Doran, who also appears in 'The Boarding House' in *Dubliners*; Alf Bergan, who is shocked to hear of Paddy Dignam's death since he is sure that he just passed him outside; Mr Bloom, who is supposed to meet Martin Cunningham to go to the widow Dignam's to help her with her insurance problems; J J O'Molloy, a barrister; Ned Lambert, an acquaintance of Simon Dedalus's; John Wyse Nolan, who brings news about a council meeting on the Irish language; and Lenehan, who has just found out he has lost money on a horse named Sceptre in the Ascot Gold Cup Race. The conversations these characters get into – which range from idle gossip about common acquaintances, to issues pertaining to Ireland's complex history and politics and the woes of horseracing – drive the events in this episode.

Not long after he arrives in the pub, Alf Bergan produces letters he claims are from individuals who have written to the Dublin High Sheriff's Office offering their services as hangmen. As Joe Hynes reads some of these letters, the newly cuckolded Mr Bloom – after pacing up and down outside for ten minutes – finally comes into the pub looking for Martin Cunningham. Mr Bloom decides to wait inside and the pub talk turns to the effects of hanging on the victim (❦ 12.455–78). Mr Bloom's explanation of the 'natural phenomenon' of the hanged man's erection is interrupted by a medical journal's report of a lecture given by the distinguished German anatomy professor, Luitpold Blumenduft – German for Leopold Flowerscent. However, because the interruption covers over what he actually had to say on the subject, the extent and accuracy of Mr Bloom's knowledge of the phenomenon in question remains unknown for the reader. After the learned interruption, the nameless narrator scoffs at Mr Bloom's liking for the word 'phenomenon' and goes on to recount a sort of 'experiment' that Mr Bloom performed on the nephew of an elderly neighbour when he and Molly lived at the City Arms hotel: Mr Bloom, apparently in an attempt to ingratiate himself with the old woman – Mrs 'Dante' Riordan who also appears in chapter 1 of *Portrait* – so as to get mentioned in her will, got her nephew 'drunk as a boiled owl' in an effort to teach him 'the evils of alcohol' (12.510–11). The experiment in aversion therapy failed spectacularly: Mr Bloom succeeded in turning the unfortunate into an alcoholic who came home drunk five times a week afterwards (12.517). This story only adds to the reader's uncertainty over whether or not Mr Bloom's knowledge of bodily phenomena is scientifically sound; nevertheless, it is Mr Bloom's firm belief in the body's natural phenomena that will be of particular help to him in episodes 14 and 15.

Other exchanges in the episode also serve to magnify the naïveté of some of Mr Bloom's political formulations on nation and nationality (𝔰 12.1414–33). The definition of the nation that Mr Bloom offers in response to John Wyse Nolan – 'the same people living in the same place' (12.1422–3) – strikes the other patrons of the bar as too simplistic: as they point out, Mr Bloom's definition – even when he revises it – can also apply to the individual. Nor is Mr Bloom's notion that a nation is 'the same people' living in the same place clear: what, exactly, would make all these people 'the same'? Race? Religion? Ability? All three? He does not say. Also problematic is his insistence that an individual's nation is simply the one into which s/he is born, thereby implying that a nation is coterminous with the borders of a particular country – in his case, Ireland. This is undermined by the citizen's conception of a 'greater Ireland beyond the sea' (12.1364–5): the Irish diaspora. Indeed, it is not even the case that the borders of a country are coterminous with the state, since the Ireland of 1904 was a country annexed by a larger monarchic state – the United Kingdom, which also included England, Scotland and Wales. Given the responses of his interlocutors, the text does not seem to be willing to let Mr Bloom's political naïveté go unchallenged.

It is also worth noting here that, until relatively recently, it had become something of a commonplace among commentators on *Ulysses* to regard the citizen – who is modelled after Michael Cusack (1847–1907), the founder of the Gaelic Athletic Association (GAA), which was dedicated to the revival of hurling and Gaelic football – as a one-dimensional (one-eyed) xenophobic and nationalistic Irish bigot with a deep hatred for the English and an intense intolerance for foreigners and anything that is not Irish.[5] It would be useless to try to deny that the citizen does not make statements that are chauvinist and xenophobic; however, on closer inspection, the text's characterization of him actually turns out to be quite nuanced: his analysis of the destruction of Ireland's economy and culture under English colonial rule is absolutely not fantasy; he seems to be vehemently opposed to corporal punishment (12.432); he expresses disgust at the brutality in military discipline (12.1330–59; curiously, Mr Bloom never actually condemns this form of discipline[6]); he advocates the conservation of endangered native Irish species of flora and fauna (12.1262–4); and, like many a modern Irish person, he has an eye towards a renewed and vibrant relationship with Europe

(12.1296–1310). Thus, in an episode rife with allusions to the dangers of metaphorical Cyclopean one-eyedness, it is perhaps better that the reader also regard the citizen with both eyes open.[7]

The text's exploration of Mr Bloom's political vision continues some pages later: after he brings up the intolerable situation of Jews in the Islamic state of Morocco at the turn of the nineteenth century – they were forced to work on holy days and their services could be bought and sold – Mr Bloom floats the notion of a universal Christian love as the meaning of life (⊜ 12.1481–501). After offering this pearl of wisdom, Mr Bloom hastily leaves the pub in search of Martin Cunningham. His sudden departure also suggests that he is not able to offer a satisfactory account of his thesis on love; and this time it is neither the drinkers at the bar nor the nameless narrator who mock the simplistic gospel of universal love, but the text itself: the text adopts a childish and sentimental diction to talk about everyone and everything loving each other – people, elephants and God (12.1493–501). Indeed, if *Ulysses* teaches the reader anything about 'love', it is surely that love between people (I'm unable to speak to the issue of elephant-love mentioned at 12.1496) is anything but simple. The love that Stephen and Mr Bloom feel and desire is complicated by competition, duty, jealousy, insecurity, fear, self-loathing, suffering, pain and so on. Indeed, Mr Bloom himself ponders the possibility of love later in episode 16, when he thinks about the fall of Charles Stewart Parnell: 'Can real love, supposing there happens to be another chap in the case, exist between married folk? Poser' (16.1379–86). The text's parody of the gospel of Christian universal love is then given a specific political and historical dimension when the citizen invokes the actions of the English general, Oliver Cromwell (1599 1658), during the siege of Drogheda (1649) in which nearly 3,500 were killed (⊜ 12.1506–9). By invoking Cromwell's religious cant, symbolized in the text by the image of the bible text 'God is love' pasted round the mouth of Cromwell's cannons, the citizen opens up a disjunction between the comforting notion of universal Christian love with what, under the flags of colonizers and civilizers, has been done in its name. The discussion is not confined to English colonialism, however: the political and colonial charge of the citizen's remarks opens up a wider discussion of European colonialism when John Wyse Nolan brings up reports of forced labour and abuse of workers on rubber plantations in the 'Congo Free State', which was then under the brutal personal control of King Leopold II of Belgium: 'Raping the women and girls and flogging the natives on the belly to squeeze all the red rubber they can out of them' (12.1542–7).

Lenehan, who remembers that Bantam Lyons told him that Mr Bloom gave him a tip for a horse named Throwaway – in epsiode 5, Mr Bloom, it will be recalled, offered Lyons his paper telling him he was just going to 'throw it away'. The riddle of Lyons's 'I'll risk it' (5.541) is thus solved: the horse won. – surmises that Mr Bloom has slipped out to collect his winnings. In the meantime, Martin Cunningham arrives, and 'confirms' the rumours (12.1573–80) that Mr Bloom has been giving Sinn Féin political strategies and ideas for securing Ireland's political autonomy (12.1635–7). The gathering, now labouring under Lenehan's misapprehension, grows openly hostile towards Mr Bloom when he eventually returns and does not stand them a drink (12.1751–91). Martin Cunningham, reading the danger, ushers Mr Bloom onto a waiting cab to go to the widow Dignam's. Mr Bloom, in response to the citizen's 'Three cheers for Israel!' (12.1791), retorts, 'Your God was a jew. Christ was a jew like me' (12.1808–9). Mr Bloom's self-identification here as a Jew should, however, be treated with caution, since it is problematic for a number of reasons: (1) the text of 'Ithaca' will suggest that there are at least two matrilineal breaks in Mr Bloom's Jewish heritage (see 17.536–7: Mr Bloom's mother, Ellen Higgins, and his grandmother, Fanny Hegarty, do not appear to be Jewish); (2) in 'Ithaca,' the reader is also told that Mr Bloom's father, Rudolf Virag (later Rudolph Bloom), converted to Christianity from Judaism in 1865 (17.1637–8); (3) 'Ithaca' also makes it clear that Mr Bloom was himself actually officially christened twice (in addition to being born to Protestant parents): once as a Protestant (17.542–3) and once as a Catholic in 1888 in order to marry Molly (17.1639–40); (4) and, to cap this all off, Mr Bloom actually admits to not being a Jew in at least two places later in the text (16.1084–5 and 17.1084–5). Given all this, it would seem that when he identifies himself as a Jew from the back of the departing cab, Mr Bloom is exaggerating his Jewish status in an effort to provoke an extreme reaction from the citizen. The citizen does not disappoint: 'By Jesus', he vows, 'I'll brain that bloody jew-man for using the holy name' (12.1811), before letting fly, in a parodic echo of the *Odyssey*, with a biscuit tin after the cab. The flight of the biscuit tin is journalistically exaggerated to the point where it destroys half of Dublin and the text closes by parodying Mr Bloom's appropriation of 'Jewishness', transforming him into 'ben Bloom Elijah' who, 'amid clouds of angels' ascends 'to the glory of the brightness at an angle of fortyfive degrees over Donohoe's in Little Green street like a shot off a shovel' (12.1916–18).

Episode 13: Nausicaa
Scene: Sandymount Strand, Dublin
Hour: 8 p.m.
Organ: Eye, Nose
Art: Painting
Technique/Style: Tumescence/ Detumescence

In Book V of *The Odyssey*, Odysseus leaves Calypso's island, falls foul of Poseidon, and is finally washed ashore on the land of the Phaeacians. He is woken by a ball that Princess Nausicaa and her entourage have been playing with. Odysseus reveals himself to Nausicaa, and decides to flatter her beauty; she is impressed and brings him to the palace of her parents who then arrange for his safe passage to Ithaca.

Episode 13 begins at 8.00 p.m., which means that nearly two hours of the day have gone missing between the end of episode 12 and this one. There is no explanation as to why this occurs: the time during which Mr Bloom and Martin Cunningham – imagine that conversation! – were in the cab as they made their way to the widow Dignam's and what occurred there is simply lost. Episode 13 is also split evenly between two narrators or narrative styles: the first half of the chapter is given over to the desires, hopes, fears and dreams of a young woman by the name of Gerty MacDowell, and is written in a sort of syrupy sentimental style that was common in women's magazines of the early twentieth century; the other narrative style used in the episode returns the reader to familiar ground: Mr Bloom's interior monologue interspersed with a third-person narrator.

Episode 13 is also where the reader begins to suspect that the dislocation of Mr Bloom's interior monologue by episode 12 may become permanent: the episode devotes just as much space to the sentimental and syrupy style of women's magazine writing as it does to Mr Bloom's thoughts. The episodes that follow episode 13 seem to confirm this dislocation: Mr Bloom's interior monologue disappears entirely from episode 14, returns in partially recognizable chunks and snippets throughout episode 15, before disappearing almost completely from episodes 16, 17 and 18 – the final three episodes of the book. Mr Bloom's interior monologue thus starts to fade as each episode of *Ulysses* becomes stylistically distinct and experimental: this suggests – when *Ulysses* is taken as a whole – that despite its apparent power to place the reader in the mind of a 'real' human being with complex thought and feelings, the interior monologue remains one of a possible number of styles at the text's disposal. Read thus, episode 13 can be said to underscore the ending of episode 11, in which the reader is made aware of a fundamental lack of 'reality' in the text that s/he is reading, while paradoxically being made aware of the peculiar 'reality' of the printed – written – object that lies in front of him/her. However, this is not to say that the reader should simply 'forget' about Mr Bloom or Stephen or any other textual figure in the text: the text certainly does not forget about them. In fact, part of the fun in reading the following episodes of *Ulysses* lies in how the text plays with the recognizable textual contours of the figures the reader has grown accustomed to. Above all, the dislocation of Mr Bloom and his interior monologue should not be felt as a 'loss': part of what *Ulysses* teaches its reader in episodes 11–18 is the shortcomings of privileging 'content' or 'reality' over style.

As the episode begins, the youthful Gerty is on Sandymount Strand – the same beach Stephen walked some twelve hours earlier in the day – with her friends, Edy Boardman and Cissy Caffrey, and their younger siblings: baby Boardman and the boisterous twins, Tommy and Jackie Caffrey. The women gather to 'discuss matters feminine' (13.12) and the syrupy sweet sentimental clichés that constitute this episode's narrative seem be a far cry from the hilariously bilious nameless narrator and the parodic exaggerations of episode 12. However, it soon becomes clear that, episode 13 shares the parodic tone of the previous episode (❧ 13.78–96). Perhaps the first thing to strike the reader in the narrative's description of Gerty is its double-voicedness: even though it is a third-person narrative, it is unquestionably coloured by Gerty's vain picture of herself. The narrative parodies Gerty's view of herself by foregrounding her acute awareness of how 'on show' she is: everything Gerty does or thinks is a self-conscious echo of a stereotypical cliché, pose, condition or ideal of femininity: she is the very specimen of 'Irish girlhood'; she takes after 'the Giltraps', her mother's side of the family (13.83); she takes products aimed at women such as 'iron jelloids' and 'female pills' (!?!) for her 'fragile' condition (13.84–6); her facial features conform to cultural ideals of beauty derived from the classical world; although her 'Cupid's bow' of a mouth evokes sexuality, she remains spiritually pure (13.87–9); she uses all manner of products, potions and folk-remedies in her extensive beauty regimen; she is in competition with her female acquaintances solely on the basis of appearance. By cataloguing Gerty in this way, the narrative lays bare not only the complex social and cultural constructions of femininity and femaleness in the early twentieth century, but also pitilessly pokes at Gerty's internalization of them. And, by foregrounding the practices and regimens of constructing and maintaining femininity, the narrative puts into question the very notion of a 'natural' femaleness or femininity.

Gerty's sense of being on show is not imagined: after the twins' ball rolls away during their game, it is thrown back by a certain 'gentleman in black' who is sitting nearby on the rocks (13.349). It is for this man that Gerty-Nausicaa performs at 13.411–16. This passage makes it clear that Gerty's whole time on the strand turns out to be an attempt at seductive performance in a theatre of romance: every blink, every tilt of the head, every glance, every minute adjustment of clothing, is a studied gesture in a complex but clichéd choreography of flirtation with the dark, exotic, sad, intellectual, mysterious gentleman on the rocks. Gerty's beach performance is ironically punctuated with both the snippets of the Litany of Our Lady of Loretto, a prayer of supplication to the Virgin Mary, and fragments of a benediction ceremony coming from the nearby church – Mary, Star of the Sea.

Gerty's performance changes somewhat when the fireworks show marking the opening of the Mirus Bazaar – a week-long fête in aid of Mercer's Hospital in Dublin – gets under way. As the fireworks travel up the sky, Gerty leans back to follow their paths; as she does so, the show for the sad, exotic-looking gentleman becomes increasingly more daring and overtly sexual as she flashes him her underwear in a scene that is also punctuated by a series of breathless 'O!'s that mark the excited reactions of those watching the fireworks explode (☙ 13.715–49). It is during this explosive interplay of sex and gunpowder that the dark foreign-looking gentleman who Gerty has been performing for is revealed to be none other than Mr Bloom, whom the text brands a brute, a wretch and a cad who has been 'At it again!' (13.746). Just what Mr Bloom has been 'at' becomes clear in a few pages.

After Mr Bloom is identified, the narrative style of the episode shifts: the syrupy narrative style of Gerty's narrative gives way to Mr Bloom's familiar interior monologue. Mr Bloom watches Gerty as she gets up to leave, her gait revealing a disability – a limp (✥ 13.771–7). Mr Bloom's assessment of Gerty as she limps away seems odd, almost as if the text is holding him at a distance: his opinion that Gerty's limp is a sexually unappealing 'defect' seems unkind and unnecessarily cruel. To make matters worse, Mr Bloom also lumps Gerty's disability with other so-called 'defects' that serve both to sexualize women and to 'make them polite' (13.776): race, glasses and celibacy. And, although he does not explain why he thinks a 'defect' is 'ten times worse in woman' (13.774–5), Mr Bloom seems to imply that a woman who is black or who happens to wear glasses – and one would have to wonder how and why one woman's skin colour is equivalent to another's weak eyesight – must compensate for these 'shortcomings' by being extra polite to men in the wan hope of securing a husband. All of a sudden, the man who was preaching the gospel of 'universal love' in episode 12 is making remarks that, to a modern ear, sound no better than the bigotry on display in the pub. Indeed, one might wonder if these indefensible remarks are not perhaps worse coming from an individual, who has been preaching 'love'.

Shortly after Gerty limps away, the reader learns what Mr Bloom has been 'at' among the rocks as he took in Gerty's one woman show (✥ 13.846–981). Just after he notices that his watch has stopped – perhaps due to dust – round about the time (4.30 p.m.) Molly and Boylan cuckolded him, Mr Bloom's attention turns to his shirt, which now feels unpleasantly cold and wet. However, it not until he tries to detach his foreskin – note this well – from his wet shirt that it becomes clear that Mr Bloom has been publicly – albeit discreetly – masturbating in view of Gerty as she flashed her knickers and the roman candles exploded: suddenly, in the light of this revelation, all those 'O!s' that punctuated the fireworks display start to take on a whole new dimension. In coming together thus, Mr Bloom, Gerty and the fireworks perform a symphony of rhythmic interplay, in which the rhythms of the body – just as they did in episodes 4 and 11 – once again intertwine with the rhythms of the world.

In his post-orgasmic state, Mr Bloom, starting to feel a little tired, contemplates revisiting the scene of his 'crime' the following day and writing a message for Gerty in the sand (✥ 13.1253–68). Mr Bloom never finishes the message he starts to write on the sand, getting only as far as 'I. AM. A.' – which could be a response to what Martha said to him in her letter: 'I called you a naughty boy' – before erasing it altogether. Mr Bloom's actions on the beach also echo Stephen's thoughts from earlier in the day in two major ways: first, Mr Bloom sees the letters he writes in the sand as forming a sort of continuum with the 'letters' – composed of lines and scars – in the rocks about him (13.1261), one chain of letters linking with another chain of letter-stones: this clearly echoes Stephen's contemplation of the signs of the world text as he walked Sandymount Strand in 'Proteus'. Second, Mr Bloom, insofar as he imagines gazing into the 'dark pool' that he saw near Gerty's foot, becomes an echo of Averroes and Moses Maimonides who, as Stephen notes in episode 2, used 'mocking mirrors' – shiny reflective surfaces that produce distorted reflections – to divine the future. In episode 13's iteration, the dark man that gazes into the mocking mirror is a Maimonides of complex and elusive Jewish-Irish heritage who is perhaps a more fitting emblem of the text's peculiar Irish art. And, it is surely no accident that this dark pool admits into *Ulysses* one of the very figures that Stephen in episode 9 says is capable of disrupting the racial and narcissistic creations of God and Shakespeare: the cuckold who is heralded here in the text through an echo of the sound of the cuckoo – a classic image of the cuckold – in the clock that Gerty hears as she leaves the beach (☙ 13.1299–306). In closing in this way, the text allows Gerty have a little bit of revenge on the 'cuckoo' Mr Bloom, who has begun a post-orgasmic snooze. And, when he awakes, Mr Bloom's path will cross Stephen's for the fourth and final time that day: Joycean cuckold and bastard finally meet.

Episode 14: The Oxen of the Sun
Scene: The National Maternity Hospital, Holles Street, Dublin
Hour: 10 p.m.
Organ: Womb
Technique/Style: Embryonic Development

In Book XII of *The Odyssey*, Odysseus and his men leave Circe's island, negotiate the perils of the Sirens and Scylla and Charybdis, before eventually arriving at the island of the sun-god Helios, which is inhabited by cattle sacred to him. Because both Circe and Tiresias warned him against harming Helios's cattle, Odysseus makes his crew – who refuse to spend another night at sea – swear to leave the sacred cattle unharmed. Inclement weather maroons them on the island, so Odysseus goes off to pray for relief and – big surprise – falls asleep. The crew, now left to its own devices, decides to slaughter enough sacred cows for a six-day feast. On his return to camp, Odysseus is horrified by what his crew has done, and makes ready to leave the next day. Helios, on learning of the feast, appeals to Zeus, who destroys the ship as it leaves the island with a bolt of lightning. Odysseus, the sole survivor of Zeus' lightning bolt, clinging to the splintered wreckage of his ship, passes once more between Scylla and Charybdis before washing up on the shore of the Calypso's island.

'Oxen of the Sun' takes place in the National Maternity Hospital, 29-31 Holles Street, Dublin, and confronts the reader, with yet another radical shift – or better yet – series of radical shifts in style. Whereas the previous episode was divided evenly between the syrupy style of women's magazine writing and Mr Bloom's interior mono-logue, 'Oxen of the Sun' features, by contrast, some 27 examples of prose style, which run the gamut from an Irish imitation of an ancient Roman hymn to the goddess of plenty and fertility (complete with triple repetitions) – 'Deshil Holles Eamus' (15.1, itself a combination of the Irish word *'deasil'*, meaning to turn right, a movement associ-ated with attracting good fortune, 'Holles', the name of the mater-nity hospital, and the Latin *'Eamus'*, 'Let us go') – to a cacophony of broken and drunken early twentieth-century slang peppered with – among other things – foreign languages and English as it might be spoken by other nationalities and races – 'Lil chile velly solly. Ise de cutest colour coon down our side. Gawds teruth, Chawley. We are nae fou. We're nae tha fou. Au reservoir, mossoo' (14.1504–6).[8] Since the technique of this episode is 'embryonic development', there is the suggestion of a parallel between the episode's changes in style and the development of a fœtus; the parallel is, however, a loose one since number of styles mimicked – 27 – does not correspond to the required number of weeks necessary for a full-term pregnancy. The looseness of this parallel suggests that the embryonic development of the fœtus in episode 14 is not simply a natural process since the fœtus develop-ing here is, not unlike the word *'fœtus'* that Stephen so vividly encoun-ters in chapter II of *Portrait*, indissociable from language. In other words, the fœtus that develops throughout 'Oxen of the Sun' is com-posed of a tissue of language and quotation, just as Stephen in 'Proteus' and Gerty in 'Nausicaa' were. The bio-linguistic development of the fœtus in 'Oxen' also ties together motifs that will already be familiar to the reader of *Ulysses*: metempsychosis – insofar as the fœtus's development seems to contain the 'memories' of the entire development of the English language – and the fluid world-text – wherein the biological rhythms of the body and the rhythms of the world interact and mingle with the rhythms of language.

The sometimes unfamiliar, difficult and archaic language used in each style also continues the text's drive towards a cracked or fractured mirroring of 'reality'; each style can therefore be regarded as similar in function to, for example, Stephen's dense theologico-philosophico-literary allusions in 'Proteus', or the Arranger's 'headlines' in 'Aeolus', in that they serve to once more draw the reader's attention to the textual surface of *Ulysses* itself. The fractured mirrored surface of the text, however, never lets the narrative disappear completely; on the contrary, it remains discernible, if encrypted 'in' the parallactically shifting mocking mirrors of these styles. Indeed, playing with the episode's encryptions is part of the fun in reading this episode. For example, when Mr Bloom calls at the hospital to inquire about the health of Mrs Mina Purefoy, who has been in labour for three days, he is 'translated' into a style that mimics the *Travels of Sir John Mandeville* – a Belgian medieval compilation of fantastic travel stories published between 1357 and 1371 and translated into English in the fifteenth century – and becomes the 'traveller Leopold' (14.26). After Nurse Callan allows him into the hospital, he meets 'the young learningknight yclept Dixon' – that is, the young doctor named Dixon – who dressed his bee-sting (which was sustained on the previous Whit Monday; see 8.429–30). However, when translated into the style of Mandeville's fantastic travelogue, Mr Bloom's encounter with an angry bee becomes something altogether more fanciful:

> And the traveller Leopold was couth to him sithen it had happed that they had had ado each with other in the house of misericord where this learningknight lay by cause the traveller Leopold came there to be healed for he was sore wounded in his breast by a spear wherewith a horrible and dreadful dragon was smitten him for which he did do make a salve of volatile salt and chrism as much as he might suffice. (14.126–31)

A similar comic effect is produced some lines later when Dr Dixon invites Mr Bloom to join him and a party of students drinking in a room beneath the maternity ward, where the simple act of opening a can of oily sardines becomes something akin to magic:

> And there was a vat of silver that was moved by craft to open in the which lay strange fishes withouten heads though misbelieving men nie that this be possible thing without they see it natheless they are so. And these fishes lie in an oily water brought there from Portugal land because of the fatness that therein is like to the juices of the olivepress. (14.149–54)

It seems, then, that the narrators of these styles both 'cover over' and 'reveal' the narrative in a manner that is often – but not always – bound by factors such as the historical state of their knowledge, their prejudices and so on. The reader should avoid trying to 'read through' these styles – doing so results in missing much of the episode's humour.

One of those drinking in the hospital is Stephen Dedalus, who Mr Bloom begins to regard with a sort of paternalistic interest. As the text makes clear, Mr Bloom's regard for Stephen is bound up with his grief at not having fathered a healthy son:

> [A]nd now sir Leopold that had of his body no manchild for an heir looked upon him his friend's son and was shut up in sorrow for his forepassed happiness and as sad as he was that him failed a son of such gentle courage (for all accounted him of real parts) so grieved he also in no less measure for young Stephen for that he lived riotously with those wastrels and murdered his goods with whores. (14.271–6)

Stephen, who is now the worse for wear because he has been drinking since he left the National Library some seven hours earlier, pours drinks for the group in a mock celebration of the Eucharist – significantly, the faux-priest Mulligan is absent; he won't arrive until 14.651 – in which he sacrifices himself to the group, urging them to 'quaff ye this mead which is not indeed parcel of my body, but my soul's bodiment' (14.282–3). Both the mock-Eucharist and its setting – the maternity hospital – prompt Stephen to produce yet another iteration of the issues that have been on his mind all day – motherhood and the problems of (artistic) creation: 'Mark me now. In woman's womb word is made flesh but in the spirit of the maker all flesh that passes becomes the word that shall not pass away. This is the post-creation' (14.292–4). Stephen here utilizes phrases from St Bernard of Clairvaux's (1090–1153) homily used for the Feast of the Blessed Virgin Mary of the Rosary. He contrasts the creative power of Mary, in whose womb God's word was miraculously made flesh – (Stephen also speculates on whether or not Mary fully understood the incestuous nature of her relationship with the God who impregnated her: Mary is also the daughter of her own Son because he is of the same substance as the Father of all things, God) – with what he calls post-creation, which he defines as the realm where flesh that has rotted or passed away lives on as words and in which the processes of divine and artistic creation meet. Stephen thus separates creation into two gendered realms: the male realm of creation where flesh becomes word, and the female realm where the word becomes flesh. It is also worth noting that Stephen seems to be extending Mary's form of creation to women as a whole; if so, then he is also suggesting that the word of God is analogous to the male seed – semen – a 'word' that nearly all women are capable of converting into flesh.

Stephen's display of witty and learned blasphemy gives way to the stark terror that a 'black crack of noise in the street' (14.408) produces. This clap of thunder – which echoes the thunderbolt hurled by Zeus at Odysseus' ship – recalls Stephen's earlier definition of God as a shout in the street (3.386). Stephen, insofar as he still fears divine retribution for his blasphemy, clearly still believes in God. That is why, despite 'Master Bloom's' assurances that the thunderclap was merely 'the discharge of fluid from the thunderhead' and 'all of the order of a natural phenomenon' (14.426–8), Stephen remains terrified 'for he had in his bosom a spike named Bitterness which could not by words be done away' (14.430–1). Stephen's 'spike' is a wound he received in the conflict between sex and religion: it was inflicted by a woman – 'a certain whore of an eyepleasing exterior whose name, she said, is Bird-in-the-Hand' (14.448–50)[9] – who turned him away from 'that other land which is called Believe-on-Me' (14.444; a reference to John 6.35) – the land of pious religious faith.

Here, an interesting difference between Stephen and Mr Bloom – a difference that the text will underline several times – emerges: on the one hand, Stephen is still in thrall to a 'perversed transcendentalism' (14.1223–4) – and the terrors that it can unleash; on the other hand, Mr Bloom is unencumbered by any such metaphysical baggage because he sees the world from a quasi-scientific perspective as a series of rationally explainable natural processes. This difference in perspective is playfully underscored in the text by the respective breast wounds that each man has sustained: Stephen's metaphysical 'spike' finds its counterpart in Mr Bloom's decidedly natural bee-sting. Thus, it seems clear that Stephen's inability to cope with his wound has a great deal to do with his perverse transcendentalism. I will return to this below.

Rattled by the thunderclap, Stephen tries to hide his fear beneath even more blasphemy. The hubbub of the conversation continues – moving through topics relating to the weather, foot-and-mouth disease, fertility, women and birth, baby Purefoy's arrival and so on – when something of peculiar significance occurs: after a brief remembrance of his youth, Mr Bloom has a 'vision' in a style that mimics that of the English romantic, Thomas De Quincy (1785–1859). Mr Bloom's vision opens with the image of a feminine equine soul – 'She follows her mother with ungainly steps, a mare leading her fillyfoal' (14.1082–3) – which quickly fades, giving way to a spectral parade of the beasts of the zodiac (≋ 14.1087–92). Mr Bloom's vision is particularly significant because there recurs in it the word that has been bothering him since lunchtime – 'parallax'. Parallax, as I suggested above, occurs when the different orbital positions of the Earth cause certain nearby stars to appear to move or change position relative to more distant stars – what Mr Bloom will later refer to as the 'socalled fixed stars' (17.1052–3). Insofar as it 'goads' the procession of the ghostbeasts of the zodiac – creatures that are themselves composed of the shapes made by drawing lines between stars – parallax can be understood as the force that makes the zodiacal beasts move in Mr Bloom's vision. This suggests something about the power of parallax: it seems to be capable of producing a sort of cosmic animation: once stars are seen to move, new lines can be drawn between them, thus creating new constellations – new animals, beasts and so on. Parallax, in Mr Bloom's vision however, is not simply concerned with life: it goads the beasts towards the *Lacus Mortis* – the lake of the dead.

In the next paragraph of Mr Bloom's vision, the text links parallax with the other word that has been on Mr Bloom's mind all day – 'metempsychosis' (≋ 14.1096–109). The 'fillyfoal' soul reappears, after the procession of the zodiacal ghostbeasts has passed, in yet another constellation – Virgo the Virgin – where it assumes the names of two females that are significant for Mr Bloom – Martha, his illicit correspondent and Millicent (Milly), his daughter. The soul – the very item that is supposed to be transferred from body to body in metempsychosis – emerges and takes feminine shape in the evershifting parallactic drift of stars. The interplay between metempsychosis and parallax is underlined by the text when Mr Bloom's vision ends with silly Milly the fillyfoal-soul's veil metamorphosing into a red triangle in the constellation of Taurus. In other words, by yoking together metempsychosis and parallax, Mr Bloom's vision suggests here that the soul is perhaps less a metaphysical object or being and more of a shifting pattern.

Interestingly, in the paragraphs that follow Mr Bloom's vision, there are unmistakable 'echoes' between it and the conversation – in the style of Walter Savage Landor (1775–1864) – between Stephen, Punch Costello (Francis), Lynch (Vincent), Lenehan and Mulligan about the Gold Cup horse race won by Throwaway earlier in the day (☜ 14.1110–73).[10] Not only is the word that Lenehan uses to signal the start of his narration of the race – 'huuh!' – the very same word that parallax uses to goad the zodiacal animals in Mr Bloom's vision (14.1088–9), it appears that the young men's topic of conversation – the Gold Cup race – has informed Mr Bloom's vision of the soul as a fillyfoal-soul: Lenehan laments backing the unfortunate 'filly' Sceptre (which was actually a colt). Still other echoes of the animated conversation about the horse race in Mr Bloom's vision are discernible in Mr Bloom's vision: Lenehan, himself perhaps succumbing to word-echoes, confuses the owner of Sceptre, William Arthur Hamar Bass, with the director of the Bass brewing empire, Michael Arthur Bass. In an effort to drown his sorrow, Lenehan reaches for a bottle of Bass to refill his glass. As he does so, Mulligan draws his attention to Mr Bloom who has been staring intently at the 'scarlet label' on the bottle – the red triangle logo still used by Bass today. Thus, it would appear that the 'ruby and triangled sign' (14.1108–9) that Mr Bloom 'saw' blazing on the forehead of Taurus was an echo of the label on the bottle of ale that the young men are drinking while discussing their poor luck on the horses. There are even echoes of Stephen's hilariously nonsensical theosophical discussion of the fates of the 'lords of the moon' who came as 'an orangefiery shipload from planet Alpha of the lunar chain' (Mars) and were 'incarnated by the rubycoloured egos from the second constellation' – Taurus – in Mr Bloom's vision of Milly's metamorphosing veil (14.1168–73).

Once these echoes are discerned, they serve to draw attention once again to the surface of the text, where it seems the very pages of the book itself are subject to a transformative parallactic drift: that is to say, Mr Bloom's vision is subjected to a parallactic shift in the text which allows the reader to discern in it the echoes of the conversation about the Gold Cup. However, this is not to say that the reader should simply 'read through' Mr Bloom's vision in order to reduce it, or subordinate it to the 'reality' of the horse racing conversation. Such a reduction would risk obscuring the fact that it is only on account of Mr Bloom's vision that the reader's attention is directed to the technique or device of parallactic metempsychosis. Read in this way, it cannot be said that the young men's conversation about the horse race is somehow more 'real' than Mr Bloom's vision, since that vision directs, programmes or teaches the reader how to read this episode by providing him or her with the tools necessary to identify and grasp the textual interplay between the vision and the conversation; 'Oxen' thus takes its place in the series of the other pedagogical scenes that are staged elsewhere in the text. It also becomes clear once more that the text has, in a way, already *read itself*: that is to say, there is a sort of playful textual 'awareness' of what has passed and what is to come.

'Oxen of the Sun' also offers the reader a reading strategy – the transformative process of parallactic metempsychosis – that can be used to (re)read the entire text of *Ulysses*. This can be made clearer by returning to Mr Bloom's vision of Milly, which shows that parallactic metempsychoses is already at work both 'in' episodes and 'between' them. In Mr Bloom's vision, Milly metempsychoses into the series of feminine figures that emerge from the conversations of Mr Bloom's companions – Sceptre, Virgo, the Queen of Heaven (one of the names for the Blessed Virgin) and so on. At the same time, the visionary image of Milly also explicitly calls on the images Mr Bloom associates with her in the fourth episode, 'Calypso': Milly's golden sandals (14.1103) recall the young sunshine girl in 'slim sandals' that runs to meet him as he returns home from the butchers, chasing away the horror he feels when he confronts the old hag's 'grey, shrunken cunt of the world' (4.227–8). (It is also worth noting that Milly here transforms the image of the hag's vagina into a vibrant, vital and fruitful one: a triangle, stained ruby-red.) Likewise, Milly's gossamer veil, which in the vision trails behind her like a multicoloured comet's tail (14.1104–7), recalls both the flowing blue scarf she wore during a boat trip around Dublin Bay (4.435–6) and the woman who waves her scarf in Lenehan's narration of the horse race (14.1130–1). Read thus, parallactic metempsychosis suggests that *Ulysses* is a book that reads itself – is 'aware' of itself as a text or book – and uses that 'awareness' to teach the reader how to read its text. At the same time, because parallactic metempsychosis is concerned with how parts of the text reflect on or read other parts of the text, the method of reading that *Ulysses* teaches the reader can only create ever more 'cracks' in the text's reflection of reality.

It would seem here that the text moves – in a way – 'beyond' Stephen's 'perverted transcendentalism', insofar as it is Mr Bloom who teaches reading by parallactic metempsychosis: this shift is particularly important because without Mr Bloom's 'scientific approach' *Ulysses* would only draw attention to itself as text woven from a tissue of dead male words and subject to rigid metaphysical and gendered oppositions between creation and the postcreation, the word and the flesh and so on. With Mr Bloom these rigid distinctions begin to fall apart; as they do so, Mr Bloom also foregrounds the reader as the site or place where the opposition of word and flesh meet: that is, words and flesh meet wherever there is a reader (you) reading (a text). Reading *Ulysses* parallactically also means that the reader no longer needs to see words restrictively in either purely paternal or postcreationist terms – indeed, it is as if to underline this point that Mr Bloom changes sex in the next episode.[11]

Words are thus transformed in Mr Bloom's non-metaphysical mode of reading; but this does not mean that somehow all pain ceases and all wounds heal miraculously. On the contrary, it simply means that one is no longer subject to metaphysical terrors. At the same time, when words meet flesh, their power to wound and re-open wounds is increased; as if to underline this, the text then offers a passage – in the style of John Henry Cardinal Newman (1801–1890) (⛫ 14.1344–55). As this passage makes clear, even though certain 'evil memories' can be repressed for a time, they are easily called from their 'darkest places' by the 'chance word' of another. Once awakened, these memories come – yet again – to the unfortunate in the guise of a dream or vision. In other words, the text seems to be at pains to point out that the ghostly forms of repressed memory are stirred by decidedly and doggedly non-metaphysical forces: the consciously and/or unconsciously overheard snippets that make up the conversations of others – their words. In other words, the ghosts return along precisely the same lines of the metempsychotic parallactic shifts in perspective that bound Mr Bloom's vision to his young companions' conversation about the Gold Cup race and drew attention to the textual surface of *Ulysses*. Such ghosts and visions, in other words, are decidedly not the product of metaphysical or esoteric doctrine; rather, they emerge from chance social interactions and situations where one encounters the words of others. Furthermore, the above passage in Newman's style can also stand as a perfect description of the technique of the episode that follows 'Oxen of the Sun' – 'Circe' – where chance words from other figures in the text repeatedly produce frightening, disorienting and funny spectres, ghosts and visions, some of which seem to test the reader's knowledge of what has occurred in the previous 14 episodes. The reading strategy that emerges in 'Oxen of the Sun' thus becomes crucial for (re)reading the entire text of *Ulysses*.

Episode 15: Circe
Time: 12 Midnight
Scene: Bella Cohen's Brothel, 82 Tyrone Street Lower
Organ: Locomotor Apparatus
Technique/Style: Hallucination

In Book X of the *Odyssey*, Odysseus tells of his adventures with Aeolus, the Lestrygonians and Circe. Having been blown back from Ithaca by Aeolus's winds, Odysseus and his crew are in understandably low spirits as they land on Circe's island. Once ashore, Odysseus kills a stag with large antlers, on which the crew feasts. Odysseus then divides his crew into two groups – one led by himself and the other led by Eurylochus. Eurylochus and his group set out to explore the island and they come across a palace where they meet the witch Circe, who transforms them all except Eurylochus into pigs. After he hears what has happened from Eurylochus, Odysseus sets off alone for Circe's palace. On his way, he is met by Hermes who offers him moly, a magic herb to protect him from Circe's magic. The moly works, and Circe entertains Odysseus and his men for nearly a year. When Odysseus makes ready to leave the island, Circe advises him first to consult the prophet Tiresias – who famously lived as both a man and woman – in Hades. When he returns with Tiresias's prophecy, Circe gives Odysseus advice on how to pass Scylla and Charybdis safely.

The style of 'Circe' differs sharply from that of 'Oxen of the Sun'; the entire episode is typographically laid out so as to resemble the printed text of a play, complete with stage directions in italics. Indeed, the sexual content and the play format lend the episode the quality of a burlesque. The episode opens as Stephen and Lynch, who have become separated from the rest of the group that were drinking in Holles Street, in an echo of their walk in *Portrait*, make their way into 'nighttown', the red-light district of Dublin. The human figures that inhabit 'nighttown' are stricken with different forms of impairment – paralysis, deformity, illness – that hinder their movement. This generalized impairment is also reflected in Stephen's and Lynch's intoxicated conversation. Amid the lewd calls of whores and bawds, Stephen's conversation (15.83–124) is a heady mixture of liturgical Latin – specifically the entrance chant for Easter mass – and a by now familiar preoccupation with the notion of self-creation, which revisits his thoughts from 'Scylla and Charybdis' concerning 'entelechy' (15.107) – the name Aristotle gives to the power a living thing has to reproduce itself. Lynch, who remains unimpressed, dismisses Stephen's thoughts as 'Pornosophical philotheology. Metaphysics in Mecklenburgh street!' (15.109). Stephen and Lynch then continue their way to Bella Cohen's brothel at 82, Tyrone Street Lower.

As Stephen and Lynch pass, the reader once again meets Mr Bloom, who has been trying to catch up to Stephen whom he last saw heading for nighttown. Mr Bloom, ever the connoisseur of unusual cuts of meat, carries a sheep's foot and a pig's trotter and is suffering from his own form of physical impairment – a stitch in his side brought on by his running after Stephen (15.163). With the reappearance of Mr Bloom, all manner of inanimate objects begin to speak, just as he observed they did in 'Aeolus' – bells say 'Haltyaltyaltyall' (15.181) and tram warning gongs say 'Bang Bang Bla Bak Blud Bugg Bloo' (15.189). Other strange things begin to occur in the text as well: just as Mr Bloom puts his hand up to alert the driver of a track-cleaning tram as it bears down on him, he sports, for a split-second, the uniform of a traffic policeman: 'Bloom, raising a policeman's white-gloved hand, blunders stifflegged out of the track' (15.190–1). Up till now there has been no mention of Bloom's owning a pair of gloves, never mind white ones. It would seem that in 'Circe' not only does everything speak, but every action or gesture performed by a character in the text is potentially powerful enough to transform and exaggerate the appearance of that character. This type of transformative exaggeration not only recalls the parallactic shifts described in the previous chapter, but also serves to alert the reader once more to the textuality of the text since Mr Bloom does not seem to be aware of the change he has undergone – he does not mention having worn policeman's gloves. A number of lines later a mysterious figure – which may or may not be a signal post – wears 'a wideleaved sombrero' (15.213–14), an item of clothing that is enough to make Mr Bloom speak in Spanish (15.216). Once again, this peculiarity passes unremarked by him. It would appear that the text is endeavouring to make the reader aware of the separation between the narrative framing of the text and the characters it enfolds since they do not appear to be aware of what the reader is. The effect of this separation is, as I mentioned above in the discussion of 'Oxen of the Sun', to make the reader acutely aware of his/her act of reading the text, to make him or her aware of the act of reading as the place where words and flesh meet in a non-metaphysical fashion.

'Circe' also puts into practice the power of the words of others to conjure visions, a power that was underscored in 'Oxen': for example, when Mr Bloom fears he may have lost his 'purse' to a pickpocket (15.246), a passing dog becomes transformed into the vision of his father, Rudolph, who forcefully reminds him that hanging around with drunks results in lost money (15.247–267). Rudolph then reminds Mr Bloom of an occasion when members of a running club brought him home muddy and 'drunk as dog' (15.266). When Mr Bloom tries to protest, Rudolph retorts, 'Nice spectacles for your poor mother!' (15.279). As soon as Mr Bloom's mother is mentioned, her vision appears to scold him, and, as she does so, Mr Bloom tries to ward off a blow which now seems to come from another female figure. This other female figure turns out to be Molly, who tells him that he must now address her by the title Boylan used on the letter delivered that morning – 'Mrs Marion' (15.305). Molly then asks her husband 'satirically' if his feet – a reminder of the sheep's foot and pig's trotter he has been carrying – are cold (15.306). When he begins fumbling in his pockets and trying to explain that he does not have Mrs Marion's lotion because he forgot that the chemist closed early on Thursdays, he feels once again the cake of lemon soap he has been transferring from pocket to pocket all day – 'This moving kidney' (15.334). The word kidney also recalls what Mr Bloom had for breakfast that morning, which results in the vision of a talking 'soapsun' that rises in the sky to remind him that he also forgot to pay for it (15.337–43). As should be becoming clear, it is chance words in the text that seem to trigger different associations that send the narrative off in wildly varying directions, thereby enacting the power of words to shift and alter other chains of words.

Mr Bloom eventually finds his way to 82 Tyrone Street Lower, where he meets one of Bella's girls named Zoe Higgins – who has the same surname as Mr Bloom's mother, Ellen Higgins – who mistakes him for Stephen's father because they are both dressed in black. During a brief flirtation with her on the steps of the brothel, Zoe puts her hand into Mr Bloom's pocket and finds his potato (first mentioned at 4.73), which she takes from him. Once in possession of his potato, Zoe then asks Mr Bloom for a cigarette. He lewdly replies that the 'mouth can be better engaged than with a cylinder of rank weed' (15.1351), to which Zoe tartly replies, 'Go on. Make a stump speech out of it' (15.1353). The scene is immediately transformed as Mr Bloom becomes a political candidate who is at first beloved by, and then reviled by, the electorate (15.1354–958). As the crowd threatens to tear him to pieces, a 'Dr Mulligan' appears, and announces that Mr Bloom is 'bisexually abnormal', has a vagina and is a virgin (15.1774–787) – itself an echo of the nameless narrator of episode 12's description of Mr Bloom as a 'mixed middling' and a menstruating woman (12.1659–60). Moments later, this 'finished example of the new womanly man' (15.1778–9) is found to be miraculously pregnant. Mr Bloom's apparent ability to change sex – a condition that allies him with the figure of Tiresias – resurfaces forcefully later in the episode when he meets Bella Cohen the brothel mistress.

Once inside the brothel, Mr Bloom finds Stephen and Lynch. Stephen is seated at the pianola, once again grappling with the artist's creation of art and himself and trading intellectual blows with Lynch – who is reduced to his cap – regarding Benedetto Marcello (1686–1739), an Italian composer who, as Gifford reminds us, tried to set the Psalms to an 'authentically' ancient music. Marcello's music – since he may have 'found' it when he visited Jewish communities or simply 'made' it himself (see 15.2087–8) – is, Stephen implies, no longer concerned with a return to its true origins. Stephen further develops his point about music's lack of authenticity by arguing that a piece of music can act as either 'an old hymn to Demeter' – the ancient Greek earth goddess – or 'illustrate *Coela enarrant gloriam Domini*' (Psalms 18.2: 'The heavens declare the glory of the Lord'). Stephen suggests, in other words, that music can be adapted to fit different forms of worship – non-Judeo-Christian and Judeo-Christian – regardless of whether or not it was originally intended for that purpose; music need have no intrinsic relation to the 'truth' or 'faith' of the system of belief that it accompanies. Such music, since it is no longer concerned with an original truth, remains open to being adapted to and by the words of others and thus exceeds the 'perverted transcendentalism' caused by the toxic interaction of Judeo-Christian belief and sexuality precisely because it predates that system of belief.

However, Stephen's next phase of argument seems to contrast sharply with the above, and this contrast can be read as an index of the extent to which Stephen remains in the grip of perverse transcendentalism. Stephen moves from Marcello's music to consider musical intervals. He argues that in a music interval 'the fundamental and the dominant are separated by the greatest possible interval which [. . .] Is the greatest possible ellipse. Consistent with. The ultimate return. The octave' (15.2105–12). Stephen here seems to have in mind a particular interval – the fifth – since in a fifth, the 'ellipse' or gap between the fundamental and the dominant is the largest possible the hand can make. The fifth would also be 'consistent' with what Stephen calls the 'ultimate return' – the octave, which always returns to the same note – due to the 'circle of fifths', in which it is theoretically possible to end on the same note on which one begins. These circular forms of music then inform Stephen's conception of identity as a transcendental and godlike – guaranteed – return to self: 'What went forth to the ends of the world to traverse not itself, God, the sun, Shakespeare, a commercial traveller, having itself traversed in reality itself becomes that self [. . .] which it itself was ineluctably preconditioned to become' (15.2117–21). The reader will recognize here a variation on Stephen's argument in episode 9 regarding Shakespeare's role as the godlike artist-father-creator of his own race who everywhere encounters himself in his creation. This time, however, Stephen extends his earlier narcissistic and theological understanding of artistic creation to how the self – every self – makes its way through the world: every self only ever journeys back to the self that it already was. In its godlike return to itself, the self – like Shakespeare contemplating his creation – need never be touched by otherness. The interval of 'otherness' it crosses – the 'not itself' of the world – is merely an ellipse that guarantees a safe return. Read thus, Stephen remains – despite his speculations on Marcello's music – caught in 'perverse transcendentalism', trapped by a theological conception of self in which there is no possibility of connecting with another; and it is this condition of being trapped that makes him all the more vulnerable to the terrors that the perverse transcendentalism can harbour – a terror that will later take the form of a vision of his mother (15.4155–247).

Mr Bloom's experiences on 16 June 1904 can be taken as a challenge to Stephen's conception of identity as an essentially theological narcissistic encounter with the self: all day long Mr Bloom has been confronting otherness: his father's suicide, the death of his son, his complex Irish-Jewish heritage, his job, his proclivities all mark him as other, as one who doesn't quite fit all the social, political, religious, sexual norms of early twentieth-century Dublin. At the same time, he marks the point of difference in Stephen's artistic speculations on God's and Shakespeare's narcissistic male creations since he has now been cuckolded by a 'bawd' – Molly. As was discussed above, bawd and cuckold are the two figures that hold out the possibility of breaking the serene mirroring of the Shakespearian artist-father-creator in his creation since, according to Stephen, they both herald the intrusion of the threatening and repulsive image of the bastard into that creation: Shakespeare can no longer properly recognize himself. Indeed, when Shakespeare does appear in 'Circe' – in a brothel mirror as Stephen and Mr Bloom gaze into it – he wears the antlers of a cuckold: '*The face of William Shakespeare, beardless, appears there, rigid in facial paralysis, crowned by the reflection of the reindeer antlered hatrack in the hall*'(15.3821–4) – an image which itself echoes the antlered stag that Odysseus kills on Circe's island. One could also argue that Shakespeare's appearance as paralytic cuckold in the brothel mirror suggests that the bastard in the text is Stephen – the very figure who acted as a portal through which the dark algebra of Averroes and Moses Maimonides finds its way into *Ulysses*. Further, due to Molly's cuckolding of him with Boylan, the Mr Bloom who returns home is no longer simply the same man he was when he left the house that morning: he is now a cuckold. 7, Eccles Street is also changed: it is no longer an entirely 'safe' haven from the rest of the world. Mr Bloom's furniture has been rearranged in his absence. He must sleep in a bed which not only bears the bodily imprint of Boylan, but is littered with his post-coital snack of Plumtree's potted meat. The bed linens he covers himself with bear traces of Boylan's semen which Molly has pointedly not cleaned up. Molly looks forward to her next tryst with Boylan and is in the midst of making her mind up about whether to leave her husband for a more satisfying sex-life.

Given all this, it is interesting to note that the cuckold is about to undergo a very particular change in the text: despite all the other changes Mr Bloom undergoes, one in particular stands out: Mr Bloom changes sex and becomes a 'woman'. This transformation is also interesting because of all the other transformations Mr Bloom has undergone in this episode, this is the only one that seems to register on him: his transformation begins when he falls under the spell of Bella Cohen – an avatar of Circe – when she makes him tie her shoe-lace (15.2804) and ends when his back trouserbutton pops (15.3440). Circe's spell falls on Mr Bloom after he has been visited by a vision of his grandfather, Virag Lipoti, who appears soon after a gramophone in another brothel starts playing 'The Holy City'. Virag's appearance after the gramophone starts up is very much in keeping with this episode's technique, where a chance word in the text provokes a vision. Virag's appearance also recalls Mr Bloom's idea of using gramophones to 'visit' a dead grandfather in the other world. Soon after the vision of Virag – whose name, given its obvious association with 'virago', has already announced the topic of gender transgression – departs, Mr Bloom hears a 'firm heelclacking tread' on the stairs (15.2734): enter Bella Cohen, 'a massive whoremistress' (15.2742) with a 'sprouting moustache' (15.2746–7). Mr Bloom, when confronted with Bella, feels somewhat threatened: he notes that she is a 'powerful being', immediately regrets having surrendered his potato to Zoe, and tries to remind himself that every 'phenomenon has a natural cause' (15.2772–96). Bella points with her fan at an open shoelace, which Mr Bloom promptly bends down to tie (15.2777–812). As he works on the knot, he indulges his fetish for garments with stays, buttons, laces, clasps and fastens (15.2813–18), and starts to fall under Bella-Circe's control: 'Awaiting your further orders we remain, gentlemen' (15.2833); just as Mr Bloom utters the word 'gentlemen', Bella becomes Bello – a being that is both male and female and part cruel brothel owner, part sadistic circus ringmaster. As Bello transforms, so too does Mr Bloom: 'he' becomes a feminine cross between a whore and circus performer reminiscent of the heroine in Molly's book, *Ruby, Pride of the Ring*.

Mr Bloom's abuse at the hands of Bello begins with a catalogue of his obsessions with buttocks and excrement (15.2838–43), after which Bello extinguishes 'his' lit cigar extinguished in 'her' ear (15.2930–9) and rides 'her' like a horse (15.2940–9).[12] Mr Bloom's abuse then takes the form of an inquisition in which he is commanded to confess to 'the most revolting piece of obscenity in all [his/her] career of crime' (15.3041–2). Mr Bloom then grows a vulva, which Bello promptly violates with 'his' fist (15.3088–9), and is put up for auction as a sex-slave. The auction fades as Bello threatens to turn Bloom into fertilizer like all the other men 'he' has killed (15.3203–13). Bello vanishes at this point and through the smoke from Mr Bloom's funeral pyre, the Nymph – whose picture Mr Bloom cut from *Photo Bits* and framed and mounted over the bed he shares with Molly – steps out of her frame and comes to stand over him (15.3232–6). The Nymph then informs Mr Bloom that from her vantage point she has witnessed all manner of shameful bedroom activity including: farting and the insertion of an anal device – the 'wonderworker' mentioned at 11.1224 – to control it (15.3274–7); the frequent use of certain shameful sexual 'words' (15.3279); the overt enjoyment of soiled 'personal linen' (15.3288); repeated noisy acts of urination (15.3292–300) and his administering of enemas Molly, something to which he readily admits: 'One third of a pint of quassia to which add a tablespoonful of rocksalt. Up the fundament. With Hamilton Long's syringe, the ladies' friend' (15.3398–400). What becomes clear in the Nymph's cataloguing of the Bloom's sex-life is the fact 'sex' for Mr Bloom involves props, mechanical devices and a measure of scatology: it is not simply focused on procreation.

In her desire to shame him, the Nymph then reminds Mr Bloom of his efforts earlier in the day to ascertain whether or not statues of goddesses have anuses (8.930–2). She haughtily informs him – in 'lofty' language that echoes his thoughts from that episode – that 'We immortals, as you saw today, have not such a place and no hair there either. We are stonecold and pure. We eat electric light' (15.3391–5). The Nymph's attempts to create a pure image of herself transform her into a nun Mr Bloom once knew, 'Sister Agatha', who shares a name with Saint Agatha of Sicily who was subjected to prostitution and then tortured by having her breasts cut off and her skin burned by live coals. All of this leads up to the Nymph's grand declaration that, as a metaphysical being, she is impervious to desire: 'No more desire. (*she reclines her head, sighing*) Only the ethereal' (15.3434–8). Mr Bloom's first reaction to this declaration is to try and stand up – a gesture that reveals that all that he has just been subjected to took place in the time it took him to tie Bella's shoelace. As he rights himself, Mr Bloom's back trouserbutton snaps – saying 'Bip!' as it does so (15.3439–3440) – and Bella-Circe-the Nymph's spell over him breaks.[13]

Once the spell is broken, Mr Bloom sets about cutting through the Nymph's metaphysical pretensions by firmly underlining female desire: 'If there were only ethereal where would you all be, postulants and novices? Shy but willing, like an ass pissing' (15.3449–51). A 'large moist stain' appears on the Nymph's robe – a clear sign of sexual arousal – and Mr Bloom, warming to his theme, argues that any metaphysical attempt to deny female desire produces cruelty, a belief he illustrates by coarsely embellishing his (erroneous) belief that a nun invented barbed wire (8.154) with the suggestion that she did so because she was sexually frustrated due to the fact that she was masturbating with too thin a crucifix: 'What do you lack with your barbed wire? Crucifix not thick enough?' (15.3464–7). The Nymph reveals her anus to Mr Bloom when she *'with a cry flees from him unveiled, her plaster cast cracking, a cloud of stench escaping from the cracks'* (15.3469–70). Triumphant, Mr Bloom sniffs the Nymph's wake, and he smells Bella Cohen as if for the first time: '(*he sniffs*) Rut. Onions. Stale. Sulphur. Grease. [. . .] (*The figure of Bella Cohen stands before him.*)' (15.3478–9). The spell broken, Mr Bloom in now self-possessed enough to ask Zoe for his potato – which the reader finally learns is actually 'a relic of poor mamma' (15.3513) – back.

Mr Bloom's passage through womanhood comes to an end with his recognition of female sexual desire, which is also the very force that – as I suggested in the discussion of episodes 9 and 14 – challenges – in the form of the bawd – the narcissistically male modes of creation – God's and Shakespeare's – that Stephen has been wrestling with for much of the book. In other words, Mr Bloom's transformation into a woman and his being held up as an example of 'the new womanly man' is indissociable from his newfound status as cuckold; indeed, as was mentioned above, Mr Bloom's/Shakespeare's reflection in the brothel mirror wears the antlers of the cuckold – actually the hatrack in the hallway – to the great amusement of the whores and their madam. The image of the cuckold gives way to the image of the paralytic Shakespeare screeching 'Iagogo!' as Mr Bloom voyeuristically enjoys his cuckolding at the hands of Boylan in a graphic vision (15.3705–858): Mr Bloom thus appears to have accepted – on some level at least – what female desire has done to him.

This is not to say, however, that Mr Bloom's recognition of female desire or his engagement with it is somehow simply 'natural', despite his repeated use of that word. As the Nymph makes clear, Mr Bloom's view of sexual desire and sexual practice is divorced from the 'natural end' of procreation, since it seems to be primarily anal-centric, involving scatological play, the use of artificial devices, mechanisms and various pharmaceutical preparations.

If Mr Bloom's ability to break Circe-Bella-the Nymph's spell has to do with a recognition of, engagement with, and acceptance of female desire, then it is possible that that same recognition of female desire might explain why his reactions to the disturbing visions he endures in 'Circe' never approach anything like the terror and violence of Stephen's reaction to the vision of his mother some pages later. Stephen's mother brings with her both an explicit denial of desire and a demand to repent and return to religion – the very forces that in episode 14 combined to produce the wound of 'perverse transcendentalism' in Stephen's breast. Stephen's vision of his mother, which is prompted by a vision of his father saying 'Think of your mother's people!' (15.4137), is also a true moment of horror in the text: '*Stephen's mother, emaciated, rises stark through the floor, in leper grey with a wreath of faded orangeblossoms and a torn bridal veil, her face worn and noseless, green with gravemould. Her hair is scant and lank. She fixes her bluecircled hollow eyesockets on Stephen and opens her toothless mouth uttering a silent word*' (15.4157–4161). With Stephen frozen with terror, the mother makes to renew his breast-wound once more by sticking her withered hand – which becomes a malignant crab's claw in an echo of zodiacal symbol of Cancer – into his chest (♋ 15.4216–23).

However, it is noteworthy that Stephen in his terror utters a word that names one of Mr Bloom's favourite substances in this episode – 'Shite!' (15.4223). This shite seems to give Stephen the fortitude he needs to begin mustering his energy to resist the metaphysical guilt and terror his mother represents (♋ 15.4231–47). Stephen's defiant word as he lashes out at the vision with his ashplant – '*Nothung!*' (German, 'needful') – invokes the name of the magic sword in Wagner's (1813–83) *Der Ring des Nibelungen* (1869–76) that eventually brings about *Die Götterdämmerung*, the Twilight of the Gods. The text seems to suggest here that Stephen's defiant resistance to his mother's vision could mark the beginning of the end of his perverse transcendentalism; at the same time, the text also mercilessly mocks Stephen's heroically significant gesture: his ashplant crumples a lampshade, causing, in Mr Bloom's sober assessment, 'not sixpence's worth of damage' (15.4290–1).

Stephen flees the brothel, followed by the whores, Lynch and Mr Bloom, who pays Bella for the damage. Stephen, drunk and obviously a little excitable, runs into two off-duty British soldiers to whom he attempts to explain that, as an Irish artist, he must mentally 'kill the priest and the king' (15.4437), the two masters – one Roman, one English – he has been wrestling with all day. The visions that spring up in the text transform Stephen's confrontation with the soldiers into a confrontation between Ireland and England: these visions seem to differ from the previous ones in the text, however, in that they are neither Mr Bloom's nor Stephen's: they are the text's. It is as if the text is having its own nightmarish visions as it plays out the troubled relationship between Ireland and England.

Moments after declaring that, 'I'll wring the neck of any fucking bastard says a word against my bleeding fucking king' (15.4644–5), one of the off-duty soldiers – Private Carr – strikes Stephen in the face, knocking him unconscious (15.4748). Drawn by the commotion, two policemen arrive on the scene, but Mr Bloom, who has now caught up with Stephen, manages to persuade them, with the help of a passing Corny Kelleher, to leave him in his care. As Mr Bloom tries to bring him round, Stephen sings once more the song he sang for his mother on her deathbed in lieu of a prayer – Yeats's 'Who Goes with Fergus'. Mr Bloom mishears the name 'Fergus' and fondly imagines that Stephen is dreaming of a girl named 'Ferguson.' As he stands in vigilant watch over the crumpled heap of Stephen reciting snippets of the Freemason's oath of secrecy to himself, Mr Bloom has the final vision of the episode: he sees his dead son Rudy, dressed in a costume that has elements of the Roman, Christian and Hebrew traditions (15.4961–7). Stephen thus seems to satisfy a deep desire of Mr Bloom's – a desire to bring a surrogate son home.

Episode 16: Eumaeus
Scene: The Cabman's Shelter, under the Loop Line Railway Bridge
Time: 1 a.m.
Organ: Nerves
Art: Navigation
Technique/Style: Narrative (old)

In Book XIII of the *Odyssey*, Odysseus returns alone to Ithaca, and is in danger of being killed on arrival by his wife's suitors if he openly declares his identity. He consults Athena, who disguises him as an old man and sends him to Eumaeus, a loyal swineherd, who receives him with kindness. After narrowly escaping the wrath of the suitors, Telemachus makes his way in Book XVI to Eumaeus to find out what has happened since he has been away searching for news of his father. Odysseus, still in disguise, tests Telemachus's loyalty before finally revealing himself. Father and son are reunited and make plans to take back their house from the suitors.

Episode 16 is the first episode of the third and final part of *Ulysses*. Its technique – narrative (old) – mirrors the technique of episode 3 – narrative (young) – the first episode of part I. Mr Bloom and his surrogate son have finally met; having steered Stephen safely – for the most part – through the hazards of nighttown after his last companion deserted him, Mr Bloom now makes it his business to try and restore a still very drunk and sore Stephen. Unable to flag a cab, Mr Bloom suggests that they go to the cabman's shelter near Butt Bridge. On their way there, Mr Bloom takes the opportunity to advise Stephen of the dangers of drunkenness and whoring. They meet 'Lord' John Corley – who also appears in 'Two Gallants' in *Dubliners* – to whom – much to Mr Bloom's dismay – Stephen lends a large sum of money. Before entering the shelter – which is reputed to be run by the former Invincible, Skin-the-goat Harris – they pass a couple of Italians gathered around an ice-cream cart arguing about money. Once inside, both men encounter a sailor by the name of D B Murphy – recently returned to Ireland aboard the Rosevean, the very ship that passed Stephen as he walked on Sandymount Strand – who claims to know Stephen's father, Simon. Murphy – whose name evokes Morpheus, the Greek god of sleep – says he once saw Mr Dedalus shoot two eggs off the tops of two bottles over his shoulder (16.389–407).

While the sailor continues to amuse the other customers with tall tales, Mr Bloom sees, for the second time that day, the whore who had asked him who Molly was and if she could do his washing. Flustered, Mr Bloom tries to avoid her eye by picking up a discarded copy of a newspaper – the last pink edition of the *Evening Telegraph*:

> Mr Bloom, scarcely knowing which way to look, turned away on the moment flusterfied but outwardly calm, and, picking up from the table the pink sheet of the Abbey street organ which the jarvey, if such he was, had laid aside, he picked it up and looked at the pink of the paper though why pink. His reason for so doing was he recognised on the moment round the door the same face he had

caught a fleeting glimpse of that afternoon on Ormond quay, the partially idiotic female, namely, of the lane who knew the lady in the brown costume does be with you (Mrs B.) and begged the chance of his washing. Also why washing which seemed rather vague than not, your washing. Still candour compelled him to admit he had washed his wife's undergarments when soiled in Holles street and women would and did too a man's similar garments initialled with Bewley and Draper's marking ink (hers were, that is) if they really loved him, that is to say, love me, love my dirty shirt. (16.706–20)

The style here is typical of the entire episode: the narrator seems tired and that tiredness sometimes confusingly reflects the tiredness of character s/he narrates: as Mr Bloom studies the pink edition, the narrator – and perhaps Mr Bloom – seem(s) momentarily distracted by the colour of the paper, asking 'though why pink' (although one could argue that the loss of the question mark at the end of this question underscores the narrator's – rather than Mr Bloom's sleepiness). The sleepiness of the narrator in the above extract also disrupts the meaning and clarity of the narrative; it is certainly not clear from this passage what dealings Mr Bloom has had with the prostitute, although her offer to do Mr Bloom's 'washing' certainly seems euphemistic. The narrator's sleepiness is also evident in his/her sentence structure: s/he starts a new thought before the previous one is finished. As a result, the text becomes corrupted by these tangents and digressions and the reader is forced to re-read the passage several times in order to separate Molly's undergarments from the jumble of undergarments belonging to several anonymous men.

Mr Bloom's and Stephen's conversation moves on from issues relating to prostitution to issues relating to the place of the soul in metaphysics and science. This conversation is important insofar as it recalls the contrast in the reaction of each man to the crack of thunder in 'Oxen' (☞ 16.748–60).[14] Mr Bloom dismisses the metaphysics of the soul in favour of the 'intelligence' – the brainpower generated by the wrinkles in the grey matter of the brain. Stephen, by contrast, offers a completely metaphysical explanation of the soul: he sardonically notes that even though the soul, according to Aquinas's *Summa Theologica* (Prima Primae, Query 75, article 6), is both a 'simple substance' and not corruptible of itself (*per se*) or by accident (*per accidens*) because it contains no contrariety, it can be destroyed by God (its 'First Cause'). Although he feels 'a bit out of his sublunary depth' due to what the narrator dubs Stephen's 'mystical finesse' (16.761–3), Mr Bloom persists in his questioning of metaphysics by turning to the issue of the existence of God (❧ 16.770–84). As these differences make clear, even though surrogate father and son have finally met, they remain poles apart on the issue of metaphysics. In contrast to Stephen's citation of the metaphysical authority of 'Holy Writ' on the existence of God, Mr Bloom, with a smile of disbelief (14.778), offers his decidedly more 'sublunary' opinion that those pieces of Holy Writ which claim to prove the existence of God – or some other authorial figure whose identity is open to question, such as Shakespeare – are nothing but 'genuine forgeries' (16.781) designed to cod the gullible. Thus the sleepily corrupted narrative of episode 16 finds itself reflected in Mr Bloom's views on the corrupt narratives of Holy Writ: and once again – as happens so often in *Ulysses* – the distinction between content and form is eroded by the text.

The issue of corrupt text resurfaces later in the episode when Mr Bloom reads Joe Hynes's article on Paddy Dignam's funeral in the *Evening Telegraph* (❧ 16.1253–61). Mr Bloom notices that the article contains a string of corrupted type – '*John Power, .)eatondph 1/8 ador dorador douradora* (must be where he called Monks the dayfather about Keyes's ad)' (16.1257–9). This textual corruption, which not only recalls Mr Bloom's earlier witnessing of how hunger can change a linear text, also marks a mind-bogglingly self-reflexive moment in the text of *Ulysses*: Mr Bloom here reads the textual corruption he himself caused in the typesetting of the newspaper article by asking about the Alexander Keyes ad (7.180–202); this textual corruption recurs in an episode that makes textual corruption into a theme, in a narrative that is itself corrupted by the sleepy narrator. Added to all this is the typographical error in the article that transforms the floral Mr Bloom into an echo of episode 14's peal of thunder – 'L. Boom' (16.1260). The theme of textual corruption recurs later when the narrator of 'Eumaeus' disrupts his/her own narrative with a violent outburst of obscene French – 'alors (Bandez!) Figne toi trop' (16.1453–4), which roughly translates as 'alright (Get a hard on!) Go fuck yourself!' – that seems to have nothing to do with Mr Bloom's surrounding thoughts on the ability of sculpture and photography to capture the female form (❧ 16.1444–55).[15]

The theme of the corrupted or 'out of place' text also lends itself to Mr Bloom's contemplation of the fall of Parnell and the divorce scandal – a situation that obviously reflects his own domestic situation since 4.30 p.m. that day. In contemplating Parnell, Mr Bloom begins to sketch a spatio-temporal force that militates against a smooth return: 'Looking back now in a retrospective kind of arrangement all seemed a kind of dream. And then coming back was the worst thing you ever did because it went without saying you would feel out of place as things always moved with the times. Why, as he reflected, Irishtown strand, a locality he had not been in for quite a number of years looked different somehow since, as it happened, he went to reside on the north side' (16.1400–6). Here, Mr Bloom states that 'coming back was the worst thing you ever did' (16.1402) because things change – even if they do not appear to change, they move on in terms of time and space – without you. Mr Bloom illustrates this by remembering how he found himself no longer at home on his return to Irishtown strand (on Dublin's Southside) after he had moved to Dublin's Northside: it was still Irishtown strand, but 'looked different somehow' (16.1405). It is surely no accident that Mr Bloom then considers the hot Spanish blood of his wife – a bawdy figure – who is the same sort of disruptive force (16.1406–10): as I suggested above, the 7, Eccles Street to which Mr Bloom is about to return will not be the same either – it, too, will have moved on without him. This spatio-temporal force – insofar as it is connected to the bawd – is related to the force that prevents the smooth return of the narcissistic male artist's reflection in his art, the return of God–Socrates–Shakespeare to himself; it is thus a force that disrupts the memory that allows the 'I' to re-find itself: 'I, entelechy, form of forms, am I by memory because under everchanging forms' (9.208–9). This spatio-temporal force also explicitly operates on the language of episode 16 itself: when Mr Bloom first recalls to himself the story of how he returned Parnell's hat, he remembers Parnell simply saying 'Thank you' to him (16.1335–6); however, when he repeats the story to Stephen some pages later, Parnell's words have changed: 'he turned round to the donor and thanked him with perfect *aplomb*, saying: *Thank you, sir*' (16.1522–3). Mr Bloom then compares the tone of Parnell's '*Thank you, sir*' to the abrupt 'Thank you' he received from the solicitor John Henry Menton after alerting him to the dent in his hat in 'Hades' (6.1026): Parnell's 'very different tone of voice' is in sharp contrast to that of 'the ornament of the legal profession whose headgear Bloom also set to rights earlier in the course of the day, history repeating itself with a difference' (16.1522–6). The spatio-temporal force Mr Bloom contemplates here thus not only changes or corrupts the text of episode 16, it also compels history to repeat itself with a difference. And, since this spatio-temporal force disrupts all returns home and causes history to repeat itself with a difference, it can be heard to echo in and through the interruptions, interpolations and digressions that repeatedly fragment the surface of *Ulysses*, disrupting over and over again the narrative's smooth and serene reflection of reality, making the reader aware of the book's – uncanny, dark, distorted, Irish – textual surface.

As episode 16 draws to a close, Mr Bloom – our Ulysses – noting the stuffiness of the cabman's shelter suggests that Stephen – his Telemachus – accompany him home – to a changed Ithaca – to 'talk things over' (16.1643–6). The things to be talked over turn out to be Mr Bloom's fantasies about a future with Stephen; a shared life in which Mr Bloom would act as Stephen's 'agent', profiting from the commercial exploitation of his knowledge and/or his talents as a writer and a singer (16.1652–61). And so, after paying for Stephen's undrinkable cup of coffee and uneatable bun, Mr Bloom links arms with Stephen – who is still very drunk and feeling poorly – and guides his 'son' back to 7, Eccles Street.

Episode 17: Ithaca
Scene: 7, Eccles Street
Hour: 2 a.m.
Organ: Skeleton
Art: Science
Technique/Style: Catechism (impersonal)

In Book XVII of the *Odyssey*, Telemachus and Odysseus go their separate ways to Odysseus's palace. Odysseus – still in disguise – enters his palace, and in Books XVII to XX, he plots to kill the suitors who have taken over his home. The next day, during a competition among the suitors to try and string his customized bow, Odysseus does so with ease. In Book XXII, Odysseus and Telemachus begin to slaughter the suitors; in Book XXIII, Odysseus finally approaches Penelope, who is slow to believe the beggar she sees is her husband.

'Ithaca' follows Mr Bloom and Stephen back to 7, Eccles Street. The entire episode is written in a somewhat disconcerting question and answer style: the sleepy narrator of 'Eumaeus' has presumably finally dozed off only to be replaced by an anonymous pair of interlocutors – they could not really be called narrators – one of whom implacably asks questions – 'the questioner' – and another who indefatigably answers them – 'the respondent'. 'Ithaca' thus has the form of a religious catechism, and it is absolutely chock-full of information: details about Stephen and Mr Bloom that have been hinted at elsewhere in the text are finally confirmed (such as the exact circumstances surrounding Mr Bloom's father's suicide [17.621–32] and the relations that exist between Stephen's and Mr Bloom's respective ages [17. 446–61]), reconfirmed (such as Mr Bloom's love of the art of advertising and non-linear writing and reading [17.392–416] and his two previous meetings with Stephen prior to 16 June 1904 [17.466–72]). The episode also strives to answer any lingering questions the reader may have, such as the number – 3 – of baptisms Mr Bloom has undergone (17.540–6), or the exact function of the mysterious 'Wonderworker' device (17.1824–33). The episode also reveals other details hitherto unknown about Mr Bloom, (such as the entire contents of Mr Bloom's library [17.1361–1407] and his complete physical measurements [17.1817–19]). Finally, the episode is driven by an almost obsessive need to catalogue and itemize everything that pops up in the narrative: for example, it provides an exhaustive enumeration of the contents of a drawer in an item of furniture in the Bloom household (17.1774–1883), an exhaustive tracing of the workings of the Dublin municipal water supply (17.163–82), and an exhaustive (and exhausting) list of the various states and properties of water (17.183–228).

Although the foregoing is doubtless hopelessly inadequate for giving the reader an idea of the sheer volume of interesting, not-so-interesting and often very useless information contained in episode 17, it should be sufficient to indicate why my discussion of the episode can concentrate on only a few of its strands: Mr Bloom's relationship to poetry and advertising, his realization about the impossibility of return, his relationship with Stephen, his thoughts on parallax and the state of his marriage to Molly.

As I suggested in my discussion of episodes 5 and 8, Mr Bloom's interest in advertising effectively allows him to see the world in terms of a multisurfaced, ever-shifting, potentially infinite text that demands to be read in ways that cannot be reduced to simple left-to-right linearity: Mr Bloom reads back and forth, up and down, even reading in radiating lines at various points during the day. 'Ithaca' underlines Mr Bloom's particularly kinetic relationship with text when it offers the reader several examples of his linguistic and 'poetic' experiments.

The first dates from 1877 – when Mr Bloom was the tender age of 11 – and was his entry for a poetry competition run by the *Shamrock* (a weekly newspaper published in Dublin from 1866 onwards):

> *An ambition to squint*
> *At my verses in print*
> *Makes me hope that for these you'll find room.*
> *If you so condescend*
> *Then please place at the end*
> *The name of yours truly, L. Bloom.* (17.396–401)

This poem is interesting primarily because it is self-reflexive: it calls attention to itself as a poem that has been published in a magazine. The second example of Mr Bloom's linguistic gymnastics is also taken from his youth; it displays Mr Bloom's ability to read and write text anagrammatically, in a manner that both recalls hunger's disruption of the linear text made by the 'H.E.L.Y'S' sandwichboard men and anticipates Mr Bloom's play with the 'Plumtree's Potted Meat' ad later in this episode:[16]

> What anagrams had he made on his name in youth?
> Leopold Bloom
> Ellpodbomool
> Molldopeloob
> Bollopedoom
> Old Ollebo, M.P. (17.405–9)

Mr Bloom's anagrammatic play with text can be read as confirming that reading *Ulysses* is not just a linear process: the reader often must 'anagrammatically' rearrange the text – not just its words, but also its events, scenes, locations, images and so on – as s/he encounters the repetitions, citations and interruptions that crack its surface. These fragments can be (re)arranged into different constellations of text and read along different lines. The final example of Mr Bloom's 'poetasting' is offered to the reader in the form of a poem he writes for Molly on Valentine's day, 1888. As is immediately obvious, it echoes the anagrammatic rearrangement just mentioned:

> *Poets oft have sung in rhyme*
> *Of music sweet their praise divine.*

Let them hymn it nine times nine.
Dearer far than song or wine.
You are mine. The world is mine. (17.412–16)

These examples of doggerel and word-play not only reveal their author to be something of a 'kinetic poet' (17.410) – itself a heavily loaded Joycean term since, from the perspective of the young Stephen of *Portrait*, 'kinetic art' is considered 'improper art' because it excites desire (222) – they also reveal his ability to read and write encoded messages along lines that move hither and thither. This hithering and thithering criss-crossed way of reading and writing reading informs not only Mr Bloom's conception of 'the modern art of advertising' (17.581–4), but also his 'boustrophedontic' encoding of Martha Clifford's name and address later in the episode: as Gifford and many others have pointed out, Mr Bloom encodes Martha's name and address by first placing an A to Z alphabet in parallel with a reversed one from Z to A. He then substitutes the letters of the name and address to be encoded with the corresponding letter in the reversed alphabet. Mr Bloom then drops all the vowels, and reverses Martha's last name, perhaps for extra security. This produces 'N. IGS./WI. UU. OX/W. OKS. MH/Y. IM' (17.1801), which can be decrypted as 'M.RTH./DR.FF.LC/D.PH.NS/B.RN' and, once the vowels are reinserted and her reversed surname is set right, 'MARTHA/ CLIFFORD/DOLPHINS/BARN' – Dolphin's Barn being an area on Dublin's Southside. When all of this is taken together, Mr Bloom's kinetic can be read as a *mise-en-abyme* of *Ulysses* itself, which also constantly calls attention to itself as a written text, making its reader aware of its playful textual surface, inviting anagrammatical and non-linear strategies of reading. In foregrounding Mr Bloom's *oeuvre*, episode 17 underscores once more these strategies for reading *Ulysses*, installing them firmly in the reader's mind as the text begins to wind down.

Later in the text, Mr Bloom finally gets around to offering Stephen a 'proposal of asylum'; however, this offer is '[p]romptly, inexplicably, with amicability, gratefully [. . .] declined' (17.954–5). Interestingly, Stephen's polite refusal is itself an echo of Mr Bloom's polite refusal of a dinner invitation Stephen extended – aged 5 – to Mr Bloom (17.470–6). Stephen's refusal causes Mr Bloom to begin to doubt his many schemes – these 'mutually selfexcluding propositions' are all detailed in the text at 17.960–72 – to profit from Stephen's talents.

This in turn prompts him to recall other misadventures – such as finding a false son in the form of a clown at a circus and the failure of a coin he had marked to return to him (17.973–88) – which once more invoke the spatio-temporal force that disrupts all smooth returns. At the same time, these memories also illuminate the problems inherent in Mr Bloom's paternal and financial interests in Stephen: his attempt to replace Rudy with Stephen and to profit from Stephen's talents fail. Stephen will not be Telemachus to Mr Bloom's Ulysses.

After Stephen's declination of the offer of a bed for the night, he makes to leave the false Ithaca of 7, Eccles Street. Both men file outside and look up to see what the respondent stunningly renders as 'The heaventree of stars hung with humid nightblue fruit' (17.1039). The sight of the heavens and the constellations prompts Mr Bloom to once more wax scientific on the stars, and he once more returns to the knotty issue of parallax, which he now displays a firm grasp of. He refines the notion parallax to include 'the parallax or parallactic drift of socalled fixed stars, in reality evermoving wanderers from immeasurably remote eons to infinitely remote futures in comparison with which the years, threescore and ten, of allotted human life formed a parenthesis of infinitesimal brevity' (17.1052–6). Here Mr Bloom notes that even the 'so-called fixed stars' are, in fact, moving – something that by 1904 had come to be widely accepted in astronomical circles. Mr Bloom's refinement of the notion of parallax here is important for a number of reasons: (1) it underlines and recalls that reading *Ulysses* involves following the parallactic metamorphosis of the words of others, something that both Mr Bloom and the text of *Ulysses* enact in episode 14; (2) if the so-called fixed stars are 'evermoving wanderers', then all recognizable constellations – whether they be composed of stars or text – are always moving, always changing; (3) this implies once again the impossibility of a return to a pristine state of affairs; (4) if the constellations are forever changing, then the reader is free to trace new ones; (5) the movement of these stars dwarfs human concerns and events.

In his contemplation of the parallactic drift of everwandering stars that dwarfs human concerns, Mr Bloom once again echoes his thoughts from episodes 5, 6 and 7 on a non-humancentric universe. At the same time, Mr Bloom's thoughts on the universe and the construction of constellations also dislocate the humancentric notion of a 'present' (☙ 17.1137–45). Since, Mr Bloom reasons, by the time the human being sees the starlight that has entered 'actual present existence', the star s/he gazes upon may no longer be there anymore; thus, referring to the star in terms of presence no longer makes sense: they are fundamentally 'unknowable'. And, it is here, in the dwarfing of the human and the dislocation of the present, that one can read yet another commentary on how to read *Ulysses*: the presence of the 'contents' of this episode – Mr Bloom's and Stephen's interactions in the kitchen of 7, Eccles Street – are themselves distanced, deferred in the catechistic to-and-fro of the questioner's questions and the respondent's responses. Read thus, the questions and answers of episode 17 do to the narration of events precisely the same thing that the stars and parallax do: they dislocate the centrality of the human and the 'presentness' of the event. However, this dislocation is not confined to this episode; as I have tried to point out above, it is something that the text of *Ulysses* has been doing from the beginning. 'Ithaca' underscores that dislocation, reaffirming it for the reader as the text draws to a close.

Interestingly, the same dislocation of the event is legible when Mr Bloom finally gets into the bed that is no longer his and Molly's. On climbing in, he encounters 'New clean bedlinen, additional odours, the presence of a human form, female, hers, the imprint of a human form, male, not his, some crumbs, some flakes of potted meat, recooked, which he removed' (17.2123–6). The question that follows his entry into the bed, however, is a slippery one: 'If he had smiled why would he have smiled?' (17.2127). Mr Bloom himself becomes a little hazy here, dislocated by the question: he does not smile, but 'would have' done had he thought along the lines of the answer the respondent offers: 'To reflect that each one who enters imagines himself to be the first to enter whereas he is always the last term of a preceding series even if the first term of a succeeding one, each imagining himself to be first, last, only and alone whereas he is neither first nor last nor only nor alone in a series originating in and repeated to infinity' (17.2127–31). In this thought, the 'event' of Molly's infidelity with Boylan is displaced. And, as if to underline that displacement, the text then offers a surprisingly long list of what appear Molly's lovers (17.2132–42): the list 'ends' on the suggestion – 'and so each and so on to no last term' – that she may take even more lovers beyond Boylan who is merely one in a long series. Here Molly is underlined as an eternal bawd who will forever disrupt the return of narcissistically reflective male art by harbouring the eternal threat of a racially different bastard.

The text then begins to wind down as Molly and Mr Bloom talk about what they have been up to that day; while they both carefully avoid telling each other about certain occurrences – such as the trip to the brothel and Boylan's visit – both seem to confront the rough shape their marriage is in (📖 17.2271–92). The problems are bad: Molly and Mr Bloom have not had vaginal sex since the death of Rudy, 10 years, 5 months and 18 days ago; they have not spoken properly since Milly got her period 9 months and 1 day ago. The narrative then limps to a close with a flurry of references to Sinbad the Sailor and eggs: 'Going to dark bed there was a square round Sinbad the Sailor roc's auk's egg in the night of the bed of all the auks of the rocs of Darkinbad the Brightdayler' (17.2328–30). Sinbad is the name Mr Bloom uses to describe the sailor in the cabman's shelter (16.858); and *Sinbad the Sailor* is also the name of the pantomime he tried and failed to write a song for (17.417–45); the roc is the huge bird that features in the 'Second Voyage of Sinbad'; the auk, which became extinct in 1844, laid a single large egg. It would thus seem that Mr Bloom is still incoherently talking about his day; the text also seems to be fusing his thoughts on Sinbad with his asking Molly for an egg for his breakfast. But the auk's egg also recalls Stephen's view of the bald head of Mr Lyster the librarian from 'Scylla and Charybdis' (9.446), a moment of the narrative in which Mr Bloom does not appear. The auk's egg here suggests that as the text comes to a close, it too is falling asleep, becoming mixed up, no longer able to keep its characters entirely separate. The episode thus ends – as does all the male narration in the book – not with a word, but with a large black dot, the roundness of which echoes both Stephen's view of the librarian's head as well as the egg that Mr Bloom wants for breakfast: ●

Episode 18: Penelope
Scene: The Bedroom, 7 Eccles Street
Time: None
Organ: Flesh
Art: None
Technique/Style: Monologue (female)

In Book XXIII of the *Odyssey,* Penelope is awoken and informed of the return of her husband, Odysseus. Penelope does not believe the news and goes to meet him. She is convinced only when Odysseus displays knowledge regarding the secret construction and immovability of their marital bed, to which they then retire.

'Penelope' ends the book and begins with the voice of the bawd complaining about the fact that her cuckolded husband has asked to 'get his breakfast in bed with a couple of eggs' the next morning (18.1–2). For the rest of this chapter, the reader will be plunged into the interior monologue of Molly Bloom. Even though the reader of *Ulysses* should be used to such stylistic jolts by now, the change in narrative style from the previous episode's catechism to Molly's interior monologue is nevertheless striking. There is an almost complete lack of punctuation: all the commas and apostrophes are missing; and even though the entire episode is composed of eight very long sentences, there is only one full-stop: the one that follows Molly's final 'Yes'. Throughout the monologue, capital letters do appear, in a mostly conventional way; however, certain words that ordinarily do without capitals get them when the word seems to have a particular significance for Molly: for instance 'Kidney' at 18.568.

The overall punctuation-free 'look' of the episode suggests that Molly's interior monologue is a flow, and as such, it echoes all the other 'flows' in the text of *Ulysses*. If Molly's monologue can be said to flow, however, its flow is not simply uni-directional: it is almost tidal in that every statement that Molly makes is contradicted by a statement she makes in another part of it: for example, with regard to her husband's fidelity, she says in one breath that she no longer cares 'two straws now who he does it with or knew before that way' (18.53–4), while in the next, she recalls a former servant, 'that slut Mary we had in Ontario terrace padding out her false bottom to excite him' (18.56–7), whom she dismissed – apparently for stealing oysters – after she found the garters Mr Bloom had bought for her (18.60–76). This situation makes it difficult to pin down what Molly really thinks since she erases what she says as she talks. Given this, it can be said that Molly's interior monologue enacts, on a narrative level, Mr Bloom's contemplation in 'Nausicaa' of the problems of trying to write in the sand: he notes that everything that is written will be erased by the rhythm of the tide (13.1266–9). And, as such a tidal woman, Molly at the end of the book thus recalls the great sea-mother invoked in the first episode and the hithering-thithering bird-girl Stephen encounters in chapter IV of *Portrait*.

The other aspect of Molly's monologue that is especially striking is its sheer carnality: she contemplates 'that tremendous big red brute of a thing' Boylan has (18.144), saying that she's never had a penis quite so big and lingers on the fact that his 'thick crowbar' (18.147–8) made her 'feel full up' (18.150). She also contemplates Boylan's sexual athleticism, noting that he must have 'come 3 or 4 times' during their time together (18.143). She then goes on to compare Boylan's relative lack of 'spunk' or semen (18.154) – as evidenced when she makes him come on her – with Poldy's apparently copious quantities (18.168).

As mentioned above, Molly's monologue is composed of eight sentences; the first (18.1–245) dwells on issues such as Boylan's sexual prowess, Mr Bloom's infidelities, the childishness of men and wives who've killed their husbands. The second sentence (18.246–534) recalls her first meeting with Boylan and upcoming visit to Belfast, one of the first stops on her upcoming concert tour, Mr Bloom's courtship, dwells on getting older and fatter, and is peppered with the images of other past suitors, one of whom, a singer named Bartell dArcy, kissed her on her 'brown part' (18.276) – her anus (cf. her thoughts about tormenting Mr Bloom at 18.1522). Molly's third sentence (18.535–95) is the shortest: it dwells on her breasts, which she thinks Boylan has made firmer by sucking them, noting that he has bitten one of them. She then recalls how Mr Bloom wanted to milk her into his tea when she was nursing Milly, and her thoughts return to Boylan's next scheduled visit on Monday. Molly's fourth sentence (18.596–747) begins with her making the sound of a train in the distance – 'frseeeeeeeefronnnng train somewhere whistling' (18.596) – which she then lets mingle, in Bloomian fashion, with the title of one of the songs she practised that afternoon – 'like the end of Loves old sweeeetsonnnng' (18.598). The noise of the train prompts her to think about how the engine-driver's job is made difficult by heat, and the thought of heat sets in train a recollection of her childhood growing up on Gibraltar. This sentence also calls attention to its own textuality when Molly – while thinking about receiving a love letter from Boylan – recalls some mistakes she often makes while writing letters:

> its a bother having to answer he always tells me the wrong things and no stops to say like making a speech your sad bereavement symphathy I always make that mistake and newphew with 2 double yous in I hope hell write me a longer letter. (18.728–31)

The self-referentiality of this passage is quite complex: not only does it reproduce textually Molly's writing mistakes in a passage about letter-writing, it also underlines how Molly's punctuation-free style is unlike speech insofar as it too does not contain 'stops'.

Molly's fifth sentence (18.748–908) dwells, for the most part, on 'what was his name Jack Joe Harry Mulvey was it yes I think' (18.819), the first the 25 suitors are mentioned in the previous episode (17.2133–42). Molly, it seems, does not go 'all the way' with Mulvey: she 'pulled him off into her handkerchief' (18.809–10), which she then kept under her pillow (18.863). On the one hand, this suggests – as a number of Joycean commentators have noted – that the 25 suitors listed in 'Ithaca' did not get all the way with Molly; at the same time, however, since Boylan is on the list, there is no way of knowing just how many of those listed she did have sex with, just as there is no way of knowing which suitors have been left off the list, which, as the list itself makes clear, is incomplete (17.2142). Molly herself notes that she 'knew more about men and life at 15' than most other women 'knew at 50' (18.896–7).

Molly's fifth sentence is also interesting because it brings her into contact with the figure of Gerty in 'Nausicaa', which should put the reader of episode 18 on guard against reading Molly as purely a 'natural' force. As the figure of Gerty illustrates, whatever 'woman' may be said to be in *Ulysses*, she is never simply 'natural'. 'Woman' is, in fact, a complex construction of socio-cultural ideas, ideals and stereotypes that is routinely soaked in all manner of natural and unnatural potions and concoctions and clad in all sorts of devices: Molly is no different. Just as episode 13 catalogued all the lotions and potions Gerty uses, the entire text of *Ulysses* catalogues – through Mr Bloom – the various lotions, creams, devices and routines that Molly uses to beautify herself. Nor do the similarities between Gerty and Molly do not stop there; Molly, as a professional singer, is every bit as self-conscious of herself as a performer as Gerty was in performing herself as an attractive young woman for Mr Bloom. This becomes clear when she imaginatively rehearses her sexuality and emotions as she sings 'Love's Old Sweet Song':

again weeping tone once in the dear deaead days beyondre call close my eyes breath my lips forward kiss sad look eyes open piano ere oer the world the mists began I hate that istsbeg comes loves sweet sooooooooooong Ill let that out full when I get in front of the footlights again. (18.874–7)

And, just as Gerty's narration revealed her to be a tissue of syrupy quotations and clichés typical of women's magazine writing at the turn of the twentieth century, so too is Molly's monologue chock-full of snippets of rhymes, poems and songs that she has performed over the years.[17] All of this indicates that Molly is not simply a purely 'natural' being: her femininity and femaleness are every bit as constructed as any other part of *Ulysses*. And, as if to underscore the textual relation of her monologue with the rest of the book, Molly ends her fifth sentence not just with an itchy vagina but with a Bloomian symphony in which her fart intermingles with the distant sound of the train and a song: 'better yes hold them like that a bit on my side piano quietly sweeeee theres that train far away pianissimo eeeee one more tsong' (18.907–8).

Molly's sixth sentence (18.909–1148) dwells upon, among other things, her difficulties with Milly who has recently started to show an interest in her appearance and in boys. Milly's interest in boys seems to be related to the arrival of her first period: as the respondent notes at the end of episode 17, Mr Bloom and Molly have not spoken properly since Milly got her period 9 months and 1 day ago (17.2289). It is thus somewhat ironic that Molly herself now starts her period, which she thinks has been brought on by the afternoon of Boylan's 'poking and rooting and ploughing' (18.1106). She is not pleased to see her period, despite the fact that it means Boylan's ploughing did not get her pregnant: 'have we too much blood up in us or what O patience above its pouring out of me like the sea anyhow he didnt make me pregnant as big as he is I dont want to ruin the clean sheets I just put on I suppose the clean linen I wore brought it on too damn it damn it' (18.1122–25). Molly's description of her blood-flow once more underscores her status as the sea-mother. As she gets up to attend to her period, she contemplates cutting her pubic hair because her skin is 'scalded' – that is, irritated through the contact with the urine in her pubic hair – and imagines that doing so would also make her 'look like a young girl' (18.1133–5), which suggests a sexual rivalry with Milly. Once out of bed, Molly mounts her chamber pot and begins to urinate loudly, remembering her own ability to urinate like a man – 'I remember one time I could scout it out straight whistling like a man almost easy' (18.1141–2) – and hoping for bubbles – 'I hope theyre bubbles on it for a wad of money' (18.1142–3) – in the superstitious belief that the bubbles are a sign that money is to come. She then underlines again the masculine tendencies of her desires by imagining being a man and getting 'up on a lovely woman' (18.1146–7).

Form and content thus merge once more in Molly's sixth sentence as her flowing, punctuation-free monologue is echoed in the bloody and urinous streams that issue from her vagina. Her seventh sentence begins by betraying some anxiety: 'who knows is there anything the matter with my insides or have I something growing in me getting that thing like that every week when was it last I Whit Monday yes its only about 3 weeks I ought to go to the doctor' (18.1149–51). Molly's flows then prompt her to return to the self-reflexive erotics of letter-writing when she recalls a letter Mr Bloom sent her during their courtship: 'my Precious one everything connected with your glorious Body everything underlined that comes from it is a thing of beauty and of joy for ever' (18.1176–8). This letter caused her to masturbate furiously – often up to four or five times a day (18.1179). Other worries flit through this sentence: Mr Bloom's involvement in Sinn Féin and the Freemasons, his habit of losing his job, their frequent flights from landlords. Molly also suspects that Mr Bloom wants her to commit adultery with Boylan – something that certainly seemed to give him immense pleasure to witness during the pyrotechnics of 'Circe' (15.3809–16) – because he has not the courage to commit adultery himself. She finishes her sentence by taking the time to criticize Mr Bloom's tongue technique during oral sex (18.1244–51) and indulging in sexual fantasies about young men and Stephen, whose intellectual refinement appeals to her. She then reckons that she is not too old for him (18.1328) and imagines that they could be lovers (18.1360–7).

Molly's final sentence (18.1368–1609) begins by contrasting Stephen's refinement to Boylan's bum-slapping antics. She once again imagines being a man (18.1381–4), expresses her frustrations at Mr Bloom's kissing her backside instead of her lips, his 'coldness' and lack of embraces (18.1400–10). She then imagines picking up strangers – gypsies, sailors, murderers – for sex (18.1410–20). Then, after briefly recalling Rudy – and noting that her desire for the sex that produced him was aroused by watching two dogs having sex outside (18.1446–8; Mr Bloom recalls the same incident at 6.77–81) – she decides to try to torment her husband tomorrow morning by giving him what she knows he likes (≋ 18.1508–32). Molly's planned temptation of Mr Bloom seems to be in an effort to make him aware that he has not been 'fucking' her vaginally like Boylan did. In other words, Molly seems to be tired of Mr Bloom's non-heteronormative desires – such as coming on her bum or her underwear, his coprophillic tendencies and so on – and the show she wants to put on the next morning comes down to her desire to 'make him want me' (18.1539): that is, to make Mr Bloom want her the way she wants to be wanted. If not, then Mr Bloom's money will be some compensation.

The general unhappiness Molly feels over the current state of her marriage and her frustrated desire to have Mr Bloom want her the way that she wants to be wanted, sets the stage for her remembrance of 'the day I got him to propose to me' (18.1573–4) on the top of Howth Head (a large peninsula located in North County Dublin) in the passage that draws *Ulysses* to its close (❧ 18.1574–609). The concluding words of Molly's monologue are, however, anything not cut and dried; on the one hand, they have often been read as Molly's final 'acceptance' of her Poldy and his desires, her final 'Yes' reliving the happy day on Howth when Mr Bloom proposed marriage. On the other hand, it is possible to read in Molly's concluding words enough to cause the reader to question whether Molly is actually accepting her Poldy and his foibles: if the reappearance of the ghost of Harry Mulvey – the young man who first kissed her under the Moorish Wall in Gibraltar (18.769) – is not enough to raise some doubt about Molly's final acceptance of Mr Bloom, then perhaps his reappearance in conjunction with her lukewarm assessment of Mr Bloom's proposal – 'as well him as another' – is. It also seems to be fairly clear that the Blooms' marriage is in trouble; as I have been suggesting, the sex life they share does not satisfy Molly, and conversation, as Mr Bloom notes to himself in episode 17, has lately dried up. And, since both parties are now acting out their marital dissatisfactions – Mr Bloom has been writing and receiving naughty letters and Molly has turned to Boylan to get the kind of sex she wants – things between them appear to have gotten worse, not better. Further, it is also possible to read in Molly's closing words – despite all her 'yeses' – the contours of a power struggle, one that mirrors the Friday morning performance she has planned for her husband: Molly effectively extracts a proposal from Mr Bloom – she says she got him to propose to her – using her sexuality. In other words, if one reads Molly's final words in the light of other parts of the book – as having a relation with the other parts of the text – it does not seem to be easy to read them as a final acceptance of her husband. But no matter what interpretation of Molly's final words the reader chooses, it is perhaps a final irony of the text that the critical speculation about the state of the Blooms' marriage and whether or not Mr Bloom will get his eggs for breakfast only serves to draw attention to the textuality of *Ulysses* one last time: there is no final resolution possible precisely because the dark morrice of the text has now run its course.

CHAPTER FIVE

THE LANGUAGE(S) AND STRUCTURE(S) OF *FINNEGANS WAKE*

Finnegans Wake was first published in 1939, the year World War II broke out; Joyce had begun working on the book not long after the publication of *Ulysses* in 1922: in all, it took him about 16 years to write. Joyce kept the title of *Finnegans Wake* a secret until just before its publication, which is why it was often referred to as simply 'Work in Progress'. Given that the book consumed over a quarter of Joyce's life, it seems somewhat absurd to try to introduce a work as complex as the *Wake* in a chapter of a book such as this. There is simply not enough time or space to do justice to the sheer volume of material that went into its composition. The best that a chapter such as the present one might be able to offer the new reader of *Finnegans Wake*, is a brief introduction that, with luck, will scratch the surface of the *Wake*'s mind-bogglingly vast network of allusions and references, its tireless citation and distortion of texts of all kinds and its endlessly inventive playfulness with all manner of natural and artificial languages. Just as reading *Ulysses* was at least a two-book operation, so too is reading *Finnegans Wake*. The second book in the case of the latter is Roland McHugh's *Annotations to Finnegans Wake* (3rd edn, Baltimore: Johns Hopkins University Press, 2005). McHugh's *Annotations* is simply indispensable for every and any reader of the *Wake*, old and new: it provides glosses for many of the *Wake*'s references and allusions to historical, mythical and literary personages, events, texts, puns and works of art, as well as translations for the fragments of the sixty-odd languages and numerous other dialects that appear throughout its pages. All editions of the *Wake* use the same pagination; references to the text will be given parenthetically in the text by page and line number (e.g., 003.01).

Speaking in the simplest possible terms, perhaps the most easily discernible structure in *Finnegans Wake* is that of a family: this 'family' consists of a father, Humphrey Chimpden Earwicker (HCE), a mother, Anna Livia Plurabelle (ALP), twin sons, Shem the Penman and Shaun the Postman, and a daughter, Issy, who at times splits into two, seven and twenty-eight other girls. These names do not remain the same throughout the text. The family appears to live above a pub in Chapelizod, a suburb of Dublin. Because the events takes place mostly at night, the book's famously difficult language is saturated by images of darkness, sleep and dreams. The book is also obsessed with arriving at the truth concerning an unspecified crime that the father has committed and the writing and delivery of a letter that promises to clear his name. The *Wake* is divided into four books: book I, which consists of eight episodes, introduces the family members; book II, which consists of four episodes, is divided between the late-evening activities of the children – their evening playtime, their homework – and the parents – tending to the pub and having sex; book III, which has four episodes, is devoted to the figure of Shaun the Postman as he delivers the letter; and book IV, which consists of only one episode, seems to deal with the approaching dawn of a new day. This overly simplified version of the *Wake*'s plot should, however, be treated with caution.

The exploration of the *Wake* that follows begins with a close look at its language with the aim of giving the novice reader a flavour of the linguistic complexity that is to be found on each of its 628 pages. It then goes on to consider how certain aspects of the language of the text can be understood to inform some of the larger structures that shape the *Wake* as a whole. One of the texts that Joyce recommended to readers grappling with the *Wake* – *The New Science* by Giambattista Vico (1744; trans. Thomas G. Bergin and Max H. Fisch. Ithaca: Cornell University Press, 1968) – is particularly helpful for illuminating those structures. In *The New Science*, Vico evolved an inventive theory of cyclical history which aimed to discover the origins of divine and human institutions among the gentile nations. To this end, he divided all human history into three ages: the age of gods, the age of heroes and the age of men. These ages were followed by a 'ricorso', a return to the age of the gods. These divisions recur throughout the *Wake*, and the book's four-part structure is based on them. Vico's cyclical philosophy is also echoed by the *Wake*'s famously cyclical structure: its opening sentence is a continuation of its closing sentence. Once these features and structures become discernible, the novice reader of the *Wake* will hopefully have the most important basic tools for grappling with the text. That being said – and I cannot emphasize this enough – due to the limitations of genre, of space, of time and so on, the approach to the *Wake* sketched here will, of necessity, have to leave out a great many of the things that make *Finnegans Wake* the often shocking, hilariously warped and profoundly unsettling gift that it is.

I

THE LANGUAGE(S) OF *FINNEGANS WAKE*:
(a) Thunder/Babel/Repetition

Without a doubt, the first thing that any new reader of the *Wake* will notice is its odd language; at first sight, it might also seem that – with the possible exception of the last pages of 'The Oxen of the Sun' – there is nothing else in Joyce's *oeuvre* that quite resembles the *Wake* or prepares the new reader for its odd mixture of foreign languages, portmanteau words, peculiar spellings and so on. However, a new reader of the *Wake* will hopefully, with a little patience, begin to realize that some of the non-linear and non-mimetic reading techniques that the text of *Ulysses* teaches the reader may be applied almost unchanged to the *Wake*. In fact, the first page of the *Wake* acts as a series of cues that serve to recall some of the techniques necessary for reading *Ulysses*. Take the first 'sentence' of the text: 'riverrun, past Eve and Adam's, from swerve of shore to bend of bay, brings us by a commodius vicus of recirculation back to Howth Castle and Environs' (003.1–3). The reader will likely notice several things about the first sentence: it begins without a capital letter, which suggests that the start of the sentence is missing, and is perhaps – like the repeated fragments found in 'The Wandering Rocks' or 'Sirens' – to be found elsewhere in the text. The next thing the reader will notice is the presence of certain Biblical proper names – Eve and Adam's; and a reader familiar with *Ulysses* will likely recognize 'Howth' as the same place where Mr Bloom proposed to Molly. This suggests that the *Wake* appears to be 'set' – like all of Joyce's other works – in and around the city of Dublin; a quick glance at page three of McHugh confirms this: 'Eve and Adam's' reverses the name of a church in Dublin called Adam and Eve's. Another thing that might stick out in the first sentence is the odd phrase 'commodius vicus of recirculation' – in which is embedded the Latin word '*vicus*', meaning street or village and suggestive of Giambattista Vico, as well as the impression that this is perhaps not the 'first' time the text has travelled in a circle: 'recirculation'. This intuition also turns out to have merit: the last lines of the book join up with the beginning: 'The keys to. Given! A way a lone a last a loved a long the [. . .] riverrun past Eve and Adam's, from swerve of shore to bend of bay' (628.15–003.02). A reader conversant with *Ulysses* will no doubt also recognize here the problematic notion of 'return' that Stephen and Mr Bloom grapple with at various points in that book. Thus, the opening sentence-fragment contains a great deal of information that would be familiar to a reader of Joyce who has never even cracked the spine on a copy of *Finnegans Wake*: familiar notions of Dublin, rivers, roads, repetition and circularity, all of which bring 'us' – the reader thus already has a place prepared for him/her in the first lines of the text – 'back to Howth Castle and Environs'. The unusual capitalization of this last location also serves to draw the reader's attention to it: I will return to this below.

Several lines later, the *Wake* (re)introduces the reader to the eponymous figure of Finnegan, the fall of whom, it would seem, is a story that is 'retaled' – repeatedly retailed and retold – all throughout history:

> The fall (bababadalgharaghtakamminarronnkonnbronntonnerro nntuonnthunntro varrhounawnskawntoohoohoordenenthurnuk!) of a once wallstrait oldparr is retaled early in bed and later on life down through all christian minstrelsy. The great fall of the offwall entailed at such short notice the pftjschute of Finnegan, erse solid man, that the humptyhillhead of humself prumptly sends an unquiring one well to the west in quest of his tumpty-tumtoes: and their upturnpikepointandplace is at the knock out in the park where oranges have been laid to rust upon the green since devlinsfirst loved livvy. (003.15–24)

This passage introduces a number of important motifs in the text: first, it sets the scene of the fall in the Phoenix Park (a corruption of the Irish '*Fionn Uisce*', meaning 'clear or white water') near Chapelizod in Dublin (Finnegan's toes seem to stick up near the Castleknock gate: 'the knock out in the park'); second, it opens an association between Finnegan and both fish and phoenixes ('parr' is a young salmon; 'Finnegan' includes a 'fin', and Finn McCool ('*Fionn mac*

Cumhaill' in Irish) is a legendary Irish hero who ate the salmon of knowledge); third, it suggests that the scene of Finnegan's 'pftjschute' (French, *chute* or 'fall') cannot be separated from multiple languages, which can be heard in Finnegan's scream as he falls: '(bababadalgharaghtakamminarronnkonnbronntonnerronntuonnthunntrovarrhounawn skawntoohoohoordenenthurnuk!)'. Finnegan's scream, it turns out, is also the stuttering sound of thunder: it is the first of ten hundred-letter thunder-words found throughout the text. The one just cited repeats the word for thunder in Irish, French, Japanese, Hindi, German, Greek, Danish, Swedish, Portuguese, Rumanian and Italian. The initial stuttering ('bababa') of the multi-lingual thunder-word also recalls the story of the Tower of Babel from Genesis 11.1–9, which goes as follows: after the flood-waters receded, the survivors left Mount Ararat and settled on a plain in the land of Shinar, where they set about building a tower whose top would reach Heaven. God was none too pleased by this, so he gave each person working on the tower a different language. This produced such confusion that it halted the construction of the tower and its builders scattered across the earth. The *Wake* seems to adopt and adapt the story of the Tower of Babel: in the *Wake*an version, 'God' does not get to remain in Heaven; as Finnegan falls, the odd 'language' that he screams in rumbles thunderously across the sky whereupon it is heard as – and thus echoes in – the different languages of those left on earth – us, the readers of *Finnegans Wake*.

The *Wake*'s roll of thunder also owes much to Giambattista Vico's *The New Science*. Vico discusses the roll of thunder and its relation to what he calls the 'first men' of the gentiles. Since the first men could only express their 'violent passions by shouting and grumbling' (NS 377), the roll of thunder seemed to them to be the expression of violent passions by the sky which they 'pictured to themselves as a great animated body' (NS 377).[1] Such men, Vico says, became afraid of this massive violent presence in the heavens, and this caused them to 'subject themselves' to its 'higher power which they imagined as Jove' (NS 1097). This terrifying god caused the first men to control their sexuality out of fear of making the god angry again:

> between the powerful restraints of frightful superstition and the goading stimuli of bestial lust (which must have been extremely violent in such men), as they felt the aspect of the heavens to be terrible to them and hence to thwart their use of venery, they

had to hold in conatus the impetus of the bodily motions of lust [340, 504]. Thus they began to use human liberty, which consists in holding in check the motions of concupiscence and giving them another direction; for since this liberty does not come from the body, whence comes concupiscence, it must come from the mind and is therefore properly human. The new direction took the form of forcibly seizing their women, who were naturally shy and unruly, dragging them into their caves, and, in order to have intercourse with them, keeping them there as perpetual lifelong companions. Thus with the first human, which is to say chaste and religious, couplings, they gave a beginning to matrimony. Thereby they became certain fathers of certain children by certain women. (NS 1098)

The fear, guilt and shame that the anger of the god – 'Jove' – produces in these men holds their bestial lusts in check ('conatus'); and, as a result, humanity first begins to take shape in these men. Thus Vico sees 'humanity' as created by the terrified reaction of the first men to the thundering God.

This terror appears some pages later in *Finnegans Wake* in a dialogue between two figures called Mutt and Jute – so named after the American comic strip, 'Mutt and Jeff', which began its run in 1907:

> Jute. – But you are not jeffmute?
> Mutt. – Noho. Only an utterer.
> Jute. – Whoa? Whoat is the mutter with you?
> Mutt. – I became a stun a stummer.
> Jute. – What a hauhauhauhaudibble thing, to be cause! How, Mutt?
> Mutt. – Aput the buttle, surd.
> Jute. – Whose poddle? Wherein?
> Mutt. – The Inns of Dungtarf where Used awe to be he.
> Jute. – You that side your voise are almost inedible to me. Become a bitskin more wiseable, as if I were you.
> Mutt. – Has? Has at? Hasatency? Urp, Boohooru! Booru Usurp!
> I trumple from rath in mine mines when I rimimirim ! (016.14–28)

The exchange between these two figures is interesting because of how closely it reproduces the terrified babblings of the first men in response to the angry thundering god: the sound of thunder has deafened (Latin, *surdus*, 'deaf') the pair somewhat, so they constantly mishear each other. Mutt, in particular has a stutter or stammer, which only serves to create more confusion in the dialogue. Mutt tells Jute that he has developed a 'stummer' in response to the thunderous roar of Finnegan's thunderous fall which, after Vico, easily morphs into the site of a battle ('buttle'; 'poddle') with a strong male figure. The strong male figure that Mutt recalls resembles Brian Boru, the Irish king who defeated an army of Danish occupiers in the battle of Clontarf (1014): 'Urp, Boohooru! Booru Usurp! I trumple from rath in mine mines when I rimimirim!' It is interesting to note that Mutt both stutters and shudders ('trumples') at the remembered image of the strong male thunderer. In other words, the terrified stuttered response to the stuttered thunder-word reproduces it – but with a crucial difference – this time he makes his own thunder (I will return to this below; it is worth noting here that repetition with a difference is, of course, one of Mr Bloom's preoccupations in 'Eumaeus' [16.1404–6; 16.1523–6]).

Reproduction with a difference also serves to draw attention to the motif of doubling that is found on the first page of the *Wake* where things go 'doublin their mumper all the time' (003.08–09). If Dublin is a site of 'doublin', then everything in the *Wake* is potentially subject to replication. That the process of doubling has a tendency to displace or erode the 'original' is explicitly underlined in another scene from episode one of book I (I.1):

Our cubehouse still rocks as earwitness to the thunder of his arafatas but we hear also through successive ages that shebby choruysh of unkalified muzzlenimiissilehims that would blackguardise the whitestone ever hurtleturtled out of heaven. (005.14–18)

Here, the roll of thunder that rocks the 'cubehouse' becomes an 'arafatas' – a combination of Arafata, the hill near Mecca that every Muslim pilgrim must visit, and a 'fart' – that resounds 'through successive ages' as a 'shebby choruysh of unkalified muzzlenimiissilehims'. Joyce is not, of course, singling out the Muslim faith here for ridicule; it is simply that this 'shabby chorus of unqualified muslims' is just another example of how mankind's stuttering doubling of the god's – Finnegan's – thundering fall/word contaminates and threatens that word. And it is this contaminating reproduction that produces an anxiety which throughout the *Wake* is voiced by the figure of Shaun the postman in his various guises.

That being said, the reader should also remain open to the possibility that there is no 'Finnegan' in the text; or rather, that 'he' is 'there' only insofar as he is not 'there': in other words, all that there 'is' is thunder – what Mr Bloom might call 'the discharge of fluid from the thunderhead', which is 'all of the order of a natural phenomenon' (14.426–8). This reading seems to be supported by the *Wake* itself: by the time the reader has 'met' the figure of Finnegan, he has already vanished, and all that remains of him is marked in the text by a stuttering roll of thunder which is heard as the sound of his screams as he falls. Nor does it seem to be possible to say that Finnegan 'appears' only to 'disappear', since Finnegan never actually presents himself in *propria persona* anywhere in the text: he is only ever spoken to through proxies or avatars. His 'fall', therefore, does not mark the 'loss' of a once pristine and potent father-god figure – simply because he was never 'there' to begin with: Finnegan only ever 'appears' 'in' – the scare-quotes are unavoidable – the *Wake* in the form of a withdrawal, in the form of a 'wake'.

The power of Finnegan's wake to actually generate text is repeatedly underlined in throughout book I: it is his 'fall' that drives the 'narrative' level of the text, which, at the end of I.1, takes on the character of a sort of 'investigation' into his 'disappearance'. This investigation is conducted by the 'Mamalujo' (a strange composite figure of the four evangelists, **M**atthew, **M**ark, **Lu**ke and **Jo**hn), who seek Finnegan in order to find out more about the circumstances surrounding his fall. At the end of I.1, the Mamalujo try repeatedly to halt Finnegan's wake (024.16–25; 027.22–30) – 'Repose you now! Finn no more!' (028.33–4). Unable to stop Finnegan's infinite regress, they turn their attentions to another, a substitute: 'be that samesake sibsubstitute of a hooky salmon, there's already a big rody ram lad at random on the premises of his haunt of the hungred bordles' (028.35–029) – 'Humme the Cheapner, Esc' (029.18–19). Having apparently given up on Finnegan as a lost cause, the four now try to dig back into Humme the Cheapner, Esc's past. However, the futility of this endeavour starts to become obvious in I.2: they are no longer looking into Humme the Cheapner, Esc's past, but into the question 'concerning the genesis of Harold or Humphrey Chimpden's occupational agnomen' (030.02–03). It would seem that what the Mamalujo are up to is actually becoming less and less clear: who are they looking for? Finnegan, Humme the Cheapner, Esc, Harold or Humphrey Chimpden? And why have they decided to look into how Harold or Humphrey got his name?

Instead of trying to clear any of this confusion up, I.2 tells the reader that Humphrey or Harold got the surname of 'Earwicker' from his occupation of catching earwigs in a flowerpot (031.1–11). He thus now bears the 'sigla H.C.E.' (032.14), short for the 'christlikeness of the big cleanminded giant H.C. Earwicker' (033.29–30).

The 'sigla H.C.E.' is worth dwelling on here: these letters function throughout the *Wake* in a manner that is not unlike the large number of alternate Hebrew names or synonyms for God found in Kabbalah, a school of thought concerned with the exegesis of the Hebrew Bible and traditional Rabbinical literature. Kabbalah, which dates from between the eleventh and thirteenth centuries, has its roots in Assyrian, Babylonian and Egyptian sources, and has influenced esoteric Christian and Theosophical studies. In Kabbalah there are many names for God, ranging from the Monogrammaton – 'H' – to the Tetragrammaton – 'YHWH' – which is often rendered as 'Jehovah' or 'Yahweh'. Permutations the Tetragrammaton were often put to use in meditations, inscribed on amulets and so on. The Tetragrammaton was also used to generate the eight-letter name of God by interspersing its letters with the Hebrew word 'Adonai', meaning Lord. The other names for God – the 12, 14, 22, 42 and 72-letter names – were derived through various formulas that were applied to the already existing names of God as well as blessings, prayers and entire Biblical verses. In many ways, the letters 'H', 'C' and 'E' in the *Wake* are analogous to the names of God in Kabbalah; although the reader does not encounter 'the sigla H.C.E.' until the second episode of book I, the Kabbalistic connection suggests that it should nevertheless be possible to read HCE's name in the text as an encrypted, wandering chain of letters that weaves its way through the text – not entirely unlike the sandwich men that Mr Bloom observes in 'Lestrygonians' who wear the letters 'H.E.L.Y'S' – recurring often, changing order and becoming interspersed with other letters: and, if the reader returns to the first sentence of the *Wake* cited above, s/he can already see HCE encrypted in 'Howth Castle and Environs'. HCE's name should also serve to alert the reader that reading the *Wake* is a complex, highly kinetic process that frequently skips over, rearranges and encrypts words and letters. This kinetic way of reading is no longer simply linear: it can move forwards and backwards and up and down; it is thus pretty much the same reading technique employed by the 'Jewish' Mr Bloom, a technique that has been shaped by in no small part by print culture and 'the art of advertising' (17.581–4).

(b) Finnegan's 'wake': Presence/Absence

Just when it seems that they have solved the mystery of HCE's name, the Mamalujo come across a ballad which purports to tell of the circumstances of his fall and disappearance: 'The Ballad of Persse O'Reilly', written by an individual named Hosty (044.24–047.29). However, the ballad not only changes HCE's name to Persse O'Reilly (which echoes *perce-oreille*, the French for earwig) and associates him with Humpty Dumpty's fall from the wall, it also accuses him of both rape (047.01–2) and homosexual solicitation in the Phoenix Park (047.09–12). The ballad thus only adds to the confusion by conflating Finnegan's thunderous fall with HCE/Persse O'Reilly's crime in the Phoenix Park, which in turn makes it possible for the reader to confuse all of these figures with each other. The situation goes from bad to worse when I.2 finally gives way to I.3's free-for-all rumour mongering and presents three very different reconstructions of the crime in the Phoenix Park, which in turn becomes the setting for a fight on a plain in Ireland. Things are further clouded when a *vox pop* is taken, and all and sundry offer their interpretations and opinions as to the circumstances surrounding the fall/crime.

I.4 then changes tack and tries to arrive at the 'true truth' (096.27) of the situation by conducting a trial. That what began as an investigation into Finnegan's disappearance has now taken the form of a trial presided over by the Mamalujo indicates how powerful the rumours and speculation of I.2 and I.3 have been. The trial, in its attempt to arrive at the 'true truth' surrounding Finnegan/HCE/Persse O'Reilly, also reconstitutes these male figures as the ever-receding paradigm for truth and meaning in the book. Despite its best efforts and its power to call forward what can only be described as unreliable 'witnesses' who 'saw' the fall/crime, the trial becomes bogged down in conflicting testimony from those witnesses and a host of other 'unfacts' (057.16). It is during the trial and investigation that the text explicitly equates truth with the unveiling of HCE's presence when it characterizes the 'true truth' as that which would finally 'unhume the great shipping mogul and underlinen overlord' (097.24). However, despite their best efforts, the judges are forced to admit their inability to arrive at the truth about Finnegan/HCE/Persse O'Reilly and decide that the best bet is to wait for his wife's letter which promises to tell the 'cock's trootabout him' (113.12). It should already be clear from this brief outline of the first half of book I, that the desire to uncover Finnegan/

HCE/Persse O'Reilly and arrive at the truth about his fall/crime/disappearance, constitutes a major structural element of *Finnegans Wake*.

But the *Wake* even as it treats Finnegan/HCE/Persse O'Reilly's withdrawal as a major structural and generative principle, also uses that withdrawal as a sort of 'lure' for the reader. This lure can be understood to play a double and contradictory function in the text. On the one hand, it suggests to the reader that there is a possibility of 'unhuming' Finnegan/HCE/Persse O'Reilly and of learning the full truth regarding his fall/crime and disappearance: the *Wake* repeatedly toys with the possibility of 'framing up the figments' of text 'in the evidential order' and 'bring[ing] the true truth to light' (096.26–7). On the other hand, even though it appears to concern itself with the inquiry into Finnegan/HCE's whereabouts after his withdrawal from the text, the *Wake* also frames that inquiry as an 'unquiry' (003.22), which creates doubt that there will ever be a successful conclusion. Finnegan/HCE's withdrawal pulls him irretrievably towards absence, and, as it does so, simultaneously thwarts the search for those 'facts' by multiplying all the distracting 'unfacts' (057.16) that overcome the search for him. In short, it would seem that both 'facts' and 'unfacts' are created simultaneously by Finnegan/HCE's 'wake'. This further suggests that the search for the 'true truth' is not simply plagued by 'unfacts' which would 'happen' to the truth 'accidentally'; rather, it suggests that everywhere in the text where there is an attempt to arrive at the truth in the form of 'unhuming' or restoring Finnegan/HCE's presence, there is also a countervailing pull towards absence. However, these tensions, because they shape the first book of the *Wake*, constitute something of a structural principle that affects the pursuit of truth/presence across the entire text. Finnegan's 'wake' is therefore legible as the structural tension between presence and absence. For this reason, Finnegan's wake cannot be reduced to either presence or absence: he is 'between' presence and absence. The text therefore plays in a strange zone of 'non-presence', which is not-simply-absent, dangling and withdrawing Finnegan as the paradigm for truth and meaning.

Finnegan's liminal position between presence/absence is further underlined in I.1, where he is served up as a phoenix-fish for ritualistic consumption, only to disappear again:

But, lo, as you would quaffoff his fraudstuff and sink teeth through that pyth of a flowerwhite bodey behold of him as behemoth for he is noewhemoe. Finiche! Only a fadograph of a yestern scene. Almost rubicund Salmosalar, ancient fromout the ages of the Agapemonides, he is smolten in our mist, woebecanned and packt away. So that meal's dead off for summan, schlook, schlice and goodridhirring. (007.12–18)

Instead of appearing in the feast of the text according to the structure of the doctrinal belief in the 'Real Presence' of God during the Eucharist, Finnegan is the 'goodridhirring' who does not 'appear' to be present at all. Finnegan does not hold out any substantial 'Real Presence' because he is 'noewhemoe'. The foodstuff he provides for consumption is precisely not flesh; it is only a 'fraudstuff'. This implies that 'Real Presence' in the text is fraudulent, a 'good red herring',[2] a false lead, and underscores Finnegan's peculiar form of 'presence' as something which never amounts to much more than a 'fadograph'. But Finnegan is not simply absent either; thus, his remains take the form of a faded photograph, and are elsewhere allied with the faded presence of a 'ghost' (024.27). Finnegan's peculiar presence/absence also shapes the *Wake*'s famously punny language: the words on its pages hover between the 'presence' and 'absence' of familiar words, phrases, titles and quotations. I.1 may thus be read as a remarkably efficient sketch of the disruptive textuality that is *Finnegans Wake*.

II

THE STRUCTURE(S) OF *FINNEGANS WAKE*

(a) Time/Body-Writing/Imagination

By withdrawing from the 'first' page of the *Wake*, Finnegan also effectively 'erases' himself: the 'fall' marks Finnegan with a 'pastness' that is not a modification of a 'present', which goes a long way towards explaining the immense difficulties that surround the book's (vain) attempts at restoring him or recovering any certitude regarding him. Finnegan's peculiar 'pastness' can also be seen in the strange temporality that is marked repeatedly in the opening lines of the book by a 'not yet':

Sir Tristram, violer d'amores, fr'over the short sea, had passencore rearrived from North Armorica on this side the scraggy isthmus of Europe Minor to wielderfight his penisolate war: nor had topsawyer's rocks by the stream Oconee exaggerated themselse to Laurens County's gorgios while they went doublin their mumper all the time: nor avoice from afire bellowsed mishe mishe to tauftauf thuartpeatrick: not yet, though venissoon after, had a kidscad buttended a bland old isaac: not yet, though all's fair in vanessy, were sosie sesthers wroth with twone nathandjoe. Rot a peck of pa's malt had Jhem or Shen brewed by arclight and rory end to the regginbrow was to be seen ringsome on the aquaface. (003.4–14)

This passage attempts to recount the peculiar time in which a series of events will have re-occurred again: very roughly speaking, 'Sir Tristram' – a version of HCE, who seems to be an amalgam of both Sir Armory Tristram, the first earl of Howth who was born in Brittany ('North Armorica', which of course echoes 'North America') and Tristan from the thirteenth century legend of 'Tristan and Isolde' – has 'passencore' – not yet – 'rearrived' on the peninsula of Howth to re-fight his penis/peninsular war; nor had the town of Dublin yet been founded on the banks of the Oconee river in Laurens County, Georgia by Peter Sawyer (the town's motto: 'Doubling all the time'.); not yet had Moses been spoken to again by the burning bush, nor had Peter yet been re-renamed by Jesus; not yet had Isaac been fooled by Jacob; nor had the double (French, *sosie*) sisters (Issy) yet been intertwined with Jonathan and Joseph; not yet had Jhem or Shen (Shem and Shaun) brewed any of pa's malt whiskey. Despite the difficulty of trying to paraphrase what is going on in this passage, it seems clear enough that what links these strange events is the fact that even though they are in the 'future', they are also already (in the) 'past'. Even though they have not happened yet, even though they are said to have *already* happened more than once, these events – the arrival of a stranger, the founding of a city, the voice of the god, the complex entanglements of sex and desire between twin brothers and sisters – constitute some of the major narrative 'events' of the *Wake*: at the same time, however, the peculiar temporality that affects them also seems to incessantly defer them, to the extent that the reader might begin to wonder if they ever really amount to narrative 'events' in the text since they never actually seem to 'happen' at all. It thus would appear that the reader is once more in the realm of possibility that Stephen pondered at the beginning of the 'Nestor' episode of *Ulysses*.

Later, in I.7, the strange temporality of the 'not yet' that seems to defer incessantly the *Wake*'s narrative 'events' is connected to a peculiar type of writing:

Then, pious Eneas, conformant to the fulminant firman which enjoins on the tremylose terrian that, when the call comes, he shall produce nichthemerically from his unheavenly body a no uncertain quantity of obscene matter not protected by copriright in the United Stars of Ourania or bedeed and bedood and bedang and bedung to him, with this double dye, brought to blood heat, gallic acid on iron ore, through the bowels of his misery, flashly, faithly, nastily, appropriately, this Esuan Menschavik and the first till last alshemist wrote over every square inch of the only foolscap available, his own body, till by its corrosive sublimation one continuous present tense integument slowly unfolded all marryvoising moodmoulded cyclewheeling history (thereby, he said, reflecting from his own individual person-life unlivable, transaccidented through the slow fires of consciousness into a dividual chaos, perilous, potent, common to allflesh, human, only, mortal) but with each word that would not pass away the squidself which he had squirtscreened from the crystalline world waned chagreenold and doriangrayer in its dudhud. This exists that isits after having been said we know. (185.27–186.09)

If the 'events' in the text remain elusive, it would seem that writing (about) them is less so. But this writing is itself peculiar; it is an insistently bodily type of writing in which the writer, 'pious Eneas', a figure for Shem the Penman, literally shits and pisses himself in response to the 'fulminant firman' – the thundering god (this is clearly a variation of the Vichian scene discussed above – the terrified response of the first men to thunder). The god's thundering word is then converted, by an alchemical/digestive process, into the writer's ink, which he then uses to write on 'his own body'. The writer's shitty words eventually harden into the protective shell of the 'continuous present tense' which is not simply present because all other history can be read in it. At the same time, the writer's words kill the world, and existence only exists after having been narrated. Thus, the present, existence and the world only come to be after the act of bodily writing.

However, it should not be thought that *Finnegans Wake* simply disables its reader by offering him/her an absent figure to pursue in a narrative where all events happen in a temporality that proves to be very slippery; on the contrary, the *Wake* enables its reader by suggesting that s/he read its text imaginatively:

> Bygmester Finnegan, of the Stuttering Hand, freemen's maurer, lived in the broadest way immarginable in his rushlit toofarback for messuages before joshuan judges had given us numbers or Helviticus committed deuteronomy (one yeastyday he sternely struxk his tete in a tub for to watsch the future of his fates but ere he swiftly stook it out again, by the might of moses, the very water was eviparated and all the guenneses had met their exodus so that ought to show you what a pentschanjeuchy chap he was!) and during mighty odd years this man of hod, cement and edifices in Toper's Thorp piled buildung supra buildung pon the banks for the livers by the Soangso. (004.18–27)

'Bygmester' – Norwegian for 'master builder' – Finnegan, a man of 'hod, cement and edifices', remains, in his wake, 'immarginable'. That is to say, despite the fact that he is both in the 'past' and in the 'future' and seems to be missing in the 'present', the reader can still 'immargine' Finnegan and how he lived as a builder. This 'immarginable' scene is also doubly self-reflexive: that which Finnegan makes and builds – 'buildungs' – echoes a chunk of the German word for 'imagination' – '*die Einbildung*'. Insofar as the reader immarginatively constructs Finnegan imaginatively constructing, the reader can be said to be exercising his/her 'immargination' in a manner that is similar to the first men Vico discusses in *The New Science*. These first men, says Vico, created their world using their 'corporeal imagination':

> [Th]e first men [. . .] created things according to their own ideas [. . .] by virtue of a wholly corporeal imagination. And because it was corporeal, they did it with marvellous sublimity; a sublimity so great that it excessively perturbed the very persons who by imagining did the creating, for they were called 'poets', which is Greek for 'creators'. (NS 376; see also 185)

The corporeal or bodily imagination that the first men used to create the world around them is, according to Vico, what made them 'poets'. The poetic images that the bodily imagination of these poets made

were themselves so sublimely powerful that they 'perturbed' the very
poets who created them: in other words, the corporeal imagination
mimics the awesome power of the gods. Vico's notion of the poetry
of a bodily imagination neatly ties together the *Wake*'s place of
the 'immargination', its description of bodily writing, and the first
men's – Mutt's, Jute's and pious Eneas's – terrified response to the
thunderous sound of the angry god. It would seem, then, that the
reader of *Finnegans Wake* – insofar as s/he uses the bodily immargination – starts to become something of a 'poet' as s/he reads the rumbling text, creating it as s/he goes. Indeed, the text has additional
advice for such a poetic reader in footnote 3, page 304: 'Wipe your
glosses with what you know.'

(b) X: The Hen's Letter

If *Finnegans Wake* can be said to have a 'plot', then that plot has to
do with a letter. This letter is the same one that announced at the end
of I.4: the letter written by HCE's wife 'A.L.P.' (102.23), which she
carries 'pelotting in her piecebag, for Handiman the Chomp, Esquoro,
biskbask, to crush the slander's head' (102.01–17). Practically the
whole of the *Wake* revolves around this mysterious 'polyhedron of
scripture' (107.08), the trajectory of which is neatly summed up later
in the text: 'Letter, carried of Shaun, son of Hek, written of Shem,
brother of Shaun, uttered for Alp, mother of Shem, for Hek, father
of Shaun. Initialled. Gee. Gone' (420.17–19). The letter is thus a sort
of motif for the desire to find and present the truth about the crime
and disappearance of Finnegan/HCE/Persse O'Reilly.

The hen's 'untitled mamafesta' (104.04) is subjected to an exhaustive exegesis in I.5, which calls its ability to finally clear things up
into question in two ways: first, its authorship seems suspect: closer
'inspection of the *bordereau* would reveal a multiplicity of personali-
ties inflicted on the documents or document' (107.24–5); second,
because it was unearthed on a 'dump' (110.26) by a hen named
'Belinda of the Dorans' (111.05), the letter has suffered staining, heat
damage and distortion:

> Tip. Well, this freely is what must have occurred to our missive
> (there's a sod of a turb for you! please wisp off the grass!) unfilthed
> from the boucher by the sagacity of a lookmelittle likemelong

hen. Heated residence in the heart of the orangeflavoured mud-mound had partly obliterated the negative to start with, causing some features palpably nearer your pecker to be swollen up most grossly while the farther back we manage to wiggle the more we need the loan of a lens to see as much as the hen saw. Tip. (111.30–112.02)

Things then only seem to go from bad to worse: the letter's addressee – who appears to be the final authority to which the letter can appeal for the truth about HCE/Finnegan – proves to be difficult to identify: 'Maggy's tea, or your majesty' (116.24) could be either male or female (or, even, for that matter, simply a tea-stain on the letter [111.19–20]). The letter's dubiety thus only seems to be exacerbated by I.5's examination of it; and the last, best hope of arriving at the truth surrounding HCE seems to turn into nothing more than yet another false-lead.

Uncannily, the *Wake* seems to feel the reader's pain at this point, aware of his/her frustration and disorientation at becoming lost in the letter's tangled, bushy undergrowth:

You is feeling like you was lost in the bush, boy? You says: It is a puling sample jungle of woods. You most shouts out: Bethicket me for a stump of a beech if I have the poultriest notions what the farest he all means. Gee up, girly! The quad gospellers may own the targum but any of the Zingari shoolerim may pick a peck of kindlings yet from the sack of auld hensyne. (112.03–08)

The text wants the reader to take heart – 'Gee up, girly!' – because the letter's jumble of words/jungle of woods is not a sacred text (the Targum is the Aramaic translation and interpretation of the Old Testament) in the hands of a couple of authorized male readers/writers (the mention of the 'quad gospellers' here suggests that the quest of the Mamalujo is to be treated, precisely as 'gospel'). On the contrary, any of the 'Zingari shoolerim' (Italian, *zingari*, gypsies; shoolerim: shoolers, vagrants, but also German, *Schülerin*, schoolgirls) may dip into the hen's sack. This reference to the hen's sack suggests that she may be more important for reading the letter than was initially suggested. This also helps to explain the reading 'tip' that the text has just offered the reader: the reader needs 'the loan of a lens to see as much as the hen saw' (112.01–02). The reader is then simply told to follow the hen's lead: 'Lead kindly fowl!' (112.09). Once the reader turns his/her attention to a bird, the hen, it starts to become clear that she is actually one of the authors – as well as the finder – of the letter: 'all schwants (schwrites) is to tell the cock's trootabout him' (113.11–12). Insofar as it involves bird-watching, reading the letter amounts to reading the auspices, just like Stephen as he watches the birds outside the National Library in chapter V of *Portrait*. The auspices also connect the *Wake* once more to Vico: according to Vico, each culture had its own Jove, and from 'the thunder and lightning of its Jove each nation began to take auspices, and taking the auspices' – which date from the first appearance of Jove as the sky – constitutes 'the first divine institution' (NS 9). For Vico, the observation of the sky while taking the auspices included the observation of birds – augury (augury gives the word 'auspice', from the Latin *avis specere*, or the observation of birds). Through the auspices it became possible to divine – from *divinari*, to foretell – what the gods had in store for mankind (NS 8). Given that human history was inaugurated by the observation of birds, it should not be surprising that the hen is a crucial component in the reader's poetic creation of the *Wake*.

The philological examination of the letter continues throughout the rest of I.5, stopping to note in detail its distinctive features, its orthography, its peculiar penmanship, its techniques and its styles. Of the letter's many unusual features, perhaps the most salient is a series of what appear to be strange 'perforations':

[T]hat the fourleaved shamrock or quadrifoil jab was more recurrent wherever the script was clear and the term terse and that these two were the selfsame spots naturally selected for her perforations by Dame Partlet on her dungheap. (124.20–4)

The 'fourleaved shamrock or quadrifoil' 'perforations' that occur where the script is clear have been put there by the hen herself – now in the guise of 'Dame Partlet' from Chaucer's *The Nun's Priest's Tale*. They are thus part of the damage to the letter noted above; these perforations also correspond to the 'wounds, four in type' (124.03) found elsewhere in the letter. In turn, these wounds seem to correspond to 'all those red raddled obeli cayennepeppercast over the text, calling unnecessary attention to errors, omissions, repetitions and misalignments' (120.14–16). These obeli (†) bring the letter into alignment with the Irish ninth century illuminated gospel manuscript, the Book of Kells: on the recto of folio 219, there are four red obeli that run down the middle of the page between the lines, and others around the margins. As such, these obeli thus correspond to the 'cardinal' and 'doubtful points' (112.07–9) also found in the letter.

In their turn, these obeli, insofar as they are also crosses, not only link up with the hen's 'four crosskisses for holy paul holey' (111.17–18) that close the letter, but also, once again, the Book of Kells: 'the cruciform postscript from which three *basia* or shorter and smaller *oscula* have been overcarefully scraped away, plainly inspiring the tenebrous *Tunc* page of the Book of Kells' (122.20–3; *basia* is Latin for passionate kisses; *oscula* is Latin for peck-like kisses). The mention of the '*Tunc*' page of the Book of Kells (124r) is important because it foregrounds a complex mode of reading: the *Tunc* page illustrates the text of the crucifixion of Christ and the two thieves – '*Tunc crucifixerant XPI cum eo duos latrones*' (Latin, 'Then were there two thieves crucified with him') – from Matthew 27.38 in a decorative line of script which itself takes the shape of a cross. This constitutes a rebus – where a picture is used to represent words or parts of words – creating a visual pun where the 'X' of the text echoes both the cipher of Christ (the Greek letter, chi: 'χ') and the cross of Christ's death. In this pun-structure, the text enfolds the 'referent' (here, the 'cross' of Christ's death, and Christ 'himself'), which now appears 'in' a decorative textual form. The mention of the *Tunc* page of the Book of Kells also makes it easier to see how the crosses/holes/wounds/kisses in the letter mimic the larger structure of the letter itself:

> One cannot help noticing that rather more than half of the lines run north-south in the Nemzes and Bukarahast directions while the others go west-east in search from Maliziies with Bulgarad for, tiny tot though it looks when schtschupnistling alongside other incunabula, it has its cardinal points for all that. (114.02–7)

Thus, the rebus-like structure of the letter invites the reader to see the part – the Xs of obeli-crosskisses – in the whole – the letter itself, which can be understood as one large cross – and vice versa.

In short, a reader of the *Wake* who follows the hen reads kinetically, following the hen's criss-crosses both back and forth and up and down, criss-crossing the text – a way of reading that should, of course, be wholly familiar to readers of *Ulysses*; such a reader also reads in a non-linear fashion by 'passing through' the 'perforations' or 'wounds' that the hen puts in the text, which open up other possible passages between its pages; finally, the reader who follows the hen reads 'hologrammatically', insofar as the 'whole' of the *Tunc*-crossed-letter can be read in its 'parts' – the wounds, the kisses, the obeli and so on. And, if part can stand for the whole in the letter, it is perhaps not surprising that the hen's 'polyhedron of scripture' (107.08) can stand for *Wake* itself. This would explain why I.5's description of the language of the letter doubles perfectly for a description of the text as a whole:

> For if the lingo gasped between kicksheets, however basically English, were to be preached from the mouths of wickerchurch-wardens and metaphysicians in the row and advokaatoes, allvoy-ous, demivoyelles, languoaths, lesbiels, dentelles, gutterhowls and furtz, where would their practice be or where the human race itself were the Pythagorean sesquipedalia of the panepistemion, however apically Volapucky, grunted and gromwelled, ichabod, habakuk, opanoff, uggamyg, hapaxle, gomenon, ppppfff, over country stiles, behind slated dwellinghouses, down blind lanes, or, when all fruit fails, under some sacking left on a coarse cart? (116.25–35)

(c) The Words of Others: 'Stolentelling!'

The final aspect of the text that I'd like to discuss here has to do with theft: in I.7, Shem, the writer of the hen's letter is said by his brother Shaun to be 'covetous of his neighbour's word' (172.30). But Shem does not stop at coveting; according to his brother, he sits in 'condign satisfaction' (172.29) in his hovel, surrounded by the echoing frag-ments and 'delicate tippits' (172.32) of 'every crumb of trektalk' (172.30) he can lay his hands on. The words Shem hoards are the very same ones that he writes all over his body in shitty ink (185.27–186.09); this gives these stolen words a 'stinksome inkenstink' that makes them seem 'quite puzzonal to the wrottel' (183.06–7). Thus, it is through the figure of the writer that the stolen words of others merge with the thunder-words of the god to become a sort of 'chambermade music' (184.04) – that is, music made in a chamber-pot. And, by rewriting the thunder-word of the god in shitty ink and the stolen words of others, Shem robs the divine word of its divinity. Shem's inauthentic doubling-distortion of the thunder-word is what seems to provoke Shaun's antipathy towards his brother and his art: for Shaun, Shem's art is unoriginal, a low form of 'bardic memory' (172.28). Shaun's annoyance at his brother grows until book III episode 1, when he angrily denounces the letter that he has to deliver:

> Every dimmed letter in it is a copy and not a few of the silbils and wholly words I can show you in my Kingdom of Heaven. The lowquacity of him! With his threestar monothong! Thaw! The last word in stolentelling! And what's more rightdown lowbrown schisthematic robblemint! (424.17–36)

Shaun's outburst here makes it fairly clear that as interesting as the letter is – and it is truly fascinating – its value does not lie in its ability to help the reader come to the final truth about the whereabouts of Finnegan/HCE and the circumstances surrounding his fall/crime/ disappearance. Rather, the letter's value lies in revealing that the divine word of the god is little more than a Bloomian 'natural phenomenon': a clap of thunder that makes you shit yourself.

Many other scenes of 'stolenetelling' are played out in the *Wake*, but I want to close my all-too-brief look at the text with the one found in II.2. In this scene – which draws on the interplay of the Same and Other in the scene of 'demiurgic' creation from Plato's *Timaeus* (36b–d)[3] – a childish creator named 'Dolph, dean of idlers' (287.18), composes poetry as he lies in his cot. He whiles his time

> chanching letters for them vice o'verse to bronze mottes and blending tschemes for em in tropadores and doublecressing twofold thruths and devising tingling tailwords too whilest, cunctant that another would finish his sentence for him, he druider would smilabit eggways ned, he, to don't say nothing, would, so prim, and pick upon his ten ordinailed ungles, trying to undo with his teeth the knots made by his tongue, retelling humself by the math hour, long as he's brood reel of funnish ficts apout the shee, how faust of all and on segund thoughts and the thirds the charmhim girlalove and fourthermore and filthily with bag from Oxatown and baroccidents and proper accidence and hoptohill and hexenshoes, in fine the whole damning letter; and, in point of feet, when

he landed in ourland's leinster of saved and solomnones for the twicedhecame time. (288.01–14)

Here Dolph uses his fingers to joyously and dextrously recount the stories he has heard from others. Unable to reproduce them perfectly, Dolph gleefully (re)composes the words of others by means of the figure of catachresis, twisting them from their originally intended meaning. Thus, in Dolph's hands, the stories become an elaborate dance of 'funnish ficts' and 'doublecrossing twofold thruths' that are no longer concerned with establishing the prior 'true' meaning of the words of others before they are catachrestically 'changed' through their 'chance' (288.01) similarity to other words. The reader is invited to hear in the chance resemblance of words a poetry that is motivated by a 'tingle' in its 'tailwords', the chime of 'bronze mottes' in complex and seductive tropes ('tropadores'): 'in the muddle is the Sounddance' (378.29–30). Paradoxically, hearing these tingling tailwords also allows the reader to hear the odd 'nothing' (288.06) that Dolph's finger-poetry says. This 'nothing' – which is not simply silence: it is more akin to the 'next to nothing' (005.01) that the 'immargination' works with (004.19) – opens up a space for the reader since Dolph is always 'cunctant' to let another 'finish his sentence for him' (288.04). What the reader 'hears', as s/he stands near Dolph in his crib, is the chiming remainder of the words of others – including Dolph's – the sounds that have been 'left over' after they have been stripped of their intended meaning. This scene, which is also hologrammatic insofar as it can be read as a scene of the *Wake*'s composition, is a fitting one to end on: it suggests that one of the most joyous, challenging, mad-dening, liberating, playful and astoundingly beautiful books ever written could not have been possible – even if it does not always treat them as sacred – without the stolen words of others or the poetic cre-ation of the reader who hears them.

CHAPTER SIX

CONCLUSION: 'WHERE ARE WE AT ALL?'

By way of a conclusion, I would like to offer the reader a brief introduction to recent exciting theoretical approaches to Joyce's work that I have found to be particularly fruitful: queer theory and postcolonial theory. I have found these approaches to be useful for opening up paths into Joyce's texts because they are engaged with ideas and issues that are of interest to new readers of Joyce in the early twenty-first century: desire, sexuality and politics. My aim in offering a brief examination of these theoretical approaches is not to provide an exhaustive discussion of them. Rather, my aim in this concluding chapter is much more modest: I want to (1) offer the reader a glimpse of a couple of the ideas that have guided some of my explorations of Joyce's texts and (2) give the reader a place to start if s/he wishes to pursue such explorations further. This conclusion is in no way intended to offer a final word on how to interpret Joyce; it should go without saying that there are, of course, many other possible approaches to his work. For a list of the other texts that have informed my approach to Joyce in this book, I refer the reader to the list of recommended readings at the end of this chapter.

I

'QUEER JOYCE'

Quare Joyce (edited by Joseph Valente. Ann Arbor: University of Michigan Press, 1998) offers its reader a good introduction to the impact of queer theory on Joyce studies. In order to give the reader a sense of what is at stake in 'quare' or 'queer' readings of Joyce – and what such readings tend to illuminate – I will consider some aspects of the arguments made by the contributors to *Quare Joyce*.[1]

The authors of the essays in *Quare Joyce*, in drawing on the work of theorists of sexuality such as Michel Foucault, Jacques Lacan, Luce Irigaray, Eve Kosofsky Sedgwick, Judith Butler, Jonathan Dollimore and others, offer challenging readings of sexuality and perversity in Joyce's texts. Broadly speaking, the readings collected in this volume share a common aim: they set about disrupting hetero-sexual and heteronormative readings of sexuality and desire in Joyce's work by viewing them through the lens of what has become known as 'queer theory'. Queer theory draws on historical analysis, psycho-analysis, deconstruction and feminism to develop a complex and nuanced way of reading and critiquing the construction of sexuality in texts and culture.

As Joseph Valente makes clear in his introduction to *Quare Joyce*, queer studies is not simply a one-trick pony: queer readings of Joyce's work explore the psychological and cultural aspects of homosexual-ity, same sex desire and homophobia in Joyce's work. Queer readings ask questions about Joyce's engagement with Victorian images and stereotypes of homosexuality, in order to examine whether Joyce's work reinforces or dislodges these stereotypes. Queer readings of Joyce also explore matters relating to the 'closet' and coming out of it – issues of secrecy, concealment, misrecognition and transgression. Finally, queer readings of Joyce's texts explore how those texts engage, reflect, construct and even obscure homosexuality and homosocial desire by considering them in conjunction with a whole host of top-ics familiar to readers of Joyce's works: the scholastic thought of Aquinas, other gay Irish literary and historical icons such as Oscar Wilde and Roger Casement, Irish colonial and British imperial his-tory, psychoanalytic, medical and sexological discourse, and so on (Valente, 1).

Queer readings tend to focus on those numerous passages in Joyce's texts where heterosexuality or heterosexual desire is put into doubt, cut across, dislocated and thwarted by other forms of desire, sexual-ity and perversity. For example, queer readings of *Dubliners* focus on the secrecy surrounding the implied perversity of the relationship between the young narrator and the old priest, Fr Flynn, in 'The Sisters' (Leonard, 77–8). Another common site for queer readings of *Dubliners* is the short story 'An Encounter'. Readings such as Margot Norris's (19–33) examine carefully the strange obvious secrecy that permeates the text of 'An Encounter', a secrecy that at once reveals and obscures the main action of the story – the young narrator's strange behaviour when in the presence of a masturbating paedophile. Still other areas of *Dubliners* that might prove amenable to queer readings would be the construction of heterosexual marriage in stories like 'A Little Cloud', 'The Boarding House', 'Counterparts', 'Grace' and 'The Dead' as a site of dissatisfaction, unfulfilment, alienation and worse.

As stories like 'The Sisters' and 'An Encounter' make clear, Joyce's texts actively engage with the construction of sexuality in and by children, even if that engagement serves to make the reader uncomfortable; queer readings of *Portrait* also examine how homosexuality and homosexual desire shape Stephen's emerging sexuality while at Clongowes. As Valente argues (47–75) and chapter I of *Portrait* clearly suggests, one of Stephen's major experiences of sexuality at Clongowes is an imperfectly grasped second-hand encounter with homosexual behaviour – the 'smugging' incident in the square – and his odd insertion of himself into a fantasized scene of being punished for that behaviour. As Vicki Mahaffey notes (125–7), the early scenes of Stephen's (perhaps traumatic) experiences with sexuality at Clongowes return throughout *Portrait* in the form of the recurrent image of being in a bath of turf-coloured water. Other queer readings of *Portrait* have tended to focus on the long and complex conversation between Stephen and Cranly in chapter V (Valente, 65–7; Castle, 177–80), in which they both seem to leave a certain same-sex desire unspoken. Obviously, this desire is never consummated; it thus remains a desire.

When it comes to *Ulysses*, queer readings can usefully illuminate the vast – but ultimately unsatisfying – network of possible sexual objects. Jean-Michel Rabaté explores Joyce's ambivalent stance towards homoeroticism (35–7), which, according to Rabaté, is neatly illustrated by a section of Stephen's discourse on Shakespeare and paternity in 'Scylla and Charybdis':

> They [father and son] are sundered by a bodily shame so steadfast that the criminal annals of the world, stained with all other incests and bestialities, hardly record its breach. Sons with mothers, sires with daughters, lesbic sisters, loves that dare not speak their name, nephews with grandmothers, jailbirds with keyholes, queens with prize bulls. (9.850–4)

Stephen, insofar as he connects homosexuality here to father-son incest, distances it from all the other forms of 'perversion' he lists; at the same time, Stephen places homosexuality – the 'love that dare not speak its name' – on the side of the other 'perversions' in which desire extends to all manner of objects in the familial, animal and mechanical realms. Homosexuality thus appears as a way of opening up a discussion of a more general 'perversion' and desire that is no longer simply focused on a heterosexual or even animate object in Joyce's work (see also Mahaffey, 124). Elsewhere, Rabaté discusses the copious links that join and sunder Wilde's and Joyce's works, as does Vicki Mahaffey (121–36). Other queer readings of *Ulysses* have focused on the ramifications of Mr Bloom's designation as a 'new womanly man' (15.1898–9), and Colleen Lamos examines the dramatic transformation of the brothel keeper Bella Cohen into the 'shemale' Bello (192–7). Jennifer Levine explores 'Eumaeus' by considering closely two of the tattoos that adorn the chest of Murphy, the old red-headed sailor that Mr Bloom and Stephen meet in the cabman's shelter: the number 16 – which is itself European slang for homosexuality – and the likeness of a Greek – a word associated in *Ulysses* with homosexuality – named 'Antonio' (101–20).

Queer readings of *Finnegans Wake* are openly invited by the remorseless ambiguity that surrounds Finnegan/HCE's fall/crime in the Phoenix Park in I.1: because the crime/fall has both homosexual and heterosexual components to it – Finnegan/HCE spies on two young women as they urinate and shows his backside to three passing soldiers (008.08–010.23) – the crime/fall fuses homosexual and heterosexual desire, making it next to impossible to separate them. As Jean-Michel Rabaté notes (42), this also has the effect of radically generalizing homosexual desire throughout the book:

> We've heard it aye since songdom was gemurrmal. As he was queering his shoolthers. So was I. And as I was cleansing my fausties. So was he. And as way ware puffiing our blowbags. Souwouyou. (251.36–252.03)

This passage's mention of 'queering shoolthers' or 'soldiers' echoes another famous passage that queer readings of the *Wake* tend to focus on: the television programme in II.3, which features the story of how a soldier named Buckley shot a Russian general as he bent over to wipe his backside with a sod of turf (337.32–355.07). The general's exposure of his backside clearly recalls the sexual ambiguity of Finnegan/HCE's fall/crime in the Phoenix Park. Robert L. Caserio examines this episode (145–8), while Colleen Lamos (203–10) focuses on Issy – the daughter of HCE and ALP who repeatedly splits in two – and her insistent association with lesbianism throughout the text.

Queer readings of Joyce's texts, because they make it possible to explore how those texts repeatedly uncouple reproduction from sexuality and insert anxiety, alienation and dissatisfaction into the pursuit of heterosexual objects and desires, are perhaps most useful to a reader of Joyce because they highlight the complexity and uncanniness of the field of desire, sex and perversion found in his texts, while offering the reader a series of critical tools for negotiating that field. It is thus not the case that queer readings of Joyce's work try and reconfigure Joyce as a 'secret homosexual' who must be outed. What queer readings of Joyce's texts highlight is the fact that in those texts desire and sexuality cannot be easily reduced to either 'hetero' or 'homo': desire, gender and sexuality remain, for the most part, mobile forces, resistant to any easy categorization. It is perhaps too simple to say that Joyce's texts are 'gay positive'; but their insistent scepticism regarding successful male-female sexual intimacy does not preclude – indeed, it often invites – readings that see in that lack of success the spectres or possibilities of still other forms of non-hetero desires. However, this is not to say that these other desires would or should be more 'successful' than heterosexual ones. In short, the value of queer readings lies in their ability to show the reader of Joyce that desire is a force that constantly confronts the reader with questions and problems relating to consent, seduction, manipulation and satisfaction in the fields of gender and sexuality.

II

'POSTCOLONIAL JOYCE'

The other recent theoretical development within Joyce studies that has proved to be as exciting and challenging as queer readings of Joyce is the movement towards postcolonial readings of Joyce. Simply put, postcolonial analyses tend to focus on issues relating to the politics of nationalism and colonialism in literary and cultural texts. In this section, in order to give the reader a flavour of the issues and topics of postcolonial readings of Joyce, I will consider two books in particular: the first is an edited collection, *Semicolonial Joyce* (edited by Derek Attridge and Marjorie Howes. Cambridge: Cambridge University Press, 2000)[2] and the second is Emer Nolan's *James Joyce and Nationalism* (London: Routledge, 1995). Once again, my consideration of these texts is merely intended to give the reader a flavour of what is at stake in postcolonial readings of Joyce.[3]

Postcolonial readings of *Dubliners* tend to explore those moments in the text where the inhabitants of the city of Dublin seem to be regarded as unsophisticated, provincial, backward or simply unmodern. In *Dubliners* these traits are often complicated by the sense that Dubliners seem to be somewhat 'grateful' for their oppression by the British Empire because it allows them to remain as they are. Seamus Deane neatly illustrates this view of Dubliners in his essay in *Semicolonial Joyce* by pointing to the short story 'After the Race' (21): the Dublin crowd that watches the fast motor-cars that represent the 'wealth and industry' of 'the Continent' race through their own little 'channel of poverty and inaction' only manages to raise the cheer of the 'gratefully oppressed' (D 35). Joyce's text, in other words, sets up continental Europe as the place of modernity, power, wealth and industry, all of which are due in no small part to imperial histories; at the same time, the countries of Europe that the racing cars represent – France, Germany and Belgium – are allied with 'Humanity' (D 39). Dublin – and by extension Ireland – in contrast, remains a place that is 'traditional', 'backward'; instead of having 'Humanity' and culture, Ireland has only an unsavoury petty and provincial nationalistic politics – a thought that is echoed by both Little Chandler in 'A Little Cloud' and Gabriel Conroy in 'The Dead'. As Deane also points out (27–33), the text's opposition of a 'backward' Ireland and its provincial political woes to a much more powerful, 'sophisticated' and 'modern' other, resurfaces in 'Ivy Day in the Committee Room', which opposes Parnell, the now dead 'Uncrowned King' (D 131) of Ireland, to King Edward VII, the crowned king of the British Empire. Now that Parnell is dead, according to Mr Henchy, it would seem that the only alternative is to embrace King Edward; not to do so is to not be 'fair', and remain one of those 'wild Irish' (D 129). However, that those who represent 'Humanity' and colonial modernity do not emerge very well from these stories suggests that *Dubliners* remains attuned, in a manner that is perhaps akin to Stephen's rejection of the pretensions of universal brotherhood (P 215), to the political power that masks itself with the ideas of 'Humanity' and 'fairness'.

Given that Parnell's ghost returns to haunt chapter I of *Portrait*, that text clearly invites an extension of the sort of postcolonial analysis carried out by Deane in relation to *Dubliners*. *Portrait* stages the complex intersections of sexuality, politics and religion in Irish society in the final decade of the nineteenth century. Politics, in the form of Parnell's ghost, cannot be kept at bay; it invades the domestic sphere and destroys the idyllic scene of the Dedalus family Christmas dinner, tearing it to shreds. As Marjorie Howes points out, Irish politics also marks Stephen's time at school, where he is subjected to forces that incessantly ask him to recognize Ireland as his 'nation' (71), and which eventually threaten to take on the religious authority of the school in a 'rebellion' (P 44). This would seem to suggest that, while young at least, Stephen and his schoolmates display the potential to be the potential heirs of Parnell in their shared desire to overthrow the school's religious authority. The fleetingness of their potential is, however, underlined ironically in chapter V of *Portrait*, when the shade of Parnell returns once again. This time, Stephen is forced to reject Davin's construction of Irish nationalism because of the narrow construction of sexuality it embraces. But, as I suggested above, and as Howes also argues (73–4), Stephen's 'rejection' of Irish nationalism is partial and ambivalent: as chapter V makes clear, he still wishes to 'hit' the conscience of the 'patricians of Ireland' (P 258) and 'cast his shadow over the imaginations of their daughters' (P 259). Thus, sex, politics and their messy entanglements, it would seem, are never really very far from the artist's mind.

As Enda Duffy points out in his postcolonial essay on *Ulysses* (37–57), most of that text was written after the shelling of the city centre of Dublin during the 1916 Easter Rising – the failed rebellion against British Imperial rule in Ireland – by a British gunboat on the River Liffey (37). The shelling, Duffy notes, destroyed several of the streets north of the Liffey along which Mr Bloom walks in 'Lestrygonians'; particularly interesting is the destruction of Little Britain Street – the setting of Mr Bloom's encounter with the citizen in 'Cyclops' (Duffy, 37–8). *Ulysses*, insofar as it reconstructs these streets, can thus be read as a partial remaking of the city in the wake of the destruction caused by an anti-colonial uprising: its text is thus consciously and unconsciously saturated by issues of colonialism.

Through the figure of Mr Bloom, *Ulysses* can also be seen to revisit the sort of political questioning of the notions of 'Humanity' and 'universal brotherhood' begun in *Dubliners* and continued in *Portrait*. For example, in episode 5 – 'The Lotus Eaters' – Mr Bloom ponders the relations between religion and colonialism – the same two masters that Stephen has been grappling with since 'Telemachus':[4]

> Same notice on the door. Sermon by the very reverend John Conmee S.J. on saint Peter Claver S.J. and the African Mission. Prayers for the conversion of Gladstone they had too when he was almost unconscious. The protestants are the same. Convert Dr William J. Walsh D.D. to the true religion. Save China's millions. (5.322–6)

Here, Mr Bloom's thoughts make it clear that imperial expansions into countries such as Africa and China are often accompanied by spiritual imperialism. This same motif returns later in 'The Wandering Rocks' where we find the same Fr Conmee ruminating on his sermon:

> Father Conmee thought of the souls of black and brown and yellow men and of his sermon on saint Peter Claver S.J. and the African mission and of the propagation of the faith and of the millions of black and brown and yellow souls that had not received the baptism of water when their last hour came like a thief in the night. (10.143–7)

Fr Conmee's patronizing way of referring to the inhabitants of Africa, India and China is ironically underlined by his thoughts about the 'colour' that their unbaptized souls would retain after death; the implication here is that those 'coloured' souls never got the chance to be washed 'white'.

Finally, another common area of focus for postcolonial readings of *Ulysses* is episode 12 – 'Cyclops' – in which Mr Bloom confronts the citizen. As I suggested above, it is perhaps more useful to regard the citizen as a thorny figure that embodies the complications and contradictions of Irish cultural nationalism in the first years of the twentieth century, rather than simply seeing him, as a lot of Joyce criticism has done, as a mindless thug. As I also suggested above, following Emer Nolan's much needed reconsideration of the citizen in her *James Joyce and Nationalism*, Mr Bloom's invocation of 'love' as a cure for all of Ireland's political ills is perhaps too naïve; Mr Bloom's political naïveté in 'Cyclops' seems all the more puzzling, especially when considered alongside his awareness in episode 5 of the role 'love' can play in colonial domination. Other postcolonial examinations of 'Cyclops', such as Joseph Valente's in *Semicolonial Joyce* (96–127), have focused on the 'masculinity' of the figures of the citizen and Mr Bloom in order to investigate how late Victorian and early Edwardian constructions of manhood could be used by colonial power to designate Irishness as both bestial and feminine for political purposes.

Just like *Dubliners*, *Portrait* and *Ulysses*, *Finnegans Wake* has also functioned as a site for postcolonial readings, and these readings, including Emer Nolan's in chapter 5 of her *James Joyce and Nationalism*, have to adopt something of a double focus: on the one hand, they attend to the *Wake*'s incessant disruption and dislocation of the notion of pristine national languages, secure national identities and so forth; on the other, they have to keep a wary eye on the coercive force of seemingly innocent notions of 'universality', 'humanity', 'civilization' and even 'love', which, as Joyce's texts make clear, can very often conceal imperial – British and/or Roman – tendencies and agendas. Thus, postcolonial readings of the *Wake* seek to, as it were, bring back into focus what Nolan calls the 'specific' Irish history that Joyce draws into his writing (141). In this way, Nolan argues, a postcolonial reading of the *Wake* would attempt to disrupt the treatment of Ireland's long history of historical invasions in which the specifics of cultural and political domination appear to be naturalized or neutralized as either an artistic or psychological 'metaphor' – something, she points out, that is quite common in analyses of the *Wake* – and thereby write Irish history and the struggle for independence back into both the *Wake* and *Wake* criticism.

***

Sex and politics, then: two ways of approaching Joyce's texts, two ways of making them alive in a way that remains wary of notions like universalism and heterosexual love that have acted as guiding lights for certain types of Joycean criticism in the past. Reading Joyce through these lenses tends to keep a reader on his/her toes, preventing him or her from ever coming to a rest. And this is perhaps

apt: reading Joyce is kinetic because, as Joyce's texts themselves constantly suggest, a reader of Joyce is already a *re-reader* of Joyce, tracing and retracing non-linear pathways through jungles of words.
Re-reading Joyce does not – and should not – make one a 'slave' to
Joyce's texts for two reasons: (1) without interested, motivated and
enthusiastic readers who are not afraid to give his texts a good shake,
there would no longer be any 'Joyce' at all – when all is said and done,
he needs us just as much as we need him; (2) it is by re-reading Joyce
that the re-reader imaginatively makes Joyce's texts anew, makes
Joyce's texts fresh, exciting and relevant. I can think of no better way
to respond to his gifts.

NOTES

1. INTRODUCING JOYCE: REALISM AND EPIPHANY IN *DUBLINERS*

1 Charles Stewart Parnell (1846–1891). Parnell was the head of the Irish Parliamentary Party which lobbied for Irish Home Rule, the establishment of an Irish legislative body with responsibility for domestic affairs. He was forced from politics due to a divorce scandal. For more on Parnell, see Chapter 2, below.

2 *Stephen Hero*, eds John J Slocum and Herbert Cahoon (London: Paladin, 1991). Cited in the text as SH.

3 It is also this aspect of *Dubliners* that opens it onto Mr Bloom's and Stephen's contemplation of the vast scales of cosmic movement in *Ulysses* and the strange presence/absence of the figure of Finnegan in *Finnegans Wake*. I will return to this aspect of Mr Bloom's and Stephen's characters in my discussion of *Ulysses* below. Given all this crossover between *Dubliners* and Joyce's later texts, it is perhaps not surprising that *Ulysses* was first conceived of by Joyce as short story for inclusion in *Dubliners* round about the same time as he began to write 'The Dead' (1907).

2. *A PORTRAIT OF THE ARTIST AS A YOUNG MAN*: THE SEXUAL POLITICS OF ART

1 The movement of 'hither and thither' is an important motif in the text: it returns on pages 148, 165 and 183–6.

2 As Deane notes, the quote should read: 'A day of dappled breeze-borne clouds'.

3 It is worth noting that when Lynch later spots Cranly in a café with Emma and her brother, Stephen writes a somewhat cryptic entry in his diary insisting that he 'discovered him. [. . .] Shining quietly behind a bushel of Wicklow bran' (P 273).

3. READING *ULYSSES* I: FROM 'TELEMACHUS' TO 'THE WANDERING ROCKS'

1 Earlier versions of the schema were given to Valery Larbaud and Carlo Linati, both associates of Joyce, in 1921. For a discussion of the Linati and Gilbert schemas and Joyce's ambivalence about making them public, see Ellmann, *James Joyce*, 519–21.

2 It has often been noted that Mulligan is conducting a black mass, which was usually celebrated using a woman's body as an altar: the woman in question here is an uneasy combination of the sea – which Mulligan repeatedly refers to throughout this episode as a mother – and Stephen's mother.

3 See Ellmann, *James Joyce*, 519–20.

4 Stephen has been in mourning for his mother for over a year. This makes him into a Hamlet-like figure, who mourns excessively for his mother, not his father. The Hamlet motif recurs throughout episodes 1–3, but it gets extensive treatment in Stephen's theory about Shakespeare in episode 9.

5 The song appears in W B Yeats's 1892 play, *The Countess Cathleen*.

6 At the time in which *Ulysses* was set, Ireland was, as a result of the Act of Union (1800), a part of the United Kingdom of Great Britain and Ireland. It remained so until in 1922 when it was partitioned and the southern 26 counties became the Irish Free State. It did not become an independent republic until 1949.

7 The text from the Preface runs: 'The nineteenth century dislike of Realism is the rage of Caliban at seeing his face in a glass. The nineteenth century dislike of Romanticism is the rage of Caliban at not seeing his face in a glass.' Caliban is, of course, the famously ugly and violent character from Shakespeare's *The Tempest*. See Gifford also.

8 I want to note here that the concept of a 'perfect', 'complete' or 'true' art is something that *Ulysses* subjects to considerable pressure throughout its text, as I will argue momentarily.

9 This is not to say simply that Ireland would not benefit from 'Hellenisation'. Such an assertion would be absurd, especially given the book's title, *Ulysses*, which would obviously be in keeping (in some part) with such a project. Rather, it seems that Mulligan's subservient version of 'Hellenisation' is what is criticized by the text.

10 Stephen, in conversation with Haines some three-hundred lines later, explicitly outlines his subservience to his colonial, religious and household masters: 'I am a servant of two masters, Stephen said, an English and an Italian . . . and a third . . . who wants me for odd jobs' (1.638–41).

11 'Silk of the kine', meaning 'the most beautiful of cattle', is taken from '*An Druimfhionn Donn Dilis*', an old Irish song about Ireland. The 'poor old woman' is a translation of '*An Sean Bhean Bhocht*', the title of another old Irish ballad about the 1798 United Irishmen rebellion.

12 Gifford gives the translation of the Latin as: 'May the glittering throng of confessors, bright as lilies, gather about you. May the glorious choir of virgins receive you'.

13 I note in passing that Maimonides's book also recalls – spookily enough – the title of the series of which the book you are now holding in your hands is a part.

14 The Italian, '*maestro di color che sanno*', is from Dante's description of Aristotle in the *Inferno*: 'master of those that know'.

15 I have here modified the Gabler edition of *Ulysses* to bring it into line with the 1922 edition which was published during Joyce's lifetime. The lines of

verse that Stephen speaks to himself lack complete iambic feet because they have an uneven amount of syllables: they are thus missing syllables and are *catalectic*. If these lines were *acatalectic*, they would not be missing these syllables. The choice of between 'A catalectic' or 'Acatalectic' produced some controversy just before Gabler's edition appeared in 1984.

16 It is worth noting here that Wilde had hit upon a similar conception of the self in his *The Picture of Dorian Gray*: the 'self' is an odd amalgam of one's ancestors and one's identification with artistic figures in art and literature.

17 Stephen is also acutely aware of how his gestures are citations of other people's as well: 'That is Kevin Egan's movement I made, nodding for his nap, sabbath sleep' (3.438–9). This also brings Stephen into contact with the construction of femininity in episode 13, which is also shown to be a series of quotations and citations.

18 The translation appears in Hyde's *Love Songs of Connacht* (Dublin 1895). Part of Hyde's translation runs: 'And my love came behind me-/He came from the South/His breast to my bosom,/His mouth to my mouth'.

19 This is thus an obvious point of connection with *Portrait*.

20 Kabala, or Kabbalah, is a Judaic form of mysticism made up of a set of esoteric teachings on the Hebrew Bible and traditional Rabbinic literature.

21 This motif returns in 'Aeolus' when Stephen hands over the remainder of Mr Deasy's letter on foot and mouth to the newspaper editor after having torn off a piece in episode 3 to write down his poem. The editor, noting that the sheet has been torn, asks if Deasy 'was short taken' (7.521). The text thus suggests that Stephen's poem is also shit.

22 An enthymeme is an informal syllogism in which one of the premises is implied or is only probable, rather than true for all cases. It is often used for comic or rhetorical effect. An example would be (with apologies to Mark Twain): There is no law against musicians with no talent. Therefore the music of Nickleback is legal. (The implication is that Nickleback have no talent.)

23 Gifford offers an annotated list of these techniques (635–43).

24 Stephen also hears these echoes when he recites to himself the piece of poetry he composed earlier on the beach: 'Mouth, south. Is the mouth south someway? Or the south a mouth? Must be some. South, pout, out, shout, drouth. Rhymes: two men dressed the same, looking the same, two by two' (7.713–16).

25 That Irishness and Jewishness are similar is something underlined by the text in episode 7: perhaps the best example of this in 'Aeolus' is Professor MacHugh's recitation of a version of a speech given in 1901 by the Irish barrister, orator and journalist John F Taylor (1850–1902) on the subject of the revival of the Irish language (7.828–69). MacHugh's version of the speech explicitly fuses Irishness and Jewishness.

26 Hugh Kenner in his *Ulysses* (2nd edn. Baltimore: Johns Hopkins University Press, 1987) notes that David Hayman was the first to dwell on this mysterious figure (65).

27 The Arranger also seems to insert a parody of Dickens at 7.763–5. This obviously anticipates the later textual intrusions in the text. I will return to this below.

28 This distancing had already begun in episode 6 when Martin Cunningham and Mr Power discuss Mr Bloom's father's suicide (6.526–34; see also 6.690–707).

29 It is also worth noting here that the three whiskeys (9.533) that Stephen had after 'Aeolus' are taking something of a toll on the coherence of his theorizing: he endows Shakespeare's father, John Shakespeare – a mere man – with the ability to pass on the mystical estate of fatherhood (9.835–6), even though he insists in practically the next breath that it is unknown to man (9. 837–9).

30 Stephen has already wondered about the 'word known to all men' (3.435); at 9.429, Stephen says that the word in question is 'love'; however, at 15.4192–3, he asks his mother if she knows what word is known to all men: she does not tell Stephen. Note that the lines including 9.429ff. are not found in any other edition of the text: they were – controversially – restored by Gabler in his edition of the text.

31 That is, fifth earl of Rutland, Francis Bacon and the third earl of Southampton.

32 One might also note that Stephen's two masters – one Roman, one English – resurface in episode 10 in the form of Conmee and Humble. They may thus be read as two of the Wandering Rocks that Stephen must avoid.

33 Over the years many Joyceans have been tempted to see Miss Dunne as the 'real' Martha Clifford – the woman to whom Mr Bloom has been secretly writing dirty letters. It is usually noted that 'Marion' is Molly's formal name and that Miss Dunne is a typist just like Martha Clifford. However, one must be careful not to rush to identify Miss Dunne with Martha: 'Marian' (not 'Marion') is also the name of a major character in Collins's novel. It would seem then, that the text is playing a game with the reader, sending the odd small wandering rock his or her way just in case the textual voyage goes too smoothly. Another famous jolt occurs later in the text when a different 'Mr Bloom' pops up: Almidano Artifoni, an Italian music teacher, walks past Mr Bloom's dental windows (10.1115).

4. READING *ULYSSES* II: FROM 'SIRENS' TO 'PENELOPE'

1 I will leave the fun of tracking down the recurrences of the textual fragments that constitute the prelude in the main body of the episode to the reader. However, wherever these fragments recur in my discussion of the episode, I will highlight them in **bold**.

2 This is, of course, not to say that the reader of *Ulysses* can always win at this game: on the contrary, as episodes such as 'Hades' and 'The Wandering Rocks' show, the text does not yield answers to every enigma. Joyceans are still asking questions about the identity of the mysterious man in the

macintosh and the relationship between Martha Clifford and Miss Dunne. Even the reader's failure to solve a riddle is accounted for by the text.

3 Further information on T Cooke and the song 'Love and War' has proven to be difficult to track down.

4 The loss of sense and the emergence of rhythm is also something Stephen grapples with in the final chapter of *Portrait*: there words disband – in a manner not unlike Mr Bloom's elastic band – themselves into rhythms without meaning, a process that allows Stephen to see the word 'ivory' to shine as a word (P 193). See also Chapter 2 above.

5 Emer Nolan's *James Joyce and Nationalism* (London: Routledge, 1995) is a landmark study in this respect. In particular, see her excellent analysis of the citizen in chapter 3. See also Enda Duffy's admirable *The Subaltern 'Ulysses'* (Minneapolis: University of Minnesota Press, 1994).

6 This may be one of the many hints given in the text regarding Mr Bloom's inclination towards sado-masochism, which emerges full force in 'Circe'.

7 On a related note, the narrator also seems to express some sympathy for the victim of a brutal lynching in the American state of Georgia, where the mob spent some time shooting at the corpse of the dead man (12.1324–8).

8 It is also worth noting that the final paragraphs of this chapter certainly do seem to herald what *Finnegans Wake* will do to English.

9 This 'whore' recalls, of course, the bird-girl Stephen encounters on Dollymount Strand in chapter IV of *Portrait*.

10 It is also worth noting here that the couple that emerges from the hedge in front of Father Conmee in 'The Wandering Rocks' has now been identified as Lynch and his female 'acquaintance'.

11 The text also plants clues about Stephen's potential to read beyond his perverted transcendentalism: in 'Scylla and Charybdis' he refers to his initials – SD – as standing for '*sua donna*' – Italian for 'his woman', while in 'Proteus' he remembers taking delight in being able to fit his foot into a woman's shoe. These two scenes can be seen in the light of Mr Bloom's change of sex in 'Circe' and his partial experiments with cross-dressing. It is also worth noting that despite his sexual fluidity, Mr Bloom still holds some stereotypical views on gender. In this respect, it seems clear that time has left its mark on the text.

12 It is interesting to note that a great deal of the olfactory imagery surrounding Bloom's encounter with Bella/Bello – dung, circuses, fish, onions and so on – recalls the language of *Sweets of Sin*, the book that Mr Bloom buys in episode 10: 'Warmth showered gently over him, cowing his flesh. Flesh yielded amply amid rumpled clothes: whites of eyes swooning up. His nostrils arched themselves for prey. Melting breast ointments (*for him! for Raoul!*). Armpits' oniony sweat. Fishgluey slime (*her heaving embonpoint!*). Feel! Press! Chrished! Sulphur dung of lions!' (10.619–23).

13 It would seem that Mr Bloom's trouserbutton is akin to the moly given Odysseus by Hermes in the *Odyssey*.

14 It will be remembered that the crack of thunder in episode 14 terrifies Stephen because he hears in its divine retribution, whereas Mr Bloom

hears only a natural phenomenon: the difference in their reactions under-lines Stephen's continuing thralldom to religion and the terrors it can hold and Mr Bloom's quasi-scientific outlook.

15 According to Gifford, the reference to Saint Joseph's sovereign thievery here may have something to do with Saint Joseph's 'usurpation' of God's place on earth insofar as he appeared to be Jesus's father.

16 Mr Bloom plays anagramatically with the name of 'Plumtree's Potted Meat', to conjure up 'imitators' of the brand: Peatmot. Trumplee. Moutpat. Plamtroo' (17.604–5).

17 It is also interesting to note that one of Molly's reasons for being annoyed with Boylan during their sexual encounter is due to his not remaining in her control during her elaborately staged scene of seduction (18.1371–5). Once again the text underlines the scripted nature of male and female sexuality.

5. THE LANGUAGE(S) AND STRUCTURE(S) OF *FINNEGANS WAKE*

1 All references to *The New Science* given here follow the convention of using paragraph numbers.

2 See also Bishop's fascinating discussion in *Joyce's Book of the Dark* (Madison: University of Wisconsin Press, 1986), pages 28, 142 and Roland McHugh, *The Sigla of* Finnegans Wake (Austin: University of Texas Press, 1976), 103.

3 Joyce filters this creation through Yeats' use of the *Timaeus* in *A Vision*. See McHugh, *Sigla*, 72–3.

6. CONCLUSION: 'WHERE ARE WE AT ALL?'

1 All citations from *Quare Joyce* are given in the text in conjunction with the essay author's name.

2 As with *Quare Joyce*, all citations from *Semicolonial Joyce* are given in the text in conjunction with the essay author's name.

3 This is not to say, however, that there are not drawbacks with postcolo-nial readings of Joyce: it can sometimes seem that postcolonialism's suspicion of the imagination and its designation of imagined solutions to political problems – something derived from its Marxist roots – as 'impotent' (*James Joyce and Nationalism*, 160) is perhaps short sighted, since it appears to assume that the imagination and the political are in simple opposition: for an attempt to reconfigure the imagination beyond such an inscription of it, see my *Imagining Joyce and Derrida: Between Finnegans Wake and Glas* (Toronto; Buffalo; London: University of Toronto Press, 2007).

4 On this point, see also Marjorie Howes's essay 'Joyce, colonialism and nationalism', pages 254–71 in *The Cambridge Companion to James Joyce* (2nd edn; ed. Derek Attridge. Cambridge: Cambridge University Press, 2004).

SUGGESTED FURTHER READING

The following list is absolutely not intended to be exhaustive: I have picked those books that have proved to be helpful for my readings of Joyce both here and elsewhere. I hope they prove to be as useful and enjoyable to new readers of Joyce's texts as they have been to me.

JOYCE'S BIOGRAPHY

Ellmann, Richard. *James Joyce*. New York: Oxford UP, 1982.
Joyce, Stanislaus. *My Brother's Keeper: James Joyce's Early Years*. New York: Viking Press, 1958.
O'Brien, Edna. *James Joyce*. London: Weidenfeld & Nicolson, 1999.

Although Ellmann's book is considered the standard, Joyce's brother's biography remains entertaining. O'Brien's biography offers a refreshing perspective.

GENERAL INTRODUCTIONS TO JOYCE'S WORK

Attridge, Derek, ed. *The Cambridge Companion to James Joyce*. Second Edition. Cambridge: Cambridge UP, 2004.
Eco, Umberto. *The Aesthetics of Chaosmos: The Middle Ages of James Joyce*. Trans. Ellen Esrock. Cambridge: Harvard UP, 1989.
Kenner, Hugh. *Joyce's Voices*. Berkeley: U of California P, 1978.
Mahaffey, Vicki. *Reauthorizing Joyce*. Cambridge: Cambridge UP, 1988.
Nadel, Ira. *Joyce and the Jews: Culture and Texts*. Iowa City: U of Iowa P, 1989.
Senn, Fritz. *Inductive Scrutinies: Focus on Joyce*. Baltimore: Johns Hopkins UP, 1995.
—. *Joyce's Dislocutions: Essays on Reading as Translation*. Baltimore: Johns Hopkins UP, 1984.

Attridge's *Companion* offers the reader several contexts for reading Joyce's works. Eco's book provides a thoroughly entertaining exploration of Joyce's debt to the scholarship of the Middle Ages. Kenner,

Mahaffey and Senn are masterful readers of twists, turns and minu-
tiae of Joyce's texts, while Nadel's book does an excellent job of looking at the Jewish contexts of Joyce's work.

JOYCE AND HIS WORK IN THE CONTEXT OF IRISH AND EUROPEAN POLITICS AND CULTURE

Hofheinz, Thomas C. *Joyce and the Invention of Irish History*: Finnegans
Wake *in Context*. Cambridge: Cambridge UP, 1995.

Leonard, Garry. *Advertising and Commodity Culture in Joyce*. Gainesville:
UP of Florida, 1998.

Mahaffey, Vicki. *States of Desire: Wilde, Yeats, Joyce, and the Irish Experiment*. Oxford: Oxford UP, 1998.

Rabaté, Jean-Michel. *James Joyce, Authorized Reader.* Baltimore: Johns
Hopkins UP, 1991.

—. *James Joyce and the Politics of Egoism*. Cambridge: Cambridge UP,
2001.

Wolfreys, Julian, John Brannigan and Geoff Ward. *Re: Joyce: Text, Culture,
Politics.* Basingstoke: Macmillan, 1998.

Taken together, all of the above books provide vital and valuable
information and analysis regarding the complex dialectical relations
between Joyce's life and texts and Irish and European artistic, political and cultural practices.

JOYCE'S INDIVIDUAL WORKS

All of the following books have informed and influenced me in reading Joyce's individual texts. I cannot recommend these books highly
enough. They should be chewed over, savoured and swallowed. Books
such as Gifford's Ulysses *Annotated* and McHugh's *Annotations to*
Finnegans Wake are absolutely indispensable for new, intermediate
and advanced readers of Joyce.

Dubliners

Norris, Margot. *Suspicious Readings of Joyce's* Dubliners. Philadelphia:
U of Pennsylvania P, 2003.

A Portrait of the Artist as a Young Man

Wollaeger, Mark A. *James Joyce's* A Portrait of the Artist as a Young Man:
A Casebook. Oxford: Oxford UP, 2003.

Ulysses

Gifford, Don. Ulysses *Annotated: Notes for James Joyce's* Ulysses. Berkeley: U of California P, 1988.

Gilbert, Stuart. *James Joyce's* Ulysses; *A Study.* London: Faber and Faber, 1952.

Groden, Michael. Ulysses *in Progress.* Princeton: Princeton UP, 1977.

Kenner, Hugh. *Ulysses.* Baltimore: Johns Hopkins UP, 1987.

Knowles, Sebastian D. G. *The Dublin Helix: The Life of Language in Joyce's* Ulysses. Gainsville, UP of Florida, 2001.

Finnegans Wake

Atherton, James S. *The Books at the* Wake. London: Faber and Faber, 1959.

Beckett, Samuel, *et al. Our Exagmination Round his Factification for Incamination of Work in Progress, with Letters of Protest by G. V. L. Slingsby and Vladimir Dixon.* London: Faber and Faber, 1929.

Bishop, John. *Joyce's Book of the Dark.* Madison: U of Wisconsin P, 1986.

Crispi, Luca and Sam Slote, eds. *How Joyce Wrote* Finnegans Wake: *A Chapter-by-Chapter Genetic Guide.* Madison: U of Wisconsin P, 2007.

Eco, Umberto. *The Aesthetics of Chaosmos: The Middle Ages of James Joyce.* Trans. Ellen Esrock. Cambridge: Harvard UP, 1989.

Glasheen, Adaline. *Third Census of* Finnegans Wake: *An Index of the Characters and Their Roles.* Berkeley: U of California P, 1977.

Gordon, John. Finnegans Wake: *A Plot Summary.* Dublin: Gill and Macmillan 1986.

Hart, Clive. *Structure and Motif in* Finnegans Wake. London: Faber and Faber, 1962.

McHugh, Roland. *The Sigla of* Finnegans Wake. Austin: U of Texas P, 1976.

—. *Annotations to* Finnegans Wake (3rd edn) Baltimore: Johns Hopkins UP, 2005.

Rose, Danis and John O' Hanlon. *Understanding* Finnegans Wake: *A Guide to the Narrative of James Joyce's Masterpiece.* New York: Garland, 1982.

Verene, Donald Phillip, ed. *Vico and Joyce.* Albany: State U of New York P, 1987.

JOYCE AND THEORY

There have been many books written on theoretical approaches to Joyce. Once again, the following list of books is not intended to be exhaustive: I have confined myself to those books and approaches that I have found useful in opening up Joyce's texts: poststructuralism, deconstruction, semiotics, psychoanalysis, postcolonialism, feminism and queer studies (for a more detailed discussion of queer and postcolonial readings of Joyce's work, see Chapter 6, above). It should be noted, however, that theoretical readings of Joyce have unfortunately produced something of a sharp, and sometimes alto-gether unfriendly division in Joyce studies. Thankfully, there have been some generous souls who have managed to combine the best from the older, more traditional exegetical studies of Joyce's work with newer theoretical approaches. Practically this entire list of sug-gested further reading is populated with their work.

Poststructuralism

Attridge, Derek and Daniel Ferrer, eds. *Post-structuralist Joyce: Essays from the French*. Cambridge: Cambridge UP, 1984.

—. *Joyce Effects: On Language, Theory and History*. Cambridge: Cambridge UP, 2000.

MacCabe, Colin. *James Joyce and the Revolution of the Word*. London: Macmillan, 1978.

Milesi, Laurent ed. *James Joyce and the Difference of Language*. Cambridge: Cambridge UP, 2003.

Deconstruction

Mahon, Peter. *Imagining Joyce and Derrida: Between* Finnegans Wake *and* Glas. Toronto: U of Toronto P, 2007.

Roughley, Alan. *Reading Derrida Reading Joyce*. Gainesville: UP of Florida, 1999.

Sailer, Susan Shaw. *On the Void of To Be: Incoherence and Trope in* Finnegans Wake. Ann Arbor: U of Michigan P, 1993.

Sartiliot, Claudette. *Citation and Modernity: Derrida, Joyce, and Brecht*. Norman: U of Oklahoma P, 1993.

Semiotics

Weir, Lorraine. *Writing Joyce: A Semiotics of the Joyce System*. Bloomington: Indiana UP, 1989.

Psychoanalysis

Brivic, Sheldon. *Joyce's Waking Women: An Introduction to* Finnegans Wake. Madison: U of Wisconsin P, 1995.

Brown, Norman Oliver. *Closing Time*. New York, Random House, 1973.

Friedman, Susan Stanford, ed. *Joyce: The Return of the Repressed*. Ithaca: Cornell UP, 1993.

Solomon, Margaret C. *Eternal Geomater: The Sexual Universe of* Finnegans Wake. Carbondale: Southern Illinois UP, 1969.

Postcolonial

Attridge, Derek and Marjorie Howes, eds. *Semicolonial Joyce*. Cambridge: Cambridge UP, 2000.

Duffy, Enda. *The Subaltern Ulysses*. Minneapolis: U of Minnesota P, 1994.

Nolan, Emer. *James Joyce and Nationalism*. London: Routledge, 1995.

Feminism

Henke, Suzette. *James Joyce and the Politics of Desire*. New York: Routledge, 1990.

Jones, Ellen Carol, ed. *Joyce: Feminism, Post, Colonialism*. Amsterdam: Rodopi, 1998.

Scott, Bonnie Kime. *Joyce and Feminism*. Bloomington: Indiana UP: 1984.

Queer studies

Valente, Joseph. *Quare Joyce*. Ann Arbor: U of Michigan P, 1998.

INDEX